ALSO BY JEFFREY A. TRACHTENBERG

Ralph Lauren: The Man Behind the Mystique

The Rain on Macy's Parade

The Rain on Macy's Parade

How Greed, Ambition, and Folly Ruined America's Greatest Store

Jeffrey A. Trachtenberg

TIMES BUSINESS

RANDOM HOUSE

Library of Congress Cataloging-in-Publication Data

Trachtenberg, Jeffrey A.
The rain on Macy's parade : how greed, ambition, and folly ruined
America's greatest store / Jeffrey A. Trachtenberg.
p.   cm.
Includes bibliographical references and index.
ISBN 0-8129-2155-0
1. Macy's (Firm) 2. Leveraged buyouts—United States. I. Title.
HF5465.U6M36 1996
3388´36138145´000973—dc20   96-16082

Random House website address: http://www.randomhouse.com

Printed in the United States of America on acid-free paper
98765432
First Edition

FOR ELIZABETH

"We built it, we bought it, and now we have to run it."

—Edward S. Finkelstein, chairman of
R. H. Macy & Co., July 1986

Acknowledgments

I would like to thank Steve Wasserman, my editor at Times Books, for his guidance throughout this project, and Peter Osnos, publisher, for prodding me to deliver the second half of my manuscript. Others at Times Books who also gave generously of their time include: Judy Schepis, Beth Thomas, Gerry Hollingsworth, Leslie Oelsner, Diane Henry, Nancy Inglis, Mary Beth Roche, and Naomi Osnos.

Many people provided encouragement and help at *The Wall Street Journal*. Paul Steiger, the managing editor, graciously extended my leave when I needed it, and never wavered in his support. I also benefited from the counsel of Byron Calame and Daniel Hertzberg, deputy managing editors; F. James Pensiero, assistant managing editor; Richard Tofel, director of international development and administration; and John Brecher, page one editor. In particular, Laura Landro, my editor at the newspaper, made this experience much better than it otherwise would have been. George Anders, with whom I wrote many stories about Macy's, was a terrific sounding board. So, too, was Alix Freedman, whose cool deliberations helped frame this story. Others who shared their time and their thoughts included Teri Agins, Laura Jereski, John Keller, Dan Kelly, Joanne Lipman, Michael Miller, Ann Podd, Patrick Reilly, Mark Robichaux, Eben Shapiro, Suzanne Vranica, and Bernie Wysocki. I also benefited from the advice of former colleagues at the *Journal* and *Forbes*, including Lisa Gubernick, Jerry Flint, Johnnie Roberts, and James Stewart.

The Wall Street Journal's librarian staff, Lottie Lindberg, Bruce Levy, and Elizabeth Yeh were always helpful. So, too, were the *Journal's* computer whizzes: Phil Chan, Tim Lemmer, James McDonald, and Richard Schuster.

I would also like to thank the late John Andrew. He loved the retail beat, and his wisdom and sure hand are missed by all who worked with him.

My agent Kim Witherspoon came up with the idea for this book and convinced me I could do it. Nancy Marx Better originally suggested my name to Kim. Martha Trachtenberg did a superb job, as a researcher and a copy editor.

Author John Rothchild provided several sources he developed while working on his fine history of Federated Department Stores, *Going for Broke.* At Federated Department Stores, Carol Sanger, Paula Cotlee, Dixie Barker, and Mary Ann Shannon shared their knowledge of the company, as did Jim Fingeroth, Michael Freitag, and Christine Lion at Kekst and Co.

I would also like to thank Henry Ferris, whose early support was invaluable; Amelia Rokicki, the research librarian at the Nantucket Historical Association; Shannon Chandley and John Golovach at the Mount Vernon Public Library; and researcher Marjorie R. Atherton. Thanks also to Alison Johns, Sam Kintzer, and Bruce Stockler for providing a warm home at *Millimeter* magazine.

This book is the result of hundreds of hours of interviews with current and former Macy's executives, directors, employees, and investors, many of whom preferred not to be identified. This story could never have been told without them.

My parents, Frances and Morton Trachtenberg, as well as my wife's parents, Joan and Elliott Sanger, were wonderful throughout, and went into baby-sitting overdrive for our sons Benjamin and Joshua.

Most of all, I want to thank my wife, Elizabeth Sanger, who read these chapters through their many revisions, and who took each sincere promise of "I'll be done in just a few more weeks" with extraordinary calm and forbearance. Her encouragement was wonderful. I couldn't have finished without her.

Contents

The Rain on Macy's Parade

Chapter I

"We built it, we bought it, and now we have to run it."

During the early evening hours of the last day of July 1986, some of the nation's most celebrated business executives gathered to toast their latest triumph, the purchase of R. H. Macy & Co.

As uniformed New York City policemen looked on, a procession of black limousines drove down Fifth Avenue, pausing in front of the Metropolitan Museum of Art to let out the presidents of international banks, insurance companies, and pension funds. Although it was the heart of the summer, a cool breeze was blowing, and some women clutched wraps around their shoulders as they made their entrances. Nearly four hundred had been invited, including former secretary of state Henry Kissinger and his wife, Nancy; Beverly Sills, the general director of the New York City Opera; and A. Alfred Taubman, the wealthy art collector whose marble-and-glass shopping malls were the envy of the real estate industry.

Here, too, was Laurence Tisch, a short, bald man who mostly shunned public displays of wealth. A financier with many interests, Tisch had a lifelong fascination with New York City department stores. So when Michael Price, who headed the Mutual Series mutual fund group, said he was investing heavily in the $3.7 billion leveraged buyout organized by Macy's senior management, Tisch indicated he was interested. "I said, 'Michael, you do the work, and if you think it's good, we'll go in,' " Tisch recalls.

Encouraged by what he heard, Tisch anted up $41 million and

bought 15 percent of Macy's preferred stock, about the same stake owned by Price. Only General Electric Credit Corp., a financial unit of General Electric Co. that now does business as GE Capital, controlled more shares.

Soon after, Tisch was asked to sit on Macy's new board of directors. He would finally get his chance to talk shop.

As night fell on Ed Finkelstein's summer gala, the Metropolitan Museum grounds were transformed into a marvelous sight. The fountains flanking the grand staircase jetted water high into the sky, while a ring of white spotlights created a bubbly, champagne effect. Many guests, making their way up the long broad staircase to the front door, paused to take a last look at the city spread out before them, a riveting vista of old money and privilege. Then they swept inside, where they were greeted by piercing blasts of welcoming trumpets. Some men, clearly amused, clasped their hands together and raised them over their heads, prizefighter style. Others grinned boyishly and shook their heads in amazement. Photographers were on hand, and as guests entered, blinding flashbulbs went off. Moments later, each couple was formally announced, their names echoing down the museum's vast hallway until lost in darkness. In turn, those already inside, the men clad in designer tuxedos, the women resplendent in exotic silk evening dresses and strings of pearls, paused and then applauded politely before resuming conversation.

In a gracious touch, Finkelstein and his wife, Myra, dressed in a red-and-pink dress, greeted each invitee on a receiving line. Finkelstein closely oversaw all of Macy's social gatherings, and his meticulous planning was in evidence this evening. In the courtyard of the museum's American Wing, seventy-five waiters and waitresses from Glorious Food, a chic catering firm, swooped down upon guests with glasses of champagne at the ready. String quartets and harpists played classical music, all part of a revelry whose six-figure cost caused some bankers to grumble into their drinks later that night that Finkelstein was already wasting their money.

The setting would have befitted a king, let along a pugnacious merchant prince. The Metropolitan Museum was founded in 1880 by business leaders and artists intent on creating an institution to rival any in London or Paris. The neo-Renaissance building stretched from

80th Street to 84th Street and housed a treasure trove of riches that reminded viewers that passion could infuse even ordinary moments with genius. Since many of the artworks were accompanied by plaques identifying their donors, the surroundings, at least for Finkelstein's crowd, were as aspirational as they were inspirational.

While the party began to gather momentum, Macy's new directors, among them Henry Kissinger, began working the crowd. Several years earlier, Finkelstein had suggested adding the former diplomat to Macy's board, only to have the nomination rejected—ostensibly because the white-shoe board objected to paying Kissinger's $250,000 fee. Now that Finkelstein had taken control of the retailing giant, however, he again invited Kissinger to join him. Kissinger, a neighbor in the green Connecticut countryside where Finkelstein spent his weekends, made a small investment in the buyout and accepted, adding his luster to one of New York's most star-studded boards. For many, that group, which included a senior partner at Goldman, Sachs & Co., the investment banking firm that raised the necessary financing, virtually assured the buyout's success.

Clearly in his element, Kissinger went out of his way to greet fellow guests. "Mr. Kissinger had something to say to everybody," says Sankar Krishnan, a former Macy's senior vice president. "He didn't appear to know much about retailing, but he was immensely charming." Krishnan, who began his career as a salesman at Bamberger's, a Macy's sister department store division based in Newark, New Jersey, had been thrilled when Finkelstein offered him an opportunity to invest $52,500. Krishnan, like all 347 executives who bought private stock in the buyout, was convinced he would earn at least fifteen times his original investment, enabling him to one day retire a millionaire.

"We were pumped up," he says. "We were going to make this thing work, we were going to earn lots of money, and we were going to live wonderfully ever after. Euphoria is the only way I can describe it. For most of us, our only disappointment was that we weren't allowed to buy even more shares."

At the appointed hour, Finkelstein's guests were summoned to dinner, where dozens of tables covered in white linen awaited them. Arm in arm, couples walked into the Sackler Wing, which houses the famed Temple of Dendur, a two-thousand-year-old structure given to the United States by Egypt in 1965. A long reflecting pool was ringed with hundreds of candles, creating a sensuous tableau of light and mystery. While the celebrants took their seats, three different wines were poured. The meal began with a cold seafood ragout, followed by a rack of veal with a Calvados sauce, sautéed apples, and summer vegetables. In between courses, some danced to the music of Peter Duchin and his orchestra. Afterward, the guests were offered a star-shaped chocolate cake or a fruit cup covered with raspberry sauce.

As the dinner drew to a close, the lights dimmed and a procession of waiters entered the room waving sparklers. Seconds later, the band broke into the rousing theme song from the movie *Rocky*. Finkelstein then rose to give the briefest of speeches.

"A simple toast to Macy's," he said after everyone had quieted. "Long may she prosper." When the crowd realized that he was done, they broke into thunderous applause.

Instead of calling it quits for the night, however, Finkelstein's guests were asked to follow their host into the nearby Grace Rainey Rogers Auditorium for what the program guide described as "The First (and Presumably The Last) Annual Leveraged Buyout Awards Cere-monies." After the guests settled into their chairs, Mike Stemen, a se-nior vice president at Macy's New York, proclaimed, "Please welcome the past master of music depreciation, the unmelancholy Dane, Vic-tor Borge."

Finkelstein had been so eager to have Borge perform that he ne-gotiated the comedian's payment himself. Yet not a single member of the audience offered a welcoming hand of applause when the en-tertainer appeared on stage.

"Thank you very much indeed," began Borge. "When the celebra-tion has died down . . . hahahaha."

Borge then proceeded to tell a series of stale jokes, each more awful than the one that preceded it. When he finally finished, popu-lar opera singer Beverly Sills mounted the stage to host the award show. A New York celebrity who had made the difficult transition from artist to fund-raiser and manager, Sills was the only former Macy's outside director invited to join the new board. In the wel-coming note in the program guide, Finkelstein wrote that "her voice, her administrative abilities, her effervescent personality and limitless energy are legendary."

As soon as she walked on stage, however, Sills began wringing her hands, perhaps in anticipation of what was to come. After a bit of canned patter, she gamely announced the first award: The Best Odd

Couple. As the audience watched in numbed disbelief, the larger-than-life faces of Laurel and Hardy, W. C. Fields and Baby Leroy, Nelson Eddy and Jeanette McDonald, and Herbert Hellman and Marvin Fenster—two of Macy's lawyers—appeared consecutively on a screen behind her.

By then it was nearly midnight, and many partygoers, exhausted by food and drink and talk, wanted to go home. Instead, they would sit for nearly two more hours as the self-congratulatory ceremony marched forward. It fell to Mark Schwartz, a bearded Goldman, Sachs investment banker, to give the event's most memorable thank-you speech. Buoyed by his moment in the spotlight, Schwartz explained how he had learned how to work with the ever-demanding Finkelstein.

In February of 1986, Schwartz recounted, Goldman, Sachs arranged an introductory luncheon at Macy's with Mutual Series mutual fund group head Michael Price. The small gathering was designed to introduce Price to Macy's top managers in hopes that he would become a key investor, one whose presence would cause others to follow. Also on hand were Jim Lane, a Goldman, Sachs investment banker and former aspiring professional soccer player; Mark Handler, Macy's president and chief operating officer; Ira Millstein, the intense, combative attorney at Weil, Gotshal & Manges who was Finkelstein's most trusted adviser; Finkelstein; and Schwartz.

The lunch went smoothly until the waiters began to serve dessert. Then Price directed a complicated financial question to Finkelstein. Instead of waiting for Macy's chairman to respond, however, Schwartz interrupted and answered it himself.

In an instant, Finkelstein turned to Schwartz and pointedly said, "If you open your mouth again, I'm going to throw you out of here."

"Jim Lane passed out, and I kept quiet for the next hour-and-a-half," Schwartz told his rapt listeners. Shortly after that experience, Schwartz continued, he joined Handler and Finkelstein for a three-week road trip designed to create investor interest in the buyout, sometimes visiting as many as three cities a day in an effort to attract investors. "Ed and Mark were real troupers," Schwartz finished. "I also learned that I wasn't going to be selling these securities: Ed was."

No speech garnered greater applause.

As the hour neared 2 A.M., the last award of the evening was finally announced: The Best Leader in History. In a tired voice, Beverly Sills read aloud the names of the nominees: General George S. Patton Jr.,

Superman, Henry V, Winston Churchill, and Macy's own Ed Finkelstein. Moments later, Finkelstein joined the diva onstage.

Beaming, Finkelstein first asked his mother to stand up. Then he praised all of those who had worked on the buyout, especially those who had put in seven-day weeks for months on end. "I'm reminded that I can't do Olivier," Finkelstein said, referring to actor Laurence Olivier. "But I'm also reminded a little bit of what Henry the Fifth said on the night before they went into battle, on Saint Crispin's day, when a small group of Englishmen took on and beat the hell out of the French at Agincourt. In Shakespeare's words, slightly moved around a little bit: We few, we happy few, we band of brothers. Those of us who bleed today shall be my brothers, and gentlemen in England today in bed will feel themselves accursed that they are not here."

Even if the words were garbled, the message was clear: the Macy's men had been to war together, slaughtered the enemy, and were now about to enjoy the fruits of their victory.

"There are three other people I want to mention and I think it's time to end the evening," continued Finkelstein. "Mark Handler indeed was a hell of a partner. When I told him that we were going forward on this early in June of 1985, he gulped, as indeed everybody did, and I asked him to go home and think about it. He came back the next day and said, 'I really have only one request: That when we make the offer, we make it in both our names. So that there's no doubt where I stand.' Great partner he was.

"Jim Lane worked on this, I can't tell you how that young man worked on this deal. About three or four months ago, Ira and I were talking about it. And we said, 'He's the guy, we've got to go with him. If he can't handle it, it's going to falter.' And he is unusual. Manipulating—I don't like that word actually—handling and developing and putting together all the variety of pieces of this tremendously complicated transaction. And he just showed tremendous ability, tremendous perseverance, all throughout, and Ira and I and everybody in this room has to feel that without Jim Lane and his ability, there's a high probability that we wouldn't have completed this deal. He's a very fine young man.

"And last, and not least, is Ira. When I started a sentence he would finish it. He thought that would annoy me, but he finished it about the way I meant to finish it myself, and we began to realize that we had different abilities but the same objectives. Without Ira and without some absolutely brilliant moves, really, in terms of his win-win development of philosophy, there's no question in my mind not only that the deal was in trouble, but that it would never have gotten done. So Ira, I salute you as well.

"One last word to my Macy's associates here, sixty or seventy of the investors. I think that we will all look back at this as the entrepreneurial decade. And I think big corporations better understand that if they don't achieve entrepreneurial status for their organization, they aren't going to keep together. I think we've done something that may be unique in terms of its size for us, but something that won't be unique when you look back at the 1980s. Because entrepreneurialism is in. What has happened is that those of you in this room from Macy's who have built this business have now bought it. We built it, we bought it, and now we have to run it. The rest of the people in this audience who have lent us this money are counting on us, so we've got to do our job well."

Concluding on that suddenly serious note, Finkelstein asked his other award winners to join him.

Up they marched. A few moments later, all burst into a rendition of "The Best of Times" from the hit show *La Cage aux Folles*, a wistful, haunting song that Finkelstein had chosen.

"The best of times is now," sang the group. "As for tomorrow, well, who knows?"

Moments later, the houselights were turned back on, signaling that the party had officially come to a close. Finkelstein left with an orange balloon in one hand and a T-shirt jauntily draped around his shoulders. On the back of the shirt, a gift from Goldman, Sachs, was a large picture of his beaming face.

If he was taking the prophetic words of his favorite song to heart as he stepped into the summer evening, not a soul knew it.

To Wall Street, Finkelstein's victory reflected the economic forces buffeting many blue-chip companies. A recent wave of mergers and takeovers orchestrated by T. Boone Pickens, Irwin Jacobs, Saul Steinberg, and others had already recast the once-sleepy broadcasting and petroleum industries. Now dozens of other asset-rich companies that had fallen out of favor were becoming potential targets.

Still, few suspected that the country's department stores would be next. For decades, such familiar names as Burdines in Florida, J. W. Robinson's in Los Angeles, and Marshall Field & Co. in Chicago had helped customers choose their wardrobes, decorate their homes, and seduce their spouses with peekaboo lingerie. At Christmas, families young and old gathered to gawk over holiday window displays. Each spring, those same windows were crowded with bikinis, beach umbrellas, and cotton towels large enough for two, cheery harbingers of warmer days to come.

It was an industry that grew lockstep with the needs of the country. As interstate highways curved their way north and south after World War II, big chains like Sears, Roebuck & Co. and Montgomery Ward left the cities in favor of new suburbs. Real estate developers spurred that growth by introducing enclosed shopping centers in the 1950s. Later came giant regional malls complete with skating rinks, movie theaters, and food courts that offered that miracle of economy, the $3.99 Chinese lunch. By the 1970s most malls were anchored by four to six major department stores, enabling retailers like Macy's to add new branches every few years.

Meanwhile, the mom-and-pop department stores that dotted the American landscape began to fade away, unable to compete on price or selection. When their lights flickered out for the last time, so did the life of many downtowns.

Many of these changes were prompted by a new school of retailers who emphasized price instead of stylish chrome racks, beveled mirrors, and comfortable dressing rooms. Eastern discount chains like E. J. Korvette's offered cut-rate prices on clothes and electronics; Marty Chase opened Ann & Hope in Cumberland, Rhode Island, the first of hundreds of New England outlet shops. On the West Coast, Sol Price made legions of friends with his Fed-Mart stores. Meanwhile, a former J. C. Penney trainee named Sam Walton wondered if he could make a living by providing friendly service and low prices to backwater towns bypassed by the big retailers. Walton opened his first shop in Bentonville, Arkansas, in 1950, calling it Walton's. After fiddling with the concept of rock-bottom prices for the next twelve years, the young merchant unveiled his first Wal-Mart in 1962.

It marked a significant change in American buying habits. The discounters, offering cut-rate prices on everything from dishwasher detergent to Italian loafers, were crowded with shoppers. Department stores, no longer nimble enough to make the quick buying decisions that translated into big profits, drew fewer customers each year. Under mounting pressure, some began placing orders with sewing rooms in

Hong Kong, Malaysia, and Thailand. But with deliveries taking as long as nine months, they often sacrificed their place as fashion leaders.

The culture was changing, too. Working women were turning in ever-larger numbers to retailers who made it easier to shop, including The Gap, The Limited, and the mail-order houses J. Crew and Lands' End. Customers could dart in and out of a Gap store in ten minutes; an expedition to Macy's lasted hours. Having prospered for decades by posing as cool arbiters of popular taste, department stores were increasingly being seen by younger customers as the places where their mothers shopped.

Ed Finkelstein didn't buy that notion for two seconds. When he hurried into Macy's Herald Square each morning, he saw the world's biggest store, a rousing, dynamic showboat of a place that swaggered, blustered, and kicked the stuffing out of everybody else. Department stores entertained, they provided essential services, and they offered more choice than anyone else in the mall. He was right, of course. As soon as Finkelstein announced his offer to buy Macy's, the shares of Federated Department Stores, Allied Stores, and Associated Dry Goods all rose on speculation that somebody would soon see their potential, too.

And bigger deals did follow. But even by later standards, Finkelstein's buyout was a bonanza for everyone involved. Shareholders received a record $68 per share for their stock. Finkelstein's lawyers and bankers were paid $165 million in fees, with Manufacturers Hanover Trust, Citibank N.A., and Bankers Trust alone sharing $75 million; Goldman, Sachs, the investment bankers who guided Finkelstein's every move, reaped $30 million; and the lawyers billed nearly $11 million. Even classy investment banker James Wolfensohn, hired by Macy's outside directors in hopes of finding someone who would top Finkelstein's offer, pocketed $5.5 million.

A gold rush was under way, one that would last well into the 1990s. American retailing would never be the same.

It was, by any standard, a marvelous prize. In a city whose character was as crisply defined by retailing as Los Angeles was by moviemaking, Macy's, located at Broadway and 34th Street, was an oasis of sensible styles and homey comforts. To be sure, Bergdorf Goodman and

Saks Fifth Avenue attracted the customers who could afford $600 silk Ralph Lauren blouses and $2,000 jeweled handbags. And when the Queen of England visited New York City during the Bicentennial celebrations of 1976, she found time to browse through Bloomingdale's, one of Macy's chief competitors. (Ensuring that the queen didn't leave empty-handed, the Bloomingdale's staff welcomed her with an Indian peace pipe.)

Yet when it came to price, selection, and sheer entertainment value, Macy's stood apart from the rest. The very size of the company's 2.1-million-square-foot Herald Square flagship made it a shaper of popular culture, and favorite of New Yorkers and tourists alike. Printmaker Wanda Gag found inspiration in a Macy's staircase. *The New Yorker* gently poked fun at the company with cartoons. For decades, the remark "Does Macy's tell Gimbel's?" signaled a question so dumb that it didn't deserve a response.

Over the years, Macy's made and sold its own aspirin and shampoo, its own bicycles, and its own horsehair mattresses. For customers with a yen to travel, it briefly offered the Air Coupe, an airplane advertised as "stall proof." When American citizens were asked to grow their own food during World War II, Macy's Herald Square auctioned live cows and sheep on the fifth floor. "Macy's is not merely the physically biggest store in the world, selling the greatest variety of items (400,000), it is also the world's largest drugstore, bookstore, furniture store and fabric and china store," enthused *Life* magazine in December 1948. The editors devoted two pages to the items that Macy's said would be its top holiday sellers. These included 77,000 pairs of nylons priced at $1.68 per pair, and 60,000 ball-point pens offered at 92 cents each.

Tens of thousands would work there, including window decorator L. Frank Baum, the author of *The Wizard of Oz;* Henry Dreyfus, who designed the rotary dial telephone; and Walter Hoving, who later headed Tiffany & Co. Others included the late lawyer William Kunstler; advertising executives Mary Wells Lawrence and Jerry Della Femina; and actor Burgess Meredith. All counted themselves fortunate. In 1971, an estimated thousand staffers wore twenty-five-year pins, while another forty-eight had been employed by Macy's for more than fifty years. Company morale was so high that the last page of Macy's annual awards dinner program was left blank for the autographs of fellow employees. "Going to work at Macy's was like joining a family," says Julia Wolff, a resident of Queens, New York, who sold ties, gloves, and men's underwear at Macy's Herald Square for forty-five years. "We all knew each other. We had clubs, we ate at each other's homes, and we went on trips together. I also made a damned fine living."

As city buffs know, Herald Square itself was a small triangle of land flanked by the intersection of Broadway and Sixth Avenue and bordered by West 35th Street to the north and West 34th Street to the south. The modest plot, named after the New York *Herald,* was graced by bronze figures of Minerva and two bell ringers, a tableau that once decorated the *Herald*'s building on the north side of West 35th Street. Although the nineteenth-century crusading newspaper was long gone, Minerva and her two helpers still kept accurate time for passersby. Infamous at the turn of the century for its bars and brothels, the Herald Square area matured into one of the city's most crowded retail neighborhoods. Six subway lines converged there, buses cruised by every few minutes, and a few blocks to the west, the Pennsylvania Railroad Station served commuters from Long Island and other points. When George M. Cohan penned the lines "Give my regards to Broadway, remember me to Herald Square," everyone knew exactly where he meant.

During the 1970s, Macy's nearby rivals included Gimbel Brothers at Broadway and 33rd Street, a nine-story department store; Franklin Simon at 33 West 34th Street, which sold a potpourri of women's clothes and accessories; Ohrbach's, a discounter at 4 West 34th Street once famed for its copies of Paris originals; and B. Altman & Co. at Fifth Avenue and 34th Street, the classy carriage trade department store renowned for its tearoom, offerings of crystal and glass, and loyal sales help. All failed to keep pace with changing tastes and habits. For most, their teary going-out-of-business sales would be the first time in years that their aisles were crowded.

Macy's survived because its buyers were smart and cunning. When Prohibition ended, the retailer wangled the first New York State liquor license, number L-1—and had arranged with a wholesaler to have a fleet of ships loaded with liquor waiting outside the twelve-mile limit. When the ban ended, Macy's shelves were fully stocked within hours. Macy's was also the first to advertise the Polaroid camera, the first to sell Panasonic products in the United States, and the first to launch Shiseido cosmetics in this country. Along the way, its merchants in-

troduced Monopoly and Scrabble, and licensed the names Howdy
Doody and Hopalong Cassidy for children's clothing. Macy's even operated its own Rube Goldberg–like Bureau of Standards to rip, pull,
and batter much of what it sold to the public. The first product tested
was a pair of rayon ladies' bloomers.

In a booklet titled "Romanticism and Merchandise," published in
1965, Macy's merchant Leo Martinuzzi posed a number of questions
that he described as "elementary" for experienced buyers. Among
them: Can you distinguish molded glass from cut glass? Is it always possible to differentiate handpainted decor on earthenware from a good
lithograph? Is there any obvious difference between hand-loomed and
power-loomed tweeds? Martinuzzi knew the answers, and during the
1950s and 1960s, so did the buyers at Macy's.

The Herald Square store became a magnet for dreamers and a destination for those making good. Every year upward of 5 million shoppers were drawn to its raucous, bazaarlike atmosphere. Once inside,
visitors were overwhelmed with nine floors devoted to food, handbags,
furs, electric razors, picture frames, TV sets, underwear, luggage, hats,
and a perplexing assortment of men's, women's, and kid's clothing.
During the early 1960s, Macy's offered a hundred different kinds of
coffee makers and a thousand different armchairs. Customer service
included scissor sharpening and free sewing lessons. The retailer developed a special relationship with its shoppers, a rapport celebrated
every year with the Macy's Thanksgiving Day Parade and a spectacu-
lar Fourth of July fireworks display. Hollywood took note of that special intimacy and captured its flavor in the movie classic *Miracle on 34th
Street*.

Dictators, too, were curious. In October 1970, Nicolae Ceaușescu,
the president of Romania, made an unscheduled forty-minute stop
at the company's Herald Square store during a state visit. The vast selection astounded him.

Store security was always an issue. Macy's own staff of former FBI
agents and New York City police roamed the floors, often in disguise.
There was also a kennel on the roof that sheltered the store's Dober-
man pinschers, guard dogs that accompanied Macy's security personnel as they collected the day's cash receipts. At night, the
Dobermans strutted across the floors with their handlers, sniffing
out malingerers who hid themselves during store hours. It was the bite
behind the smile at the front door.

According to one tale, an elderly woman lingered past closing hours, realized her mistake, and took an express elevator down to the first floor. When the doors opened, she came face-to-face with shotgun-wielding guards flanked by matching Dobermans. Instantly the dogs leaped up from their haunches, baring their teeth. The old woman moaned and then keeled over in a dead faint. Seconds later, the doors closed and the elevator began another ride up.

In his book *Hunting Mister Heartbreak: A Discovery of America,* Jonathan Raban wrote:

> The department store was the great treasury of New World culture. It was a splendid edifice—a many-storied exhibition hall, part opera house, part classical temple. It aimed, or at least pretended, to house a whole civilization within the space of a city block. Ranged in order, section by section and floor by floor, according to a system of classification as ingenious and arcane as that of the Brothers Roget in their "Thesaurus," were the prestigious materials and objects of American society, its domestic arts and sciences; its inventions, foods, customs, furnishings and accoutrements.

Macy's Herald Square, which boasted thirteen thousand tons of structural iron and steel, thirty-three hydraulic elevators, and the city's largest private generator when it opened in 1902, was as fine an example of that ideal as any in the city.

In an era dominated by specialty stores like The Limited and The Gap, cut-price manufacturer outlet malls, and such discounters as Wal-Mart and Kmart, it is easy to scoff at the concept of customer loyalty to a department store. But Macy's shoppers were both faithful and vocal. When the company's senior management tried to close Macy's state-chartered savings bank in the 1960s in hopes of introducing charge cards, a move that spurred additional spending at other department store companies, thousands of elderly Macy's customers said no. Instead, they insisted on having purchases deducted from their low-interest Macy's Depositor's Account, much as they had done for decades. Customers deposited money in the account, and made purchases against those funds. "Shoppers refused to do business any other way," says David Yunich, a former Macy's vice chairman.

By 1986, Macy's was one of the nation's most important and powerful department store companies. While it sold mostly clothes and accessories, Macy's was also famed for its televisions and other electronics, its home furnishings, its housewares, and its enormous furniture department. There were buying offices in nineteen countries, an executive training program that was regarded as the best in the industry, and a credit card operation so important that it accounted for more than half of all consumer purchases. Macy's also boasted its own stable of more than one hundred house brands, such as Austin Grey and Morgan Taylor, and its own designers. This business enabled Macy's to eliminate the markup charged by outside manufacturers, creating higher profits for Macy's and savings for its shoppers. Because it was so hard to anticipate styles nine months ahead of time, however, many retailers limited their private label lines to such staples as sheets, dress shirts, and blazers. Not Macy's. While private label goods accounted for only 6 percent of sales in fiscal 1980, they generated about 20 percent of revenues six years later and were still growing as a percentage of the whole.

This colossus of a business would soon enter Florida, Louisiana, and Texas. Although the neighborhoods were new, Macy's name was a part of the American imagination, assuring its stores a warm reception.

In its grocery catalog for 1923–24, Macy's promised customers ordering its 64-cent, double-layered chocolate cake, that they were purchasing the "most toothsome" dessert anyone could desire, mostly because Macy's used "the best materials, the most careful mixing and baking, and all at less cost than you can make for yourself."

Sixty-two years later, only the price had changed.

Certainly few retailers boasted a more colorful history. Rowland Hussey Macy, the company's founder, hunted whales in the Pacific, panned for gold in northern California, and went bankrupt at least four times. A tightwad with a brittle temper, Macy sported a five-pointed star tattooed on his arm, a memento, he said, of a mysterious evening light that guided his ship to safety one foggy night. Later he put that star between his last name and the letter S, creating one of the country's best-known trademarks.

Macy was an original Yankee showman, a snappy blend of brass and street smarts who enjoyed celebrating a good day with a huge cigar. He opened his first store in Boston in 1843, and though he had little to show for his next twelve years as a merchant, he developed sound ideas about what his customers wanted and how to satisfy them. At a time when most retailers refused to put prices on the goods they sold, forcing shoppers to bargain over every purchase, Macy followed good Quaker tenets by marking his prices in plain sight. One of six children, he valued a dollar and instinctively sympathized—much as retailer Sam Walton did a century later—with customers who hungered for bargains. He kept his costs low by buying and selling for cash, and then advertised that his goods were always "cheap" or "marked down."

These simple principles of fairness, price, and promotion served Macy's for more than a century.

Rowland Macy was an evangelical discounter with disdain for all that was ordinary, tidy, and safe. He beckoned not to those growing rich from a new era of industry and public transportation but to the working class. Retailing, with its promise of cotton sheets, warm winter coats, and children's black patent leather shoes, has always been a polite battleground of class struggle, squaring as it does the privileges of those who have with the aspirations of those who dream.

Macy, who once wrote in his ledger, "I have worked for two years for nothing. Damn. Damn. Damn. Damn," understood the yearning in that equation as well as anyone.

Although he opened and closed four stores between 1843 and 1855, Macy never lost confidence in himself. After earning money in Wisconsin real estate, he moved to New York City in 1858, rented a sliver of a store at 204–206 Sixth Avenue, near the corner of 14th Street, and opened a "fancy" dry goods shop on October 28. First day sales were only $11.06, a reminder that the neighborhood was well north of the busy shopping district that surrounded City Hall.

Macy, though, had learned from his earlier mistakes. Penning a series of newspapers ads, he turned disappointment into triumph.

"Cheap Ribbons!!! You want them, of course. Go to Macy's," barked the first, which appeared on November 25, 1858, in the *New York Tribune.* In later ads, Macy repeated key words and phrases, such as "Our goods shall be sold cheap! Our goods shall be sold cheap!" His good-humored efforts drew the eye like a beacon, and when New Yorkers discovered that his prices were as good as promised, his new store flourished.

Over time, Macy acquired the leases of eleven of his neighbors. The effect was a patchwork-quilt-like department store whose offerings of clothes, jewelry, toiletries, plants, toys, and dolls were displayed in a labyrinth of odd-shaped rooms. By 1861, Macy's department store was accepting mail-order business; two years later, it held its first annual clearance sale. Shoppers who lived in the borough of Brooklyn, or across the Hudson River in the New Jersey communities of Hoboken and Jersey City, were promised free delivery.

Despite his new prosperity, Rowland Macy never lost his love of a sharp deal. In 1873, he was approached by Isidor and Nathan Straus, two Bavarian-born brothers who sometimes supplied his store with small lots of china. Rowland Macy's ancestors had moved to the United States in the seventeenth century to escape religious persecution; two centuries later, Lazarus Straus, the father of Isidor and Nathan, had come in hopes of finding political freedom. A liberal democrat, Lazarus had supported the constitutional reform movement that blazed across Europe in 1848. Disappointed by the outcome, he emigrated four years later. Friends helped him find a peddler's cart before setting him loose in the back roads of rural Georgia. Soon afterward, he settled in Talbotton, Georgia, a beehive of a town one hundred miles south of Atlanta. After opening a dry goods store, Straus built a house in 1854 and sent for his wife, Sara, and their four children: Isidor, Hermine, Nathan, and Oscar. This energetic German reformer then set about fitting into his new community. He enrolled his children in a Baptist Sunday school, raised his own chickens, and purchased slaves to help his wife with domestic work at home, much to the embarrassment of later generations.

Although loyal Southerners, the family was driven out of town by the anti-Semitism that flared up after the start of the Civil War. A local grand jury called to investigate war profiteering issued a report that blamed all of the town's problems on unnamed Jewish businessmen. Lazarus Straus, the only Jewish merchant in town, denounced the findings as biased. He then closed his store and moved to Columbus, Georgia. (The Strauses, however, would not be forgotten. In 1958, long after time had obscured the reasons for their departure, a bronze plaque was erected in Talbotton directing tourists to their original home. "Straus and his sons, Isidor, Nathan, and Oscar, are among those men in American Jewry of whom all Jews are most proud," it reads. This may have been true. However, by then most of his family had become Episcopalians.)

After the Civil War ended, the Strauses moved north to New York, buying a small wholesaler of china and crockery in lower Manhattan. Then, in the fall of 1873, brothers Isidor and Nathan asked Rowland Macy if they could rent space in his department store. It was a simple plan, they explained. They would take all the risk while paying a fixed percentage of their sales as rent.

With a recession under way, Rowland Macy decided it was his kind of deal. He promptly offered the Strauses 2,500 square feet of prime selling space—in the basement.

The following March, L. Straus & Sons opened a china department chockablock with plates, saucers, tureens, cut-glass vases, majolica, and glassware of every conceivable size and description. Within a few months, they advertised that theirs was the "most extensive assortment" of its kind ever displayed in America. The brothers knew what they were doing, too, because their area became the most popular in the store.

All of which only enhanced Rowland Macy's reputation as a skilled businessman with an eye for value.

There would be only one disappointment in his life as a retail magnate, but as his papers indicate, it darkened his later years and changed the course of his company's future. His problem was his son, Rowland Macy Jr.

Overshadowed by his father, Rowland Jr. rebelled to no apparent purpose, drinking heavily. During the Civil War, intent on starting over again, he ran away from home and enlisted in the Union Army under an alias. Less than two weeks later, he deserted. His real name came to light in the subsequent court martial proceedings. His father pronounced himself humiliated, and the two never fully reconciled.

In a will signed in February 1877, shortly before he died, Rowland Macy wrote, "I am grieved to say in this solemn manner that my experience has been such with my son, Rowland H. Macy, Junior, that I cannot entrust him with the care or management of any property. He has never succeeded in supporting himself."

Instead of bequeathing his company shares to his only son, Macy sold his stock to relatives. He also directed his executors to establish a small trust for Rowland Jr. It is a sorry fact that Macy worried about doing even that much because he feared Rowland Jr. would drink the money away.

Events justified that concern. A little more than a year later, Rowland H. Macy Jr. was found dead in a Boston hotel room. His death certificate attributed his passing to "Convultions [sic] and delirium tremens." He was thirty-one years old.

In the years that followed, Macy's changed hands several times until two of the founder's relatives, Charles Webster and Jerome Wheeler, took control in 1879. Soon afterward, however, the pair had a falling out, and the business began to suffer.

The Strauses, by contrast, were proving themselves superb merchants. After opening their shop at Macy's, they made similar arrangements with such retailers as R. H. White's in Boston and John Wanamaker's in Philadelphia. They also grew their wholesale company, importing china from Europe while expanding into silverware and other areas of home furnishings. Meanwhile, baby brother Oscar Straus was establishing a diplomatic career that would be capped in 1906 when he was named to the cabinet of President Theodore Roosevelt.

Recognizing their growing importance to Macy's, Jerome Wheeler sold the Strauses his 45 percent stake in January 1888. Soon after, they also acquired a half-interest in Wechsler & Abraham, a distinguished Brooklyn department store that they promptly renamed Abraham & Straus. Both businesses thrived, and when Charles Webster, their remaining partner at Macy's and a longtime supporter, told them in 1896 that he wanted to retire, the Strauses were able to borrow the necessary funds and buy him out.

A little more than three decades after leaving Talbotton, Georgia, in anger and shame, the family had become one of the country's foremost retailing clans.

For more than a decade, the Straus brothers managed Macy's and Abraham & Straus. Then tragedy struck. On April 15, 1912, the HMS *Titanic* sank, claiming among its victims Isidor Straus and his wife, Ida. During the Senate inquiry that followed, survivors testified that Ida Straus was offered a seat in a lifeboat but refused, saying that she preferred to stay with her husband. Her body was never recovered. New York City later dedicated a small park in their memory on the Upper West Side, where Broadway crosses West End Avenue at 106th Street.

A year after their deaths, Nathan Straus agreed to sell his Macy's stock to his late brother's three sons: Jesse, Percy, and Herbert. To raise cash, the trio sold their interest in Abraham & Straus, ending their relationship with the only department store business that carried their name. (In 1929, Abraham & Straus joined with Filene's of

Boston and F. & R. Lazarus & Co. of Columbus, Ohio, and formed Federated Department Stores, Macy's most important competitor, and later, its owner.)

The Straus brothers then concentrated their energies on Macy's. Even when Jesse served as the U.S. ambassador to France from May 1933 to August 1936, he made valuable contacts for the company, among them the Taittinger family, which later bottled champagne under the Macy's brand name, Étoile Rouge.

The Strauses would continue in control until Jack Straus, Jesse's eldest son, retired as chairman in 1968. "Mister Jack," as he was obsequiously addressed by employees, was succeeded by Donald Smiley, a tough lawyer with a strong financial background.

For the first time in the century, a Straus family member wasn't in charge.

Twelve years later, in August 1980, Smiley stepped down and was replaced by Edward Finkelstein, who had headed up the company's New York division. Finkelstein lacked Smiley's financial sophistication, but he was a keen political strategist, and six years later, he was able to use his leveraged buyout to strengthen his control over Macy's and its employees. Although he invited 346 other Macy's executives to buy stock in the company's leveraged buyout, investors had to assign their voting rights to Finkelstein as a precondition to purchasing their shares.

For the first time in his career, he would no longer have to report to anyone. This included the new board, since directors outside the company, such as Larry Tisch and Henry Kissinger, were outnumbered by executives who worked at Macy's, all of whom were loyal to their boss. In exchange for a personal investment of less than $5 million, Ed Finkelstein had seized control of one of the premier department store companies in the world.

The leveraged buyout also had one other effect: it severed the emotional ties between Macy's and various Straus heirs, some of whom were invited to become investors. They declined. Fittingly, however, the Straus and Macy families have remained linked even in death. Thirty minutes north of Herald Square, bordered by Van Cortlandt Park on the west, and the Bronx River on the east, is Woodlawn Cemetery, a resting ground of four hundred acres in the Bronx where New Yorkers have buried their dead since 1863. It is a beautiful but solitary landscape, a vista where white oak, weeping beech, and umbrella pine shelter solitary monuments and mausoleums. Some of these tombs, like financier Oliver Belmont's replica of the Chapel of St. Hubert at Château d'Amboise in France, are intricate, dazzling constructions. Elsewhere the grounds are dotted with simple tombstones, weathered by decades of sun and hard rain.

Isidor Straus and other family members are buried here in a depressing, moss-covered U-shaped mausoleum. In the front, flanked by a bronze filigreed fence, is a seven-oared Egyptian funeral boat that sits atop a massive stone base. The name "Straus" has been carved into the front facing, and on the back are these poignant words: "Many waters cannot quench love, neither can the floods drown it." The verse comes from the Song of Solomon.

Only a few hundred yards away is the grave site of Rowland Macy. The retailer is buried high on a ridge, his family plot marked by a twenty-foot Victorian granite monument crowned with an urn and graced by icanthus leaves. Nestled close-by are his wife, Louisa Houghton Macy, and his son and namesake, Rowland Hussey Macy Jr.

If, as Isidor Straus's Egyptian funeral boat seems to suggest, life is a treacherous journey, the presence of these two families so close to each other suggests it can also provide a comforting sense of closure.

Chapter 2

"Why can't we do this deal? It's not that complicated."

It started the way so many things do, over an early morning cup of coffee.

On May 15, 1985, two men met at the Knickerbocker Club in Manhattan, a haunt of old New York families that Nelson Rockefeller once rescued from the wrecker's ball because he didn't want his apartment view spoiled. Both were Macy's directors and acquaintances of long standing. Between them, though, lay nuances of judgment and style defined by the Knickerbocker Club itself, a place so discreet that its name did not appear on the entrance at 2 East 62nd Street.

J. Richardson Dilworth was a money man whose influence was felt from Wall Street to Washington, D.C. Tall, thin, and born into a family that traced its American roots to the eighteenth century, Dick Dilworth was a skeptic by nature, a blue blood by birth, and a liberal by choice. He lived in Princeton in a sunlit home bordered by pachysandra and stately trees, and counted former diplomat George Kennan among his friends and neighbors. He had been married to the same woman for forty-five years.

Dilworth spoke in the low, persuasive voice of a counselor of the rich. He spent five years as a Kuhn, Loeb & Co. investment banker specializing in the iron ore and steel business, and another seven as a partner. When Chrysler nearly collapsed in the early 1980s, Dilworth, a director, deftly oversaw the delicate bail-out talks that followed. He was also a trustee of the Yale Corporation, a close adviser to the wealthy Rockefeller family, and by dint of two dozen years on the board, the senior outside director at Macy's.

With his pedigree and gracious manners, Dick Dilworth could say, although of course he didn't, that he knew almost anyone worth knowing. Here, in a secretive club founded more than a century earlier by the son of Alexander Hamilton, he felt right at home.

His guest that day had moody brown eyes and a frank, commanding manner that suggested strength of purpose. Edward Sidney Finkelstein lacked Dilworth's glittering array of social connections. But Macy's chairman and chief executive was a formidable presence in his own right, a gifted, charismatic leader who oversaw ninety-five department stores in fourteen states, nineteen foreign buying offices that stretched from Hong Kong to Paris, and a valuable portfolio of shopping center properties.

Macy's made money, and lots of it, by selling midpriced lines of clothes, furniture, home furnishings, and electronics. Although the retailer stumbled during the early 1970s, Finkelstein nursed it back to life by focusing on young, affluent customers who wanted fashion, not bargains. By the early 1980s, Macy's was dominating more timid rivals with huge assortments and endless runs of newspaper ads.

Finkelstein was an imposing figure when he spoke about the company he loved, his eyes flashing, his glasses sliding halfway down his face. Although he gained weight when under pressure, Finkelstein retained the subtle menace of a schoolyard athlete, and he was still capable of punishing players half his age—on the tennis court and off. Harvard-educated, his life as a retailer had been framed by rock-and-roll singers and editors of women's fashion magazines who decoded Ralph and Calvin. On his watch, Macy's, one of the city's first discounters, had become a fashion-driven, upscale retailer.

Finkelstein led Macy's to record sales and earnings during the early 1980s. But by the close of 1983, the future appeared cloudy. Such discounters as Wal-Mart Stores, Toys "R" Us, and Kmart were promoting national brands at low prices Macy's was struggling to match. Thirty years earlier, department store chains made brand names the backbone of their marketing strategies. Now those same brands were being used to lure away the customers. Such competition, coupled with large, fixed overheads, forced Macy's and other department store companies to increase the space allotted to men's, women's, and children's clothing, all high-margin businesses.

Slowly but surely, one-stop shopping, the golden promise of the department store industry, was being whittled away.

For his part, Ed Finkelstein didn't intend to surrender market share it had taken years to achieve. And in January 1984, he opened secret merger talks with William Arnold, the chairman of Associated Dry Goods, a New York retailer whose divisions included Lord & Taylor in New York; J. W. Robinson in Los Angeles; Caldor's in Norwalk, Connecticut; and Loehmann's in Riverdale, New York. Associated, with about $4 billion in revenues, was a tempting target. Macy's had been trying to establish a foothold in southern California for twenty years without success, while the discount chains—Loehmann's and Caldor's—would have given Macy's two strong businesses in the fastest-growing segment of retailing.

And as Finkelstein told Arnold, there were solid reasons to merge. They would save millions of dollars almost immediately by merging their distribution centers, their back-office operations, and their buying staffs. In theory, the savings would translate into lower operating costs that could be passed on to shoppers in the form of lower prices, making the combined company more competitive.

When Bill Arnold, quietly battling cancer, expressed concern about the future of his own handpicked management team, Finkelstein promised to find them jobs. The Macy's chief even said he'd name Redmond J. Largay, Associated's president and chief operating officer, as head of Macy's struggling Midwest division.

Arnold liked what he heard, so much so that he even sketched out a new board of directors for the merged companies.

And then the deal fell apart. In a late Sunday afternoon phone call, Arnold told Finkelstein that his cancer was getting worse, and that he no longer had the strength to see Associated through such a marriage. He was sorry, but they would have to call it off, at least for a while. Finkelstein was disappointed, but said he understood.

"It was a game stopper," says Peter Solomon, an investment banker who represented Associated during the negotiations, and who later invested in the Macy's buyout. "Give Ed credit. He saw that the department store business was shrinking. Later he told me that frustration led to his decision to buy Macy's."

Several months later, Bill Arnold retired. Associated would eventually be taken over following a brief fight, but not by Macy's.

Ed Finkelstein wasn't the only retailer that spring whose efforts to buy a bigger partner ended in failure.

In April 1984, Leslie Wexner, the quirky, art-collecting chairman of The Limited, based in Columbus, Ohio, launched a $1 billion takeover bid for Carter Hawley Hale Stores, Inc., the Los Angeles-based retailer. The move took Wall Street by surprise. A chronic underperformer, Carter Hawley Hale operated the specialty store chain Contempo Casuals; Bergdorf Goodman, the elegant Fifth Avenue retailer; and Neiman Marcus, the luxury department store group. Despite its promise, however, Carter Hawley Hale never succeeded in delivering the profits its shareholders expected. For the fiscal year ended January 1984, for example, The Limited earned $71 million on $1.08 billion in revenues, while Carter Hawley Hale earned less money on three times the sales, reporting profits of $67.5 million on revenues of $3.63 billion.

Considered by many to be one of the best merchants of his generation, Leslie Wexner opened his first store at the Kingsdale Shopping Center in Columbus in 1963. "It was the coolest place in town," says Carol Farmer, a retail consultant who shopped there as a teenager. Wexner rang up $160,000 in sales his first year and never looked back. More daring and self-assured than his contemporaries, Wexner spun his fashion ideas into a trendy retail empire of nearly one thousand stores nationwide. Company lore had it that at least fifty of his employees became millionaires because of their stock holdings, including some warehousemen.

Leslie Wexner was a wonder at forecasting the fashion tastes of teenagers. Waging a takeover fight was another matter. Instead of accepting Wexner's offer, Philip Hawley, Carter Hawley Hale's chairman, quickly orchestrated a buyback of company shares to keep them out of Wexner's hands. Hawley then sold $300 million worth of convertible preferred shares to General Cinema Corp., a soft-drink bottler and motion picture theater owner based in Chestnut Hill, Massachusetts. General Cinema, now known as Harcourt General Inc., also gained an option to buy the Walden Book Company, one of Carter Hawley Hale's most desirable divisions.

Within days, the battle was over. Disheartened by the unexpected turn of events, Wexner returned to Columbus in a snit. (He made a second run at Carter Hawley Hale in November 1986, but was again rebuffed. In its fight to remain independent, however, Carter Hawley Hale added so much debt that it eventually filed for Chapter 11 bankruptcy protection; the retailer's pension fund, which had invested heavily in Carter Hawley Hale stock, was devastated.)

Several seemingly unrelated issues now began to weave themselves together. As interest rates dropped, insurance and pension fund investors began buying high-yield junk bonds, making it easier for corporate raiders to raise funds. At the same time, Japanese management styles were coming into vogue, reflecting the booming Asian economy. As steel mills closed and the Big Three auto makers laid off workers, the American public began to show interest in fast-growing Japanese companies and their management styles.

American business culture was about to change. And few understood this more quickly than Herbert and Robert Haft of Washington, D.C. This intimidating father and son team operated the Dart Group, a holding company whose assets included the Crown discount bookstore chain; Trak Auto, an auto parts discounter; and considerable real estate.

Herbert Haft was a gifted retail pioneer who helped pave the way for the rapid growth of the discount store industry. Despite this, his tough, secretive manner made him few friends in the retail business that he had helped transform. By contrast, his oldest son, Robert, was accessible, gracious, and generally liked. A graduate of Harvard Business School, Robert Haft successfully transformed his thesis of "bigger, more, less expensive" into Crown Books, launching his career as a retailer.

The two Hafts first made national headlines in early 1985 when they acquired a block of shares in May Department Stores Inc. May, a well-managed business based in St. Louis, operated Hecht's in Washington, D.C., Kaufmann's in Pittsburgh, and Meier & Frank in Portland, Oregon. Although most doubted that the Hafts had the finances or the management skills to capture May, the department store retailer quickly put a large block of shares in friendly hands. Rather than launch a costly takeover fight they probably would have lost, the Hafts sold their shares for a $1.4 million profit.

Although the Hafts were chased away, Ed Finkelstein understood the significance of their bid. Size and performance would no longer be enough to guarantee the independence of any company.

By the spring of 1985, Macy's most senior executives were speculating that they would be raided next. Although the retailer's board had considered a poison pill, the matter was finally tabled without any action being taken. It was a highly principled stand, but one that didn't provide any comfort to the company's top managers.

Following one late Friday afternoon bull session, Macy's top in-house lawyer, Marvin Fenster, put together a leveraged buyout primer for Finkelstein and Mark Handler, Macy's president and chief operating officer. In his memo, Fenster explained that raiders typically borrowed against the assets of the companies they wanted to take over. If they succeeded, they then sold many of those same holdings to reduce debt.

Divvying up Macy's, whose holdings included four regional shopping centers and interests in six others, would be child's play. "There was not a doubt in my mind that we could be bought for the value of our real estate alone," says Fenster.

Then the April 29th issue of *Business Week* hit the newsstand.

In a smart and prescient story, the magazine identified Macy's, Allied Stores, and May Department Stores as likely takeover targets. Leveraged buyouts, takeovers, and mergers set a ten-year record in 1984, the magazine noted, and the pace was likely to accelerate in 1985. Retailers, with their rich real estate holdings often valued on their books at only a fraction of true worth, would prove irresistible.

Several days later, Finkelstein called Dick Dilworth and requested a private meeting. Dilworth agreed and suggested a breakfast at the Knickerbocker Club.

The two men were seated in the dining room on the club's second floor, only a few steps away from a view of General Burgoyne surrendering his troops at Saratoga. After they ordered, Finkelstein broached the subject that had brought them together.

Macy's was in a dangerous situation, he said. The company's stock was selling at less than $50 a share, down from nearly $65 in 1983. "What happens if an outsider shows up on our front door tomorrow?" Finkelstein finally blurted out. "What I want to do is talk with someone at Goldman, Sachs. I'd like to understand all my choices, including the possibility of buying the company."

"All right," Dilworth replied. "But maybe you should talk to more than one group of bankers and see what they have to say." Dilworth personally believed that it was reckless to consider replacing years of hard-earned equity with debt. But in light of the mood on Wall Street, he decided that Finkelstein was probably right about having to be prepared.

After finishing their meal, the two men walked outside. Finkelstein's chauffeured Mercedes was waiting at the corner, and he offered the older man a ride to his Rockefeller Center office. The last Dilworth saw of Macy's chairman that morning, he was disappearing in a cavalcade of traffic edging its way down Fifth Avenue.

Later that day, Dilworth called Donald Smiley, a fellow Macy's director, and repeated the morning's conversation. Smiley said he understood and hung up.

Several weeks later, Sidney James Weinberg Jr. of Goldman, Sachs & Co., left his office at 85 Broad Street and went uptown to visit Ed Finkelstein at Macy's Herald Square.

Sidney's father was a legendary Wall Street figure whose good judgment and trading skills had transformed Goldman, Sachs into one of the top private investment banking companies in the world. A confidant of some of the most powerful businessmen of his time, Weinberg had served on such prestigious boards as Ford Motor Co. and General Electric Co.

His youngest son, John, joined Goldman, Sachs immediately after graduating from Harvard Business School in 1950 and matured into one of the firm's most influential partners. In 1976 he was elected co-chairman of the company; eight years later, he took the reins by himself. His older brother, Sidney, who went by the nickname "Jimmy," also graduated from Harvard Business, but instead of joining Goldman, Sachs, he took a job at a division of Owens-Corning Fiberglas, Inc., where he worked for the next sixteen years. Although Jimmy Weinberg was elected a partner at Goldman, Sachs in 1967, two years after joining the firm, he was always more comfortable as a relationship banker than as a number-crunching deal maker. Macy's, where he had once worked in the curtain and drapery department, was one of his most important accounts, and he and Finkelstein knew and liked each other.

After Finkelstein welcomed Weinberg into his office, he emphasized how important it would be to keep everything they discussed completely confidential. When Weinberg said he understood, Finkelstein quickly opened up. Although he hadn't made up his mind, Finkelstein said, he was thinking about taking Macy's private through a leveraged buyout. He knew how such a bid would look to shareholders, Finkelstein continued, and he was set on paying top dollar. He didn't want anyone to ever say that he had stolen the business.

What he needed to know now was whether Goldman, Sachs would help him.

In the spring of 1985, Goldman, Sachs was one of the few surviving private partnerships on Wall Street. But what also set the firm apart was its refusal to participate in hostile takeovers, a long-standing policy that had cost it millions of dollars in fees.

Orchestrating management-led leveraged buyouts, however, was another matter. In the early 1980s, prompted by the success of Kohlberg Kravis Roberts & Co., and Forstmann Little & Co., Goldman, Sachs began advising executives how to acquire their companies. In some cases Goldman, Sachs invested in the buyouts it organized; in others, it raised the necessary capital in exchange for a fee. When this fledgling business began to show promise, the firm put it in the hands of Alfred Eckert III, a brash ten-year veteran who never left home without a fistful of Montecruz $2 cigars jammed into his jacket pocket.

Jimmy Weinberg would need someone to oversee Finkelstein's buyout. After returning to Goldman, Sachs's offices on Broad Street, Weinberg asked Eckert to step into his office. A few minutes later, he asked what he thought about Macy's chances of going private.

"The deal is going to cost a ton of money," Eckert said. "I'm not sure we can raise that much."

"I think it's something we ought to consider," replied Weinberg, peeved by Eckert's reaction. "Can't you at least think about it?"

The next day, Eckert, dressed in a spiffy blue suit, a white shirt with French cuffs, and one of his fifteen pairs of black Bally loafers, went with Weinberg to Macy's to meet Finkelstein.

The three men had barely finished shaking hands when Finkelstein turned to Eckert and said, "Why can't we do this deal? It's not that complicated."

Oh great, thought Eckert, this is going to be really fun.

The Macy's team that Eckert assembled at Goldman, Sachs included Jim Lane, a vice president of finance; Rita Reid, an associate in the leveraged buyout department; and Robert Kaplan, an associate in private finance. As they were sketching out their plans, Finkelstein called and invited Eckert to dinner. "If you're going to be my guy, I want to get to know you," said Finkelstein, in a conciliatory voice.

A few evenings later, Eckert, Finkelstein, and Mark Handler were standing on the terrace on the south side of Macy's thirteenth floor, admiring the glow of the city spread before them. After Eckert and Handler shared a round of vodka martinis, a uniformed waitress began to serve dinner. Throughout the meal, Finkelstein talked at length about Macy's real estate holdings, suggesting that the retailer's stores could be sold and leased back, or used as guarantees for some kind of mortgage-backed security.

After querying Eckert on how he thought Goldman, Sachs would structure the buyout, Finkelstein relaxed and began to talk about the attendant politics. Robert Schwartz, the chairman of the Metropolitan Life Insurance Company, sat on Macy's board, and Finkelstein was confident that Met Life would be a willing investor in his deal. Finkelstein was also on the board of Chase Manhattan Bank, and though the bank had shied away from investing in leveraged buyouts in the past, Finkelstein felt Chase might look more favorably on his deal.

Throughout the dinner, Mark Handler listened quietly. Handler, who was so good looking that some referred to him as the Clark Gable of Macy's, had been close friends with Finkelstein since 1958, when they worked together in the fabrics department. Since then, Finkelstein had guided Handler's career, ensuring that Handler was given opportunities for promotion. The two were so close that they even dressed alike.

Now, during a lull in the conversation, Handler leaned toward Eckert and said he had a question. When Eckert nodded, Handler asked him how old he was. Eckert replied that he was thirty-six.

Handler, nonplussed, slumped back in his chair and said, "Arghhhh."

By the time the last plates were being cleared away, Eckert decided that while Handler had some street smarts, he had no interest in the details of what would almost certainly be the biggest financial investment of his life. (Handler says he can't recall this meeting.)

Finkelstein, though, seemed to be keeping up nicely.

Three weeks later, Goldman, Sachs cobbled together a plan that called for Macy's chairman and other senior executives to buy the retail institution for about $3 billion. It would be the biggest leveraged buyout of a retail company in history. And not one of Macy's outside directors, including Dick Dilworth, knew a thing about it.

Chapter 3

"It was obvious that Ed was going to be a star."

Ed Finkelstein was a Barnumesque showman who relished shaping public taste and opinion. He worked on the hushed thirteenth floor of Macy's flagship store, safely sequestered behind $50,000 bulletproof glass doors that he had installed at the entrance to the executive corridor. Although the doors were designed to keep out irate shoppers and grandstanding union executives, secretaries found them so difficult to pull open that they often walked to the rear of the floor and entered via a normal door after punching in a secret password: 10001.

The five-digit number was Macy's zip code.

Each evening one of Finkelstein's three chauffeurs picked him up on West 34th Street and whisked him away, sometimes to the opera or the ballet, more often to a favorite restaurant such as the Four Seasons or the "21" Club. The trio of drivers, dressed like prep school students in gray slacks and blue blazers chosen for them by a Macy's merchant, were also professional bodyguards. All had trained in antiterrorist diversionary tactics at a driving school in North Carolina, reflecting the fear that American chief executives were tempting targets for kidnappers.

Safety, however, was only one reason for their double duty. The Internal Revenue Service treated the use of corporate chauffeurs as taxable personal income but accepted bodyguards as a legitimate expense—as long as they were part of a designated security program.

All three of Macy's drivers were on the payroll as employees of the company's security department.

The Macy's chief was a brooding, heavyset man with large, sympathetic brown eyes and a poet manqué's love of language. Macy's, he would intone, catered to shoppers, not consumers. His merchants didn't "market" anything, either. Instead, they picked and sold merchandise. His pet peeve, though, was the use of the word "must" in an annual review; for example, "Mr. Ward must improve his communications skills in order to be promoted."

As Finkelstein frequently reminded his associates, no one had to do anything.

Engagingly curious, Finkelstein would signal a good mood by asking colleagues about the books they were reading or the movies they had seen. Like all good merchants, he often pushed Macy's junior staffers to expand their personal horizons and develop their tastes. When young buyers would return from Paris fashion shows, excited about what they'd seen on the runways, he sat patiently, hearing them out. Then, almost casually, he asked what they most liked at the Louvre.

If they hadn't visited the famed museum, he "let them have it," in the words of one admirer.

Finkelstein held sway over 55,000 employees with a personality that slipped easily from bravado to bonhomie to chilling, withering tirades. Often he pummeled associates at the weekly Monday morning executive meetings, using his loud, powerful voice to scream, demand, and belittle. What he liked even better was when his staff turned on each other: this meant they cared. Those who couldn't tolerate it quit. Others accepted their beatings in silence and then stepped into the hallway while someone else took his licking. Often, only hours after such outbursts, Finkelstein would invite his victim into his office, put his arm around the person's shoulder, and offer encouragement. It was a captivating performance that left his listeners dazed, drained, and, more often than not, grateful. Robert "Bobby" Friedman, who was president of Bamberger's until August 1980, when he succeeded Mark Handler as the New Jersey division's chairman, jokingly referred to this experience as meeting "Mr. Zig and Mr. Zag." (Friedman was no softy, either. When a job applicant innocently asked him how he was feeling, Friedman turned and sneered, "A little fucking better than you. At least I have a job." Mr. Friedman declined comment.

Each year, senior vice presidents made a formal presentation to Finkelstein and Handler outlining their new objectives. At one such gathering, Dan Bergman, a former senior executive at Bamberger's, began by analyzing the use of retail space by gross margins rather than sales volume, the accepted Macy's yardstick.

Finkelstein listened for two minutes. Then he said, "Excuse me. Unless I'm missing something, the question arises as to why any chairman who thinks he is a merchant would let his director of stores step outside the responsibilities of his job to the extent where it could undermine the function of the entire organization. I wonder what I've got here, whether you people know what you're doing, and what's going on. I'm surrounded by maniacs."

When Finkelstein finally calmed down, Robert Friedman, to whom Bergman reported, said, "I guess Dan's done with his presentation." Finkelstein agreed that yes, he was finished, and the meeting came to a close.

Everybody then rose and trooped over to another side of the room for a cup of coffee. Bergman remained behind, shaking and wondering whether his career was finished. A minute or two later, though, Finkelstein came up to Bergman and asked if he had eaten yet at Le Bernardin, a new fish restaurant on East 51st Street. The restaurant was supposed to be great, Finkelstein continued, but he had decided not to go until he knew whether Bergman had been there or not.

Bergman understood then that his job was safe.

Few women at Macy's rose to positions of authority in such a macho atmosphere. One exception, however, was Barbara Bass, a respected merchant in the Macy's California division who resigned in 1980 to join Bloomingdale's. When Finkelstein expressed surprise after she rejected a last-minute offer of a top assignment at the Macy's New York division, Bass decided she owed him a frank explanation. "You run a boy's club," she said. "Since I don't use your locker room, that's going to be a problem for me."

If he was sometimes difficult, Finkelstein could also be both understanding and generous. After he was named chairman, one of his first decisions was to expand the health care benefits for the company's senior vice presidents, a group known as the "75 Club." "As soon as they got in, Mark and Eddie raised the per diem allowance for travel and decided that administrators could travel business class," says Dan Bergman. "If that wasn't available, you were allowed to fly first class."

Bergman would usually have criticized such excess. Soon after Finkelstein and Handler took office, however, he was asked if he would like the free use of a car. Bergman promptly rented a $21,000 BMW. A fellow Macy's executive, Bergman says, leased a $35,000 Mercedes. Twelve months later, Finkelstein decided that all seventy-five of Macy's senior vice presidents should enjoy a free car. Having learned a lesson, however, he limited the monthly rental stipend to $600.

Much to the astonishment of Sankar Krishnan, a senior vice president at Bamberger's, members of the "75 Club" were also allowed to put in for related expenses, including gasoline, monthly garage bills, and insurance. "We didn't have to pay a dime," says Krishnan. "I knew we made some foreign car dealers very happy." When the tax laws changed, Finkelstein made sure to cover the additional expense. By the time Krishnan left the company in 1988, he was being reimbursed $1,400 a month for his car. "They took care of us," he says.

High living became acceptable behavior at Macy's under the premise that whims could be indulged as long as profits increased every year. Besides, Finkelstein wanted his staff to eat and socialize together because he believed it nurtured stronger company ties. Often he hosted elaborate dinners himself, including one Christmas soiree at the posh Four Seasons restaurant. After his fellow executives sat down, Finkelstein raised his glass and toasted what had been yet another profitable holiday performance. Then he asked, "How many of you have bought new first homes or second homes this year?"

A number of hands went up.

Finkelstein looked around carefully, nodded his head in approval, and said, "Well, I guess the rest of you don't need raises."

Everyone laughed—but there was a nugget of insight in that joke. Finkelstein wanted Macy's staffers to spend their money because he knew it would encourage them to work even harder the following year. Many approved of his rough-and-tumble style, too. They appreciated his willingness to let his top merchants take big risks, and that he rewarded them if they succeeded. There was also pride in knowing that Macy's was outperforming Federated Department Stores and May Department Stores, the retailer's two most important competitors.

"Ed gave you style," says Ted Newman, a former Macy's senior vice president for personnel. "It was an attitude that said: as long as we're doing well, there's no reason we shouldn't all enjoy it. And that created great closeness and great affection for the company. Whatever happened later, I think you'll find that the people who worked at Macy's were very happy there. Herbert Mines, who once worked in personnel at the company, used to say that Macy's staffers always asked one question that no one else ever asked when they were looking for a job: will I like the people?"

On weekends, Finkelstein and his wife escaped to Flying Brook Farm, a lush country estate that he purchased in April 1982 for $419,500. A two-hour drive from New York City, the 105-acre property in Litchfield, Connecticut, featured gently rolling hills, manicured lawns, and a twelve-room contemporary house complete with a paneled library, huge picture windows, and a climate-controlled wine cellar. Elsewhere on the grounds were a colonial "saltbox" built in 1740; a swimming pool; a tennis court; a henhouse; a man-made waterfall; and a pond-side picnic area. In a decision that others would later question, Finkelstein allowed Macy's own design staff to help order and choose the furnishings for his new home. One former Macy's employee says he was told to go to Finkelstein's former house in Westport, Connecticut, to photograph the furniture in it so that decisions could be made as to which pieces would be kept, and which would be sold.

A gracious host, Finkelstein's social circle widened to include many celebrities who had second homes in the area. "We went to some of the same dinner parties but most of his friends in New York were pals from his home in Litchfield," says Leonard Lauder, chief executive of Estée Lauder, the cosmetics company. "These were people like Abraham Ribicoff, Jim Hoge, Bill Blass, and Henry Kissinger." Others Finkelstein befriended included the late Lady Slim Keith; the late tennis star Arthur Ashe; the late actress Audrey Hepburn; Geraldine Stutz, a former president of Henri Bendel; and Walter Cronkite. Jim Hoge, a former publisher of the New York *Daily News,* says Finkelstein loved to stand outside and watch the sun set over his waterfall and pool while he tended to his guests. "Ed was always congenial," says Hoge. "His wife, Myra, was quieter, a supporter and confidante to her husband. We'd have a drink, talk, and then go home early, like everyone in the country."

On Monday mornings, Finkelstein would sometimes arrive at the office clutching supermarket-type egg cartons. On the top of each was an adhesive label that read Flying Brook Farm in burgundy and white, Macy's signature colors. Inside were eggs laid by his own hens, a reference to his own past. Finkelstein then dispensed those eggs in plain brown cartons throughout the Macy's executive floor, much as teachers awarded gold stars in grade school. No notes were attached. They were just eggs, eggs from Ed.

Those lucky enough to receive eggs let them sit all day on the desks of their secretaries. Everyone understood. Eggs were a sign of Finkelstein's favor. But those who didn't get them sulked. Such was the importance of these eggs that when a much-admired top executive quit, word spread that one of his complaints was that Finkelstein had not rewarded him with eggs often enough.

"Who got eggs and who didn't get eggs, and how often somebody got eggs, was probably the most important thing at Macy's," says one former staffer. "Eggs were a sign you were loved, and being loved was what it was all about. If you got eggs one week, and somebody else got them the next week, you weren't concerned, because you already had your eggs. But if you never got eggs, you started to worry."

As some knew, those eggs were a sly reminder of Finkelstein's childhood. Although family lore had it that the Finkelsteins once advised the czar in Mother Russia, in Passaic, New Jersey, where they put down roots before the turn of the century, they sold butter and eggs.

Maurice Finkelstein, the youngest of eleven children, was born in Passaic in 1899. Twenty-four years later, he married Eva Levine, moved to New Rochelle, New York, and opened a wholesale butter and eggs business with his brother Louis. The two partners did business as Windsor Dairy and Spencer Farms, names that conjured up the lush English countryside and the promise of better days to come.

Edward Sidney Finkelstein, Maurice and Eva's only son, made his entrance into the world on March 30, 1925. Several years later, the family moved to nearby Mount Vernon, New York, where the tracks of the New Haven Railroad neatly divided the city in half. The newer, more affluent homes were to the north, with the less attractive, two-family houses and apartment buildings to the south. The Finkelsteins lived on the south side, in a small, tight-knit neighborhood, in a home they rented. "We never thought of ourselves as poor, and we never went hungry," says Thelma "Timmy" Weinberg, née Finkelstein, who was born nearly six years after her brother. "But the times were tough. One of our next door neighbors worked for a railroad that went out of business, and I don't think he ever had another job."

Today Mount Vernon is a community struggling to overcome crime and drugs. But during the 1930s, this New York City bedroom community promoted itself as "The City of Homes," an open, friendly place where newcomers were welcome. There were five synagogues in town, including the conservative Jewish Center of Mount Vernon, where the Finkelsteins were active members.

There is a dreamy quality to most childhoods, especially those recollected decades later, and that is how many of Ed Finkelstein's earliest friends remember their youth. "This was a generation that listened to its parents, that didn't drink, and didn't smoke," says Herman Geist, a prominent Westchester attorney who first met Finkelstein in third grade. "Not that we didn't horse around. Eddie and I were bar mitzvahed together, and I still remember him patting a Hebrew school teacher on the back with a chalk eraser and then climbing out of a window to escape."

There were two local high schools. One, Edison, specialized in vocational classes. The second, A. B. Davis, was a well-regarded collegiate high school whose graduates include music man Dick Clark and Ralph Branca, who as a Brooklyn Dodgers pitcher would give up one of baseball's most famous home runs to New York Giants slugger Bobby Thomson. In 1942, the year that Ed Finkelstein graduated, Davis students won twelve of the twenty-five Regents scholarships awarded in the county.

It was a world in which Ed Finkelstein excelled. Although his sister says their parents never pushed them to study, Finkelstein was elected to Tau Epsilon Pi, an honor society for students who maintained an 85 average for two years. He was also chosen president of Omega Delta, one of two Jewish fraternities in his high school, and voted most likely to succeed by his peers. "Eddie was a smart guy in what was a fantastic class," says Joel Freedman, a business executive who graduated with Finkelstein. "We had the first person to score a hundred on a state Regents examination. A black student, Wesley Parker, translated the Gettysburg Address into Latin for fun." Years later, at Macy's, Finkelstein re-created that world by surrounding himself with sharp

Jewish guys willing to spend weekends at his country place, swimming in his pool and playing doubles on his tennis court.

Finkelstein dated Eila Rader during his senior year, sometimes taking her to New York City to hear band leader Tommy Dorsey at the Café Rouge. "Eddie was always one of the boys, self-confident, handsome and thin," says Rader, who still lives in Westchester. "I remember his mother as pretty. His father was heavy and portly, the way Eddie became later in life. When we dated, Eddie liked to spend Sunday with his parents, and we'd pop in on them during the afternoon. He and his family were very close, very loving."

Finkelstein won a partial scholarship to Harvard. He was the first member of his family to attend college. A photograph published in the *Maroon and White* high school yearbook of 1942 shows a wavy-haired young man wearing a jacket with wide lapels, a shirt with long collar stays, and a tie with a geometric pattern. He has a faint smile, dark eyes, and the look of someone who hasn't yet tested his limits.

That May, his class was the first to hold its graduation ceremony during the day instead of at night. With the country at war, Mount Vernon was doing its part by saving electricity.

Finkelstein entered Harvard as a member of one of the college's largest freshmen classes. He lived at Kirkland House, studied economics, and waited on tables to earn pocket money. Recalls Dr. Daniel Shields, a physician in Maine, "Ed always saw the bright side of everything. The country was at war, and we were all nervous because we knew we were going to go. But he worked hard, studied hard, and kept smiling the whole time. You could trust him as far as you could anybody in the world."

Like many classmates, Finkelstein joined the Navy's V–12 training program. He eventually served as a ship's radio operator before he returned to Harvard and graduated cum laude in 1947. Finkelstein earned his MBA (with distinction) from Harvard Business School in June 1948, moved to New York City, and joined Macy's training squad.

Shortly afterward, he met Myra Schuss on a blind date at a music festival in Tanglewood, Massachusetts. He married her in August 1950, a month before his father died. Schuss, a bright, introspective woman who would later earn graduate degrees in education and clinical psychology, was raised in New York City, where her father operated a small retail store. Later her parents moved to Mount Vernon, buying a house only a block away from where Eila Rader grew up. "Her family was intellectual, and Myra was bright and attractive," says Rader. "He couldn't have found a nicer girl."

The young couple's first son, Mitchell, was born in May 1952; a second, Daniel, was born in October 1954; and a third, Robert, followed in January 1958. Sadly, the two younger children each suffered from chronic illnesses. Daniel was diagnosed as a diabetic when he was two years old, while Robert was born with cystic fibrosis, a serious, often fatal, genetic lung disease that requires constant medical attention. Robert also suffered from diabetes.

"Of course it affected Ed and Myra," says Thelma Weinberg. "They had to study and learn how to care for their children. But they did what they had to do. Nobody gets out of this life unscathed."

Finkelstein would have a storybook career at Macy's, part Horatio Alger, part Knute Rockne. Lean, big-shouldered, and blessed with a God-given flair for the dramatic, he was soon buying dress linings and managing the sixth-floor fabrics department at Macy's Herald Square, where the formaldehyde fumes from new fall woolens stung the eyes each summer. "It was obvious that Ed was going to be a star," says Richard Echikson, a New Jersey–based retailing consultant who worked for Finkelstein as his assistant during that period. "He confided in you, he brought you along, and because he was on the fast track, you were too."

Finkelstein was moving fast because Herbert Seegal was pushing him. Seegal, an intense, reserved Bostonian, joined Macy's during the spring of 1953 in the role of a senior merchant, the first outsider in decades to be given a major job. On his first day at work, Seegal noticed each piece of office furniture was tagged and numbered, as though it had been readied for an auctioneer's gavel. When he asked why, he learned that Macy's was so pressed for cash that it had hocked all of its assets, including his desk and chair.

A workaholic who considered himself a sophisticated ladies' man, Seegal was most comfortable when talking about the business. A secretary he once dated complained that Seegal barely said a word through dinner until she asked him about Macy's. Then she couldn't shut him up. Despite his overwhelming interest in work, however, he refused to socialize with anyone at Macy's, explaining, "I can't eat dinner with somebody on Friday night and then fire him on Monday."

Seegal talked tough, but he was a gifted teacher. In one training class, he pulled out a pocket handkerchief and neatly placed it on the floor. Then he got down on his knees, put his hands together, prayer-like, and said, "This is what you have to do sometimes. Don't be afraid to beg manufacturers for markdown money if you need it." On another occasion, he was discovered lying faceup at the Herald Square store, as still as a corpse. When a nervous fellow executive bent over to take his pulse, Seegal lifted his head and said, "See that spotlight? It's in the wrong place. It should be focused directly on the mannequin."

There were, in the beginning, some sweet moments. New to the city, Seegal spent hours each day darting into offices, asking secretaries where they bought their last blouse, their last sweater, their last pair of shoes. Then he studied each department, walking the floors with Jack Straus, Macy's chairman, arguing over how to choose and price assortments. Seegal disliked Macy's style of displaying handbags and other accessories on huge tables, and arranging them in long, separate rows by price.

Seegal believed that money was the last thing on a customer's mind when she bought something she intended to use every day. If she wanted a key case, she was more interested in the number of keys it held, whether it was made from cotton or leather, and its color, he insisted. And if she happened to see a case she liked sitting next to a matching handbag, she just might buy both. Intent on proving his theory, Seegal built a series of handsome display islands. Then he pulled together an assortment of wallets, key cases, and handbags, and matched them by color.

When sales nearly doubled during the first month, Jack Straus pronounced himself amazed.

More often, though, Seegal went home at night glum and frustrated. "Macy's was struggling, trying to pay its bills, always trying to sell cheap goods with double truck ads in the *Daily News*," he says. "I wanted to sell goods at full price, and what I needed were cohorts, people to help me."

Seegal would never be the warmest star in the Macy's constellation, but he was a master at recognizing talent and putting a stamp on a business. When it became clear that most of the older Macy's managers didn't like the idea of a "kid" telling them what to do, he began hunting for younger managers to convert into protégés. He found three working in the fabrics department: Ed Finkelstein; Mark Handler, Macy's future president; and Herbert Friedman, who would later become chairman of the Macy's Atlanta division.

Years later, of course, Seegal would say that Finkelstein was his greatest discovery. "Ed was eager and bright, and even though his [fabrics] business was going down, I could see that he had spark," says Seegal, who retired as president of the Macy's corporation in August 1980, after turning sixty-five. "All he wanted was somebody to talk to about the business."

Seegal also liked Finkelstein's swagger. By tradition, company employees addressed Jack Straus as "Mister Jack." Finkelstein, though, refused to go along, and instead made a point of loudly greeting Straus by his first name. The behavior amused Finkelstein's friends, but it also established him as a man intent on making his own way.

There were many ambitious Ivy League graduates at Macy's during the early 1950s. Finkelstein, though, would be remembered as one of the few who willingly nurtured younger employees. Generous, smart, and good-natured, he built relationships that lasted decades. "Ed recruited people and pulled them close to him," says Elliot S. Jaffe, chairman of Dress Barn Inc., a women's specialty store chain based in Suffern, New York, who worked at Macy's during that period. "When he lived in Westport during the 1950s, he had a baseball team of guys who would literally show up at his house on Saturday mornings and play ball."

When Herb Seegal was named president of Bamberger's in 1962, he made Finkelstein his top merchant. Finkelstein, in turn, brought Mark Handler with him across the river. One former Macy's executive says the depth of that friendship became clear at a divisional staff meeting in Kansas City. Finkelstein and Handler had flown out to give annual performance reviews, with Finkelstein opening the morning meeting with a polished speech about consumer spending. Handler followed, apparently half hungover from the night before. Reaching into his pocket, he finally pulled out a tattered sheet of paper, looked up, and said, "Okay, I'm not going to win any awards for neatness." Finkelstein looked on approvingly throughout, nodding his head with respect.

A year after moving to Bamberger's, Finkelstein and Seegal named Philip Schlein, a talented baby-faced twenty-six-year-old, to be their administrator of lingerie and accessories. Together with Mark Handler, the new Bamberger's team transformed the New Jersey division into Macy's biggest moneymaker.

"Ed had the ability to see things in three dimensions, so he knew how he wanted the stores to look in terms of light, layout, and departments," says Joseph Nagy, a former Bamberger's executive. "When Jack Straus was in charge, you could stand anywhere in a store and see a sea of clothing racks. Ed and Herb changed that by offering the customers niches tailored to specific needs. It was the start of boutique retailing."

Seegal and Finkelstein would make a formidable team. When they started, Bamberger's was earning a 6 percent pretax profit, the highest in the company. When they both moved on to bigger jobs seven years later, Bamberger's was enjoying pretax profits of 10 percent. They did it by devoting more space to cosmetics, redesigning the Young Men's area, and aggressively promoting consumer electronics. Despite their success, however, the two men gradually drifted apart. Seegal was abrasive and dominating, and Finkelstein, a forceful personality in his own right, grew tired of his role as student. Senior Macy's executives noticed, and when Seegal was promoted to a new job at the Macy's New York division in 1969, Finkelstein was transferred to San Francisco as president of Macy's California. In New Jersey, Mark Handler succeeded Finkelstein as president of Bamberger's, while Phil Schlein replaced Handler as a senior vice president.

Seegal shrugged off the strains in his relationship with Finkelstein and saw to it that his protégé was given an odometer at his going away party, a tribute to Finkelstein's record of having commuted from Connecticut without missing a day's work in five years. "Nobody outworked him," says Seegal.

In his new post, Finkelstein reported to James Lundy, a twenty-two-year Macy's California veteran who had been named divisional chairman at the same time that Finkelstein was promoted. Shortly after arriving at the Macy's offices in San Francisco, however, Finkelstein made it clear that he had no use for him.

"Ed began to make a lot of trips back to New York, and he didn't keep me apprised of what he was doing," says Lundy. What irked him even more was Finkelstein's habit of greeting the office secretaries and then closing his door. Lundy, who always kept his own door open, eventually realized that he was being frozen out of day-to-day affairs. Although Fredrick G. Atkinson, Macy's top personnel manager, made three trips to San Francisco in an effort to patch over the differences, it became obvious that Lundy and Finkelstein would never get along. Lundy was then fired.

"That was all right," he says. "I wasn't having any fun anymore."

With Lundy gone, Finkelstein renovated the Macy's Union Square store in downtown San Francisco. He tossed out the store's budget lines, replacing them with more expensive clothes. He also built new fixtures in an effort to attract more affluent shoppers. At the same time, he chose a new team of buyers and merchants. Twelve months later, the California division was on the rebound; before he left, pre-tax profits had climbed from 3 to 8 percent. "Ed didn't tell you how to get from point A to point B, but he made you want to come in every day and work like hell," says Al Artieres, a former senior vice president at Macy's California. "Jim Lundy was a good man, but Ed built a fire under you."

The turning point came in November 1972, when Macy's California opened The Cellar, an arcade of boutiques crowded with kitchen gadgets, chopping blocks, cutlery, plates, and housewares. Twinkling lights were strung along the ceiling, creating a cheery, holiday mood, while coffee mugs were displayed on carpenter nails, a reminder that San Francisco was a city of dedicated coffee drinkers. The walls were constructed from weathered barn siding, and old kitchen tables and hand-cranked cornhuskers were placed throughout to enhance the country mood. The customers loved it, and The Cellar was soon hailed as one of the city's most exciting retail experiences.

Many would claim credit. Orris Willard, a skilled construction engineer who built Macy's West Coast stores on time and under budget, says he conceptualized The Cellar while vacationing in Hawaii. "I wanted it rustic, not spit and polish," says the former senior vice president. "I told Ed that I had a new idea for selling housewares, and he let me go ahead. That was his contribution." Al Artieres says he developed the concept after being inspired by the wide boulevards of Paris, Mexico, and Berlin. "Ed always takes credit for everything," he grumps. Bob Huck, a retired San Francisco architect, says it was his idea to present merchandise in a series of small shops.

When a newspaper article about The Cellar appeared in *Home Furnishings Daily,* a trade publication, Finkelstein sent the clipping to Willard, along with a note that read, "Will. For your collection of your accomplishments." Willard, a pack rat, kept both. Years later, while on a trip to New York, he visited Finkelstein and said, "Ed, I've heard so much about how you did The Cellar that I wanted you to have this." Willard then handed him the original article, reprinted in color and laminated in plastic. He also gave him a copy of the note Finkelstein had written years earlier.

Willard says Finkelstein threw the note in the garbage can. The plaque, however, was prominently displayed for years.

Impressed by Finkelstein's resourcefulness, Donald Smiley, Macy's chairman, brought him back to New York in December 1973. Smiley was so eager for Finkelstein to return that he rented him a Fifth Avenue apartment and put a car and driver at his disposal. The company's New York division was losing money, and the Herald Square flagship was so dilapidated that Herb Seegal wanted to close several of the 100,000-square-foot floors and rent them to furniture dealers. There were even discussions about converting part of the building into a parking structure.

"I told Ed that we had more space than we needed," says Seegal. "His answer was: when you have the space, use it."

Every great downtown store has a signature statement. At Macy's Herald Square, it was the fifty-three bargain tables scattered across the main floor. Bowed under stacks of 19-cent irregular cutlery, $3 men's shirts, and $199 fur coats, the tables generated an impressive $10 million a year in revenues. Jack Straus considered the tables so important that he had a daily sales tally taken at 1 P.M. By mid-afternoon, slow sellers were dispatched to the bowels of the world's largest department store, presumably never to be seen again.

Ed Finkelstein, though, didn't return to New York to oversee a failing variety store. Declaring that Macy's needed a new "ambiance," he ordered that the tables be removed.

In quick succession, Finkelstein also closed the first-floor drug department, the liquor department that sold Macy's brand Old Whaler bourbon and York House scotch, and the budget dress department squirreled away in the basement. Even the pet shop—where hundreds of parakeets had escaped over the years, raining down their modest droppings on unsuspecting customers—went the way of the dodo bird.

It was a daring strategy. In 1974, Macy's Herald Square generated only $165 million in revenues, with the bargain tables, the drug business, and the budget dress area contributing $10 million each, or roughly 20 percent of the total.

Much as he had done in California, Finkelstein was hitching his future to baby boomers and their enthusiasm for designer labels and pasta makers. After persuading Smiley to invest $15 million in new fixtures and remodeling, Finkelstein launched a major rebuilding effort that included the sixth floor, which then offered mostly housewares, and the basement, with its tacky budget store.

"It was an intense period," says Gordon Cooke, who joined Macy's in 1975 as a senior vice president in charge of sales promotion. "Ed would take everyone out to the yacht club at Montauk and get the biggest table he could find. Then he'd lay out different views of each floor, talking about traffic patterns and what he thought Macy's should look like. Ed was a master of this, of perceiving what kinds of businesses Macy's should be in, what Macy's should concentrate on, and how customers would perceive the decor of the store. I used to think that was the kind of work other people did. Ed felt it was the key."

Intent on polishing Macy's public image, Finkelstein also brought back Macy's Fourth of July fireworks as part of the nation's Bicentennial celebrations. Gordon Cooke arranged for a tie-in with the Walt Disney Co. and persuaded the French government to donate the fireworks. In his enthusiasm, he even agreed to fly in kleig spotlights and backlight the Statue of Liberty. He also ignored the fact that he was way over budget. One morning, however, Finkelstein called him to his office. "I walked in, very nervous, and Ed asked me to sit down," says Cooke. "He said, 'Listen, if I don't know about something and someone tells me, I can't defend you. I might have done exactly the same thing if I were in your shoes. But it would have been a lot easier for you if you had me as your partner.' " Macy's, he added, would find the extra $200,000.

Finkelstein understood Macy's couldn't compete with the city's top retailers when it came to designer clothing. However, the Herald Square store was still admired for its home furnishings, and he decided to capitalize on that while creating a new fashion business.

As part of the refurbishment of the sixth floor, Finkelstein built floor-to-ceiling shelving that flanked the perimeter walls. He then filled those shelves with hundreds of yellow, red, and blue towels, creating a rainbow of color. He also added a mind-numbing array of comforters, pillowcases, pillow shams, down-filled pillows, polyester pillows, decorative pillows, coordinated window treatments, mattress pads, blankets, and fitted and flat sheets in twin, full, queen, and king sizes.

It was dramatic, it was fun, and it became the industry standard: shoppers who walked in looking for a single item often left clutching full shopping bags. Finkelstein even coined a phrase to describe his merchandising strategy. Macy's was "distorting" the business, he said. Any store could sell a set of sheets. But only merchants could create a fantasy world. Early in his career, Finkelstein had emphasized the need to show customers the merchandise. Now he was proving it.

The new sixth floor opened in September 1976, followed by a new version of The Cellar. Joseph Cicio, Macy's design major domo, created a wide, brightly-lit, terra-cotta center aisle surrounded by boutiques that sold small electronics and fancy imported kitchen gear. It even included a pharmacy, The Apothecary, which had been relocated from the first floor. This version of The Cellar proved an even bigger success than the original in San Francisco.

Then Macy's got lucky. When Alexander's and Korvette's opened for business on Sundays late in the fall of 1976, Finkelstein insisted on following suit. Bloomingdale's, though, fought the Sunday openings, and its opposition provided Macy's with an opportunity to lure affluent Upper East Side shoppers to Herald Square. Soon newspaper ads were reminding readers that the RR and N subway lines stopped at Macy's Herald Square as well as 59th Street and Lexington Avenue. Choirs, marching bands, and bagpipers were also invited to perform, creating a carnival-like sense of excitement throughout the store.

When P. J. Clarke's opened a stylish new restaurant, all of New York finally noticed. "Retailing was heating up in the city," says Marvin Traub, the former chairman of Bloomingdale's, a unit of Federated Department Stores. "We didn't feel we'd gotten worse. Rather, we thought our competition, particularly Macy's, had gotten better."

When the Macy's board of directors met in the summer of 1980 to elect a new chairman, Ed Finkelstein was the only serious candidate. "He was viewed as exceptionally talented and deserving of the job," says Harold Shaub, a former chief executive of the Campbell Soup Company and an outside director at the time. "I regarded Ed as a damned good merchandiser, and I had every reason to believe he was a good administrator as well."

Only Donald Smiley and Herb Seegal, each of whom had reached the mandatory retirement age of sixty-five, expressed doubts. Both questioned whether Finkelstein had the discipline and maturity to run the business, suggesting that the board might want to hunt for other candidates. One reason for their concern involved a well-publicized incident that took place in 1975, when Finkelstein told Smiley that he was so tired of being criticized by Seegal that he would quit if Seegal ever walked into his office again. He was drawing a line, Finkelstein said, and he didn't want Seegal crossing it.

"I heard about that meeting, but Don never mentioned it to me," says Seegal, still annoyed nearly two decades later. "If he had, Ed and I would have had fireworks. Smiley knew that, so he calmed Ed down without angering me."

Despite the reservations expressed by Smiley and Seegal, Finkelstein was blessed by the full board. Finkelstein in turn named Mark Handler to succeed Seegal as Macy's president and chief operating officer. If Finkelstein knew that Smiley and Seegal had singled out Handler as a possible candidate to be chairman, he never mentioned it.

During the years that followed Herb Seegal's retirement, he was never invited to attend a Thanksgiving Day Parade, or to any other Macy's event. When other company executives saw that he was no longer welcome, they too began to shun him.

"I never could put it together in a mosaic that made sense," says Seegal. "Why would anybody frighten people to the point that they were unnerved to talk to me? One guy walked right past me at the opera. Another discovered that we were at the same dinner party and trembled so much that he couldn't finish his drink. It was pathetic."

In the spring of 1986, months after Finkelstein announced his intentions of buying the company, his investment bankers sponsored a sales presentation in Los Angeles to excite potential investors. Among the crowd was Robert Straus, whose brother, Jack, had served as Macy's chairman for decades. Instead of joining Macy's, Robert had gone on to invest in a variety of media properties. Yet he had a life-long interest in the company, and he wanted to hear what Finkelstein had to say.

During a break, Robert approached Finkelstein, introduced himself, and said, "I understand you're a protégé of Herb Seegal." Instantly Finkelstein's smile disappeared. "That's not true at all," Finkelstein said. "He didn't teach me a thing."

Straus quickly apologized and walked away. At day's end, he decided not to invest.

To his credit, Finkelstein was often at his best when others were involved in a personal crisis. When doctors discovered that Sankar Krishnan had a polyp on his colon, for example, Finkelstein, who was a trustee of St. Vincent's Hospital in Greenwich Village, arranged for a top surgeon there to perform the operation. Finkelstein also took Krishnan aside and said that Macy's would provide him with a private room and twenty-four-hour-a-day nurse. When Krishnan expressed concern about the costs, Finkelstein assured him that Macy's would pay for anything not covered by the company's insurance plan.

Four days after Krishnan underwent surgery, Finkelstein knocked on his hospital door and walked in. He was visiting his son, Robert, Finkelstein explained, but he wanted to say hello.

Krishnan was still so weak that he could barely speak. But Finkelstein lingered for an hour, talking to Krishnan's wife, Susan, and entertaining them both. "Ed didn't have to do that," says Krishnan. "It showed how much he cared, and I was very appreciative. In those days, that's how Macy's operated."

Krishnan's rise through the company's ranks reflected Macy's reputation as a meritocracy. Born in Coimbatore, India, a textile center, Krishnan earned a master's degree in chemical engineering at the University of Waterloo in Ontario, Canada, before moving to the United States in the summer of 1970. Anxious to find a temporary job before looking for a position in his field, Krishnan went to work at the Newark Bamberger's, where he counted pillows in the sub-basement. A few weeks later, he applied for a position as a junior budget analyst. When he completed his first task in one day instead of a week, he was hired. Krishnan quickly moved up the ranks and held key posts at Macy's Midwest and then Macy's South. By 1981, he was doing so well that when the chief financial officer's job opened up at Macy's South, he expected it would be offered to him. Instead, the post went to someone else.

Krishnan flew to New York to see Finkelstein. After he explained how angry and disappointed he was at being passed over, Finkelstein shrugged and said, "It's a big company, and people will get recognized at the appropriate time." Instead of ending the conversation, however, Finkelstein began to reminisce about how he had struggled to become a senior vice president. And before the meeting ended, he suggested that something good would happen to Krishnan in the near future. "I went in feeling angry, and left feeling very good," says Krishnan. "I didn't get anything, but Finkelstein was a good listener. What really mattered to me was that he had shared something of himself." Five months later, Krishnan was named senior vice president and controller of Bamberger's.

There would be other instances in which Finkelstein extended himself on behalf of those far below him on the company ladder. He once interceded with the police on behalf of the child of a favorite elevator operator. He also saved the job of a longtime employee who had been put on notice immediately after reporting that $20 in change was missing from her register. "I felt so badly I thought the world was going to come to an end," says Julia Wolff. "My name had been dirtied. A few minutes after I was put on notice I saw Ed. I went over to him and cried like an infant. Then I said, 'Can you help me?' The matter was dropped right away. He was a beautiful person, a real man." Such stories made their way throughout the company, burnishing Finkelstein's reputation as someone who cared about those who worked there.

Finkelstein did not stint when it came to his own needs, either. Occasionally the company's board of directors challenged him, but not often, and only rarely with success. In 1982, for example, he suggested that it was time for Macy's to buy a corporate jet. The company was expanding into new markets, he said, and a plane would be a welcome addition for real estate staffers who were spending long hours hunting for potential store sites.

Donald Smiley, the former chairman, argued that Macy's had survived for decades without such extravagances. Jack Straus, who preceded Smiley as chairman, also thought the plane was a waste of money and told one confidant that he thought Finkelstein was getting "too big for his britches." After mulling it over, though, the board gave its approval. Macy's was making so much money that the directors could afford to indulge their chairman.

In due time, Macy's acquired a blue-and-white Gulfstream II from

Chase Manhattan Bank for about $8 million. After Dick Dilworth interceded, the sale also included the right to have the plane piloted and serviced by the Wayfarer Ketch Corporation, a Rockefeller-owned company that maintained the Gulfstream II when it belonged to Chase. Wayfarer Ketch derived its unusual name from *The Wayfarer,* a yacht that had once belonged to the Rockefeller clan. What interested Finkelstein, however, was not the service company's blue blood pedigree but the fact that it also managed planes owned by Time Inc., Chase Manhattan Bank, and the Rockefellers. As Finkelstein knew, an old boy's arrangement enabled Wayfarer's clients to borrow aircraft from one another as needed, exchanging equal amounts of flight time on their planes in lieu of cash.

Ed Finkelstein didn't need the services of another jet. But he was often able to borrow a helicopter on weekends and fly in style to his country estate in Connecticut, landing in the grassy pasture across the road from his house. (Dick Dilworth argued strongly against Finkelstein and Handler riding in the same plane together, since an accident might eliminate Macy's two most senior executives. Finkelstein considered the notion a foolish waste of time, particularly since the two so often visited the same location. Eventually a study was done on the accident rate per 100,000 miles flown for general aviation and the two Macy's executives continued to fly together. For his part, once Jack Straus accepted the idea of Macy's owning a plane, he argued for one with four engines, not two.)

For two years, Macy's made do with the former Chase aircraft. Then Finkelstein decided that he wanted a faster, larger, better-equipped plane. What he had in mind was a ten-passenger Gulfstream III, the Cadillac of the private jet industry. The price tag was about $14 million, with maintenance adding another $1 million a year or so in costs. This time the board expressed its doubts. Macy's had already built a new luxurious boardroom modeled after one used by Chase Manhattan, and there was the sense that the spending was getting out of hand. But like many Fortune 500 companies that purchased jets during the 1980s, Macy's directors concluded that such perks were necessary to keep its talented chief executive in place.

"Sure, you think of Sam Walton, working from his simple desk," says Stephen DuBrul Jr., a Macy's director at the time. "But Ed was a professional manager, not an owner. Macy's was making a lot of money, and it wasn't an issue we wanted to go to sword's point over." The former Chase plane was subsequently sold to a ministry owned by Jimmy Swaggart.

Macy's new Gulfstream III was delivered with its interior bare, and its exterior aluminum skin painted dusty green with zinc chromate to prevent corrosion. In quick order, Joseph Cicio, Macy's tastemaker, oversaw the installation of a fully-equipped galley; certain chairs that folded down, enabling users to stretch out and sleep; and four chairs that were built, padded, and upholstered to Finkelstein's specifications. One of the chairs was lugged up to Finkelstein's office so that he could give it a "test seating."

Afterward, the jet's exterior was painted white with burgundy stripes on the tail. Burgundy was Macy's official color and graced its shopping bags as well as its charge cards.

According to one figure, Macy's was then advised to stock Melmac plastic plates and glasses. Most small jets aren't equipped with dishwashers, which means that dirty dishes are offloaded and cleaned by powerful, high-temperature commercial machines.

But hard plastic doesn't create a sense of elegant living. So Cicio instead stocked the jet with Lenox china, Christofle silver-plated flatware, and Orrefors crystal glasses. As predicted, the expensive glasses and plates often chipped and cracked while being cleaned, and had to be replaced at considerable expense. (One Macy's former executive denies that plastic plates were ever mentioned and notes that many corporate jets use good china and glasses.)

James York, a Macy's director who headed up the company's real estate division, found it all rather amusing. Although York was responsible for approving every site selection, he never once flew on a Macy's aircraft. Instead, he used commercial airliners. "I traveled that way for more than forty years without a problem," he says.

Soon after Macy's directors agreed to purchase the Gulfstream III, Finkelstein made yet another request. The one-bedroom apartment that Macy's provided for his use at 800 Fifth Avenue was no longer big enough, he said. As chairman, he needed a home that would be more appropriate for entertaining. More importantly, he wanted Macy's to buy it for him.

Finkelstein was then earning $781,000 in salary and another $150,000 in deferred compensation. Although he wasn't the highest-paid executive in the retail industry, it was a generous package by company standards, and after much discussion, the board decided that if

in needed to host dinner parties at home, he could rent a
? or formal hall. The company would then reimburse him.
but Finkelstein persisted, and the board finally bought him a new
place to live. In April 1985, Macy's paid $2.6 million for a two-story
carriage house at 77 East 77th Street. The landmark building featured
a huge living room and an eat-in breakfast area separated from the
kitchen by a hand-laid brick archway. There was also a bar and sauna
in the basement, while the upstairs master bedroom boasted his-and-
hers walk-in closets and an octagonal-shaped bathroom that included
a stall shower, a toilet behind a glass door, and a bathtub.

In a rather considerate gesture, the board also gave Finkelstein the
right to purchase the property at the original price. Or, if he preferred, Finkelstein would share in the profits when the building was
sold. At the time real estate prices were climbing 5 to 10 percent a
year. "We wanted to keep Ed enthused and motivated to do a good
job," explains Harold Shaub. "Looking back, we might have gotten
into a smoky area."

But when Finkelstein suggested making Henry Kissinger a director,
the Macy's board finally put their collective foot down. And meant it.

Finkelstein and Kissinger, the former secretary of state, were neighbors in western Connecticut and were becoming close social friends.
Retailing was becoming an increasingly global business, and Finkelstein decided that Kissinger would be a welcome addition to the
board.

Although there was some logic in this, the suggestion didn't sit well
with Finkelstein's fellow directors, most of whom were shocked by the
$250,000 fee that Kissinger commanded for his services. After con-
siderable debate, the board suggested that if Finkelstein wanted additional information about global markets, he should tap resources
at Warner Communications or Chase Manhattan, companies where
he served as a director. To allow their chairman to save face, however,
the board said they would allot $25,000 a year for Finkelstein to take
Kissinger to lunch. (Kissinger declined to comment on this story.)

Briefly stymied, Finkelstein returned with a new candidate—
Lawrence Eagleburger, a former Kissinger aide in the White House
and State Department. Eagleburger was then president of Kissinger
Associates, a consulting firm, and as Finkelstein explained, his retainer
was only $175,000 a year.

The board hooted down Eagleburger, too. (Finkelstein would have the last laugh, though. After he bought Macy's, all but one of the company's outside directors were dismissed. Henry Kissinger was one of the first to be invited to replace them.)

To be sure, Macy's could afford the cost of a new jet, or buy its chairman a townhouse. And Finkelstein did very well by Macy's shareholders during his first five years as chairman, far better, in fact, than some retail chief executives who earned higher salaries. Yet his style of doing business created a new set of expectations inside the company, especially when whispers of expensive, high-level junkets to Hong Kong and France began to circulate through the ranks. Whether such stories were true or fair became irrelevant; what mattered was that line managers believed them and began to take certain liberties of their own.

"Even the people at the divisional level lived like kings when they traveled," says Sankar Krishnan. For example, when Krishnan worked at the former Macy's Midwest division in Kansas City, a group of senior staffers went to the Lake of the Ozarks for a long-range planning session. They buzzed around the sleepy hardscrabble countryside in a pack of Porsches and Mercedeses, roaring up to restaurants and demanding lobsters for dinner. If the tasty crustaceans weren't on the menu, the Macy's men asked that they be flown in for the following night's consumption. "We were working hard, and the company was making a lot of money," says Krishnan. "With rank goes privilege."

At the same time, some began to notice a darker side of Finkelstein's personality, a side Al Artieres, the former Macy's California senior merchant, says he occasionally experienced during the early 1970s. Although Artieres describes himself as one of Finkelstein's "greatest fans," he says it was apparent that Finkelstein resented being crossed. "Sometimes, in meetings, I would tell him that I thought he was wrong about something. Then he'd look at me with a facial expression that made me think, 'Oh, Christ,' " says Artieres. "It wasn't a look you wanted to see too often."

By the mid-1980s, say former executives, Finkelstein rarely brooked any criticism, particularly when it came to Macy's growing reliance on its house brands, clothes that the company designed itself, manufactured in Hong Kong, and sold under such labels as Alfani and Charter Club. In theory, private label clothes enabled retailers to benefit from higher profit margins because the process eliminated the middlemen—manufacturers—and therefore a level of cost. Macy's, for example, might pay $40 for a Liz Claiborne blouse that would then sell for $80. However, Macy's could take that same blouse to Hong Kong, have it copied and manufactured for $20, and then sell it for $70. Customers benefited from the lower price, while Macy's enjoyed larger markups.

The problem was that if the private label goods didn't sell, Macy's had to absorb all of the loss. By contrast, store buyers often asked manufacturers whose goods didn't sell for "markdown money," funds that could be applied toward future purchases.

"Ed always talked about how our initial markup percentage was skyrocketing," says one former merchant who asked not to be identified. "But I said, 'Ed, you don't make your markup when you put your price on the goods, you make it when you sell the goods.' If a blouse cost twenty dollars, we marked it at seventy dollars. But if we only sold five percent of the goods we received, we had to keep reducing the price." And every time the price was cut, the profit margin decreased.

Finkelstein became so enthusiastic about private label merchandising that he moved his oldest son, Mitchell, to Hong Kong, to oversee the business. Mitchell, a serious tennis player, had worked overseas before, and his father believed his presence would end any possibility of corruption in a community where "personal gifts" were prevalent.

At the same time, it was common knowledge inside the company that one of Macy's highest ranking in-house designers was Jane Justin, otherwise known as Mark Handler's sister-in-law. The result was that Macy's senior merchants found themselves in a bind. If they didn't like the quality of the private label merchandise they received, or couldn't sell it once it was in the stores, they couldn't complain.

And anyone who thought otherwise had only to remember what had happened to Phil Schlein.

Soft-spoken Phil Schlein succeeded Ed Finkelstein as president of Macy's California in December 1973. A modest but poised Wharton graduate who joined Macy's in 1957, Schlein worked his way up to a group manager's job at the Parkchester, New York, branch store before being named a buyer. Herb Seegal had noticed that certain suppliers were making dresses and coats for women who stood five foot four inches or less, a category some were calling "petites." Few companies were making petites sportswear, however, and Seegal asked Schlein to go into the garment market and have them produced. Working closely with Finkelstein, Schlein built a $1-million-a-year sales business.

By the time Schlein arrived on the West Coast, The Cellar had already opened and the California stores were attracting a new crowd of affluent shoppers. Schlein continued to steer the division in that direction, working to make Macy's fashion message consistent in each department in terms of quality merchandise. Four years later, Finkelstein called Schlein and asked him to put twenty-two-year-old Daniel Finkelstein in the Macy's California training program.

"I'd known Dan since he was a youngster," says Schlein. "He was quiet and sensitive, and I didn't think it was necessarily a good idea for him to get into the retail business. But we gave him a spot." Dan, a diabetic, was so self-conscious about his father's clout that he insisted on pronouncing his last name "Finkel-stine" instead of "Finkel-steen" as his father did.

In the years that followed, Dan Finkelstein rose steadily from trainee to assistant buyer to buyer to group manager, causing some to grumble that he was receiving preferential treatment. His father, however, was so concerned at what he perceived as Dan's slow progress that in 1983 he met with Schlein to discuss it. Before the meeting was over, Finkelstein had even chided Schlein for not inviting Dan to lunch on a regular basis, adding that if Schlein's daughter had worked for him in New York, he would have nurtured her development on a continuing basis.

Schlein, stung by the criticism, said, "Ed, I've watched Dan, I've put him only with good people who could train him and where he could learn a lot. But I didn't think you wanted me to be obvious about the association." Finkelstein quieted down, and Schlein felt the issue had been settled.

One of those who questioned Dan Finkelstein's abilities was Ron Beale, a senior merchant for electronics, housewares, carpeting, and furniture. Ed Finkelstein had hired Beale in 1970 as a rug buyer, and Beale expanded that business from $1.8 million in revenues when he started to $24 million in 1984. "Ed was a pretty straightforward guy in the beginning," says Beale. "He understood presentation, standards, and the importance of carving out a niche that was a cut above the other department stores in town." When Beale was hired, for example, the Macy's California rug department consisted of cheap wall-to-wall bathroom sets wrapped in plastic, and low-quality cotton scatter rugs. With Finkelstein's approval, Beale replaced them with fine imported rugs from India, Pakistan, and China. "We became masters of our own destiny," says Beale. "Ed let you do what you had to do in order to get to the right level."

Despite that, Beale was irritated by Dan Finkelstein's rapid rise inside the company. "Dan is a nice young man, a gentleman, and very bright," says Beale. "And he would have been a great professor or a lawyer. But he doesn't have the personality for a merchant. He isn't gregarious or outgoing, qualities which are essential for a job like that. And they pushed him. He'd be given a review, and if it wasn't what Ed wanted, they'd make the person redo it. Dan's salary was also out of whack. If everybody got a $2,000 raise, he got $10,000. And if you showed any feelings about it, you were fired."

Becky Gould, who was in charge of executive personnel at Macy's California, says she was aware that other employees shared similar views. While describing Dan as "ethical and caring," she declined to discuss whether management employees at Macy's California were under pressure to promote him or change and improve his job reviews. "I think at times Dan was embarrassed, but he never said no," says Gould. "Was he as good as some of the others? It depends in what field. I think he was very good with statistics and in terms of organization. In terms of merchandising, people had very mixed feelings."

When questioned about Dan's rise in the company, Ed Finkelstein on several occasions strongly insisted that his youngest son was promoted solely on merit.

Macy's California thrived under Phil Schlein. In January 1981, *Women's Wear Daily,* the retail industry's trade paper, described the division as "the dominant upper-moderate department store in Northern California" and noted that sales had grown from $244 million in 1974 to $620 million six years later. Yet by early 1984, Schlein heard through the grapevine that Ed Finkelstein was dissatisfied with his performance. There was also a suggestion that Finkelstein was jealous of Schlein's new wealth. At the suggestion of Dick Dilworth, Schlein had joined the board of a small start-up company called Apple Computer. In the years that followed, he earned millions of dollars on the Apple stock options.

In any case, the relationship between Finkelstein and Schlein began to cool rapidly. At one point, Finkelstein even sent him a letter complaining that Schlein was "marching to his own drummer."

The problem, Schlein now believes, was that he strongly objected to Macy's dependence on its private label program. "Ed wanted us to be more aggressive in terms of our private label purchases," says Schlein. "But I felt we were charging too much while offering too little to the customer. Macy's California had its private label program, one that offered customers the kinds of fashion looks they wanted. Ed had even complimented us for it. But then he changed. He wanted more commonality among divisions, he said, because there were pricing advantages. And I understood that. But we were being asked to buy more Macy's private label goods than we thought we could sell."

The summer of 1984 marked the beginning of the end of Schlein's career. A forty-day strike at Macy's California that started in July crippled sales just as the vital fall selling season was beginning. In addition, the division had a difficult time absorbing several large stores that Finkelstein acquired after a nearby rival went out of business.

To make matters worse, word had gotten back to New York that dope had been smoked at several parties Schlein hosted at his Napa Valley home during a period when his marriage was under strain. "We'd have a big party once a year, and on several occasions there was marijuana," says Schlein. "There was never anything more than that involved."

By the late fall of 1984, many had heard that Schlein's job was in jeopardy. Yet Schlein says he wasn't concerned. He had been a director of the corporation since 1977, and he and Ed had been good friends for more than twenty years.

In late November 1984, he flew to New York for a board meeting, where he was formally reappointed to the board. A few hours later, however, Finkelstein called Schlein into his office and fired him. Schlein was fifty years old and had been employed by Macy's for twenty-seven years.

"He said he had differences with me over Dan, over Apple, and particularly over merchandising," says Schlein. "Ed wanted me to be more aggressive with private label goods, and I thought we already had too much of it. We were also trying to develop a culture based on servicing the customer, and he was opposed to using commissions in order to incentivize sales people. Maybe I was a little naive. I'd been getting some feedback from some peers that I should temper myself a little bit in terms of my positions, particularly relating to Dan."

Shortly after he was fired, Schlein sued Macy's over his severance package. The suit was finally settled, but only after a series of ugly charges. The entire experience, he says, was deeply troubling.

"It was a very sad period for me," says Schlein. "I got raises every year. So I was surprised."

Soon after Schlein left the company, Ed Finkelstein attended a small executive party in San Francisco. Stuart Widdess, director of stores at Macy's California and a fast-rising executive, turned to Finkelstein and said, "Now that Schlein is gone, who do you have to challenge you? Who's going to raise questions?" Finkelstein looked at him and replied, "I don't need anybody to challenge me."

Phil Schlein would later have a successful career in San Francisco as a venture capitalist. What most disappointed him following his ouster from Macy's, he says, is that former colleagues immediately stopped talking to him, apparently because they feared angering Finkelstein. "There were two weddings that were held six months or so after I left, both of which I had been verbally invited to attend," says Schlein. "Then I was disinvited. They were simply scared to have me."

Years later, Schlein did hear from one of those men whose daughter had gotten married that spring. It seemed he was looking for a new job, and he wanted to know if Schlein could help. Schlein said he would see what he could do.

Chapter 4

"Before we go any farther, I'd like to know a lot more about this."

A few minutes before the Macy's board meeting of June 25, 1985 started, Ed Finkelstein signaled to Stephen DuBrul Jr. to join him outside.

DuBrul was chairman of Macy's finance committee, a group that consisted of Macy's most powerful directors. DuBrul, who had the rakish good looks of Paul Newman in *The Color of Money*, all trim and blue eyes, was a veteran investment banker. He had started at Lehman Brothers during the 1950s, when the firm's blue-chip client roster included Gimbel Brothers, Federated Department Stores, Macy's, and Associated Dry Goods. By the time he was thirty, he was a director of May Department Stores.

DuBrul would later move to rival Lazard Freres, and then to Washington, D.C., where he served as chairman of the Export-Import Bank of the United States during the Ford Administration. After the Republicans lost the 1976 presidential election, he returned to New York City and hung up a shingle at 610 Fifth Avenue. Soon afterward, Macy's chairman Donald Smiley invited him to become a director.

Since joining the board, DuBrul had spent hundreds of hours walking through the company's stores, talking to customers and shoppers. This gave DuBrul something of an edge, since he didn't have to ask Finkelstein about company morale, or whether the bathrooms were clean, or whether spring fashions were selling. Since DuBrul had looked for himself, he knew the answers.

After he and Finkelstein stepped into the hallway, Finkelstein asked how DuBrul was feeling. Then, almost before DuBrul responded, Finkelstein said he intended to take Macy's private in a leveraged buyout. He knew this was coming as a shock, Finkelstein continued, but he hoped that he could count on DuBrul's support.

"We've never had a finance committee meeting on this," replied DuBrul. "How can you bring something this important up now, in this way?"

"I'm sorry I didn't tell you earlier," said Finkelstein. "I was told you had a conflict of interest."

"Oh?" asked DuBrul. The words hung between them like a broken promise. No one had questioned DuBrul's integrity before, and he didn't like the way it sounded. Rather than start an argument, however, he nodded that he understood and walked back into the boardroom.

DuBrul was seething.

The seventeen men and women who served as directors of Macy's were an eclectic group of academicians, celebrities, bankers, heads of major companies, and retired chief executives. Six worked at Macy's, including Finkelstein; Mark Handler; James York, president of the real estate division; Herbert Friedman, chairman of Macy's Atlanta; Robert Friedman (no relation to Herbert Friedman), chairman of Bamberger's; and Arthur Reiner, chairman of the Macy's New York division. Two were retired Macy's veterans: Donald Smiley, a former chairman, and Ken Straus, who had stepped down as chairman of the company's private label division at the start of the year. Jack Straus, Ken's father and Macy's honorary chairman and director emeritus, was also present.

Macy's outside directors included DuBrul; Harold Shaub; Lawrence Fouraker, a former dean of the faculty at the Harvard Business School; Robert G. Schwartz, the chairman of the Metropolitan Life Insurance Company; J. Richardson (Dick) Dilworth; and Robert G. Stone Jr., chairman of Kirby Exploration, an oil and gas firm. There were also three women: Martha Peterson, president emeritus of Beloit College in Wisconsin; diva Beverly Sills Greenough, the general director of the New York City Opera; and Barbara Scott Preiskel, the former general counsel to the Motion Picture Association of America, a trade group.

As soon as they were seated, Finkelstein said, "I have an important

statement, and I'd prefer to make it from the speaker's podium."
When no one objected, he walked to the side of the boardroom and
began to speak.

As they knew, he said, rival retailers were aggressively raiding the
company's most talented merchants. Some had left, while others were
convinced only at the last minute to remain. Macy's had traditionally
been something of a training ground for the retail industry, but now
that the company's stock price was selling at less than $50 a share, the
stock options that had once motivated the most senior and talented
executives were practically worthless.

At the same time, the country was becoming more entrepreneurial, he continued, a spirit Macy's needed to embrace. After giving this
a lot of thought, he'd concluded that the best way to do this was to
encourage the merchants who'd built the business to become full
partners.

And the only way to do that was through a leveraged buyout, one
in which each of the company's top managers participated.

Waiting outside in the hallway were lawyers from Weil, Gotshal &
Manges, and investment bankers from Goldman, Sachs & Co. said
Finkelstein, gesturing toward the door. With the board's permission,
he would invite them inside and let them explain the details.

When Finkelstein finished, the room was as quiet as an empty con-
fessional.

Then DuBrul jumped out of his seat.

"I feel like I've come in at the second act," he said, his voice rising.
"Before we go any farther, I'd like to know a lot more about this. I'd
also like everybody who works directly inside Macy's, with the exception of Ed, to leave. I'm calling an executive session."

As DuBrul sat down, confusion registered on the faces of his fellow directors. Ken Straus, sitting directly across from his father, saw
Jack Straus's jaw visibly slacken. Even though the Straus family owned
less than 5 percent of Macy's stock, Jack Straus had expected the family's ties to the company to last at least as long as his lifetime. Now that
this relationship was threatened, he was speechless.

The momentary quiet was broken by Finkelstein. "This is a personal
affront to me," he said, raising his voice in an effort to regain control.
"I think you should be at least willing to listen to what we have to say."

For the first time in years, no one paid him any attention.

One by one, Macy's directors turned to each other and asked what it all meant. When it became obvious that Finkelstein was unable to quiet the room, his five fellow management directors, including real estate man James York, who had no prior warning of Finkelstein's proposal, did exactly as DuBrul asked. They rose and filed out. This brought the formal board meeting to a close.

At the request of Macy's outside directors, Finkelstein remained. They were confused, they said, and they wanted a clearer understanding of his motives.

As Finkelstein began to explain his proposal, Martha Peterson, the former president of Beloit, grew increasingly apprehensive. Peterson believed that corporate directors, like college administrators, were obligated to work for the future of the institutions they served, not to line their own pockets. She also knew that many Macy's shareholders were former employees who took pride in their long association with the company. She didn't think it made much sense to push those people out while turning Macy's into a private, heavily debt-laden business that might be forced to sell its assets or lay off workers in order to reduce costs. Peterson had been invited onto the board by Donald Smiley, a fellow director on the board of Metropolitan Life. Although she didn't know very much about retailing, what she saw fascinated her. At the insurance company, directors were expected to think in terms of sixty years. At Exxon, where she also served as a director, the time frame was twenty years. But at Macy's, merchants bought and sold goods in sixty days or less. The consumer-driven retail business apparently didn't lend itself to long-term planning. A mathematician by training, Peterson had been the only woman on Macy's board at the time of her election. Although she didn't expect to do much in the way of retail conceptualizing, she had spent many years in the Midwest, and she believed she could fairly express a sense of what people "out there" thought, a voice that reflected the needs of everyday shoppers. Now she found herself wondering what "they" would think of all this.

After Finkelstein finished speaking, his fellow directors stood and left the board room. Instead of returning to their offices, however, the outside directors moved across the hallway into the old boardroom—later converted into Finkelstein's personal office—to talk among themselves.

As soon as the door closed, Donald Smiley raged that he wanted Ed Finkelstein fired on the spot. During his years as chairman, from

1968 to 1980, Smiley had chosen the majority of Macy's outside di-
rectors. This alone would have made him the most influential figure
on the board. But Smiley was also one of the few senior executives at
Macy's to win acclaim in outside business circles. He sat on the boards
of Metropolitan Life Insurance Company, the United States Steel
Corp., and RCA Corp., and served as a trustee of the Metropolitan
Museum of Art, a socially prestigious post. He also belonged to the
Union League Club in New York, the Blind Brook Club in Port
Chester, and the Indian Harbor Yacht Club in Greenwich, Connecticut. Smiley even owned a small island in Long Island Sound off Greenwich known as "Wee Captain's Island," and since he didn't have a
telephone there, on several occasions the Coast Guard had to be sent
to retrieve him.

Smiley was blunt, firm, and tenacious, a lawyer whose financial
know-how and negotiating abilities propelled him into the chairman's post. That he rose to the top in a company dominated by merchants made his success that much more impressive. Although Smiley
didn't talk about it himself, Ken Straus and several other directors felt
that Smiley's ability to win the trust of Macy's bankers during the early
1970s had meant survival at a time when Macy's was being widely out-
performed by rivals.

Not many who worked at Macy's liked Donald Smiley. But because
he treated everyone with the same arrogant indifference, he was
widely respected. "Don was a common man, and so self-confident that
he was smarter than anybody else that he never pulled rank," says Dan
Bergman, the former Bamberger's executive. "We'd go up to his place
after work for a drink, and he'd yell at me about the fucking liberals
destroying the country. He could also be incredibly rude. He once
told a roomful of people that the reason I never married was that I
was too selfish to share. He didn't think any particular dignity came
with his office. He was just Don."

The board knew that Smiley had once viewed Ed Finkelstein as
Macy's most talented merchant. During an annual meeting in the late
1970s, an irate shareholder asked why Macy's was providing Finkelstein with a Fifth Avenue apartment which cost $15,000 a year at a
time when Smiley's own Central Park South address cost only a third
of that amount. Even though Smiley was chairman and Finkelstein
merely a divisional president, Smiley loyally answered that Finkelstein had more important social obligations than he did.

Gradually, however, Smiley soured on his successor. Smiley had been raised in Davenport, Iowa, where his father owned a small market, and he held conservative, Midwestern values. Smiley disapproved when Finkelstein showed early signs of enjoying the perks of executive life. Later, when Finkelstein began roaring up to the annual Macy's Thanksgiving Day Parade accompanied by a police escort, Smiley didn't bother to conceal his disdain, particularly since he rejected the idea of a car and driver for himself; he used the New Haven Railroad when commuting from Greenwich. Otherwise, he took the subways when traveling around New York City.

After Finkelstein's name first surfaced as a candidate for Macy's top post, Smiley reminded listeners, he had questioned whether Finkelstein was too much of a merchant to succeed in a job requiring keen financial skills. Now that Finkelstein was threatening to destroy Macy's balance sheet by adding billions of dollars in debt, Smiley's fears were being realized.

Before sitting down, Smiley added that he had always liked Mark Handler, Finkelstein's best friend inside the company. Maybe they could meet privately with Handler and sound out his interest in becoming chairman.

Moments later, Jack Straus seconded Smiley's proposal to fire Finkelstein. Straus didn't have a formal vote, but he was so angry that he wanted to call the Weinberg brothers at Goldman, Sachs and tell them that they would never do business with Macy's again. (John Weinberg later insisted that Straus's anger was misplaced. Goldman, Sachs had been approached by Macy's chairman and acted at the company's request, he said. It wasn't the job of Goldman, Sachs to take the board's temperature.)

After Straus quieted down, Stephen DuBrul asked, "How many of you here knew about this?"

When he learned about Dick Dilworth's breakfast with Finkelstein, and Dilworth's subsequent call to Smiley, DuBrul felt an even deeper sense of betrayal. He and Finkelstein were not close friends. But in recent years, DuBrul had often taken a subway to Herald Square so that he and Finkelstein could have lunch and talk over Macy's direction.

Looking back, DuBrul realized that during the prior twelve months Finkelstein had often chatted about hostile takeovers and leveraged buyouts. Not once, however, did Finkelstein ever suggest that he was thinking about buying Macy's himself. Now DuBrul felt as thought he'd been manipulated.

As other directors continued to talk, DuBrul also thought back to a private dinner that had taken place several weeks after Finkelstein was named chairman. It was Finkelstein's first opportunity to outline his agenda in a friendly social setting, and DuBrul expected him to either discuss his strategy of building new stores in the South, or perhaps to address Macy's ambitious private label program.

Instead, Finkelstein had arrived clutching a badly typed four-page speech that he delivered in an awkward, disjointed style, much to everyone's discomfort.

It was a defining moment of character, DuBrul now felt. Finkelstein, by right of the years he'd spent at the company and on the board, should have been able to speak easily, without notes, an equal among friends. Instead, there was something that night that reminded DuBrul of Richard Nixon's uneasiness in the White House, an inherent insecurity about the legitimacy of his place at the table. (Finkelstein's admirers, however, say that the Macy's chief frequently prepared notes in advance of important meetings or telephone conversations, believing they eliminated the possibility of being misunderstood.)

Now that side of Finkelstein's character was being exposed again, DuBrul decided, first in his failure to give the board fair warning, and then by violating Macy's rules of corporate governance. Finkelstein knew that any significant issue involving Macy's capital structure had to be brought first to the company's finance committee, which DuBrul chaired. Clearly this would have included an offer to buy the company.

Instead, Finkelstein had concealed his intentions in hopes of taking the board by surprise. (Marvin Fenster, Macy's former in-house counsel, says that Finkelstein, in his role as chairman, was entitled to raise any subject he wanted with the board.)

Something else also bothered DuBrul. As hard as he tried, he couldn't think of a single key Macy's executive who had left the company in the last two years. To the contrary, DuBrul felt that Macy's had a solid bench of bright, aggressive young merchants. And since Macy's board had already approved more than $1 billion in spending on new stores and remodeling, opportunities for further advancement and higher salaries had never been better.

DuBrul and the retailer's other directors had always known that

Macy's might one day be raided. No one, though, ever suspected that such a raid would be led by someone inside their circle.

Before the impromptu gathering of outside directors ended on that June day in 1985, cooler heads prevailed. Their first obligation was to protect the assets of the corporation, and if they forced Finkelstein to resign, or fired him outright, Macy's stock would plummet, wiping out millions of dollars in shareholder value. Several directors also feared that Finkelstein would then return with outside money and launch his own tender offer for the business. (That same possibility was also discussed among several inside directors.)

Besides, what would Macy's do if Finkelstein left and took all of his top merchants with him? They needed time, they agreed, time to study what a buyout would mean for Macy's, its employees, and its shareholders. They didn't want to say yes, but they didn't want to be forced into saying no, either.

Finally, Dick Dilworth agreed to go to Finkelstein's office and explain their concerns. Forty-five minutes later, he returned and said that Finkelstein understood and was temporarily willing to forgo his formal presentation. However, he still wanted the Macy's board to hear what his lawyers and investment bankers had to say, and he wanted to schedule that meeting as soon as possible.

As the outside directors headed toward the elevators, Finkelstein spotted Martha Peterson and caught her eye. "This is going to be a difficult decision," she said. "You've given us a lot to think about."

"I hope we're going to merit your support," Finkelstein replied politely.

Peterson didn't answer. Although she served on a number of boards, Peterson was now wrestling with difficult questions of loyalty. Was she responsible to Finkelstein, or to Macy's shareholders? And would investors be better served by taking a cash premium for their stock, or by keeping it and sharing in future dividends and profits? Like many on the board, Peterson didn't know very much about how leveraged buyouts work. She wasn't sure about her legal obligations, either. Before she gave Finkelstein her blessings, she intended to find out.

•   •   •

Nobody left that day more agitated than Jack Straus, Macy's honorary chairman. A thin rail of a man who never weighed more than 145 pounds, Straus stood a shade under six feet tall. Even his three children described him as a human toothpick. He had a receding hairline, jug-like ears, and poor vision which he overcame with thick-lensed glasses.

Straus was born on January 13, 1900, in New York City, where he lived at 49 East 74th Street in a dark, five-story building. When he was only two years old, he held a silver trowel at ceremonies marking the laying of the cornerstone of the Macy's Herald Square flagship store. It was a fitting start to a career that spanned sixty-four years, a period in which he never missed a single Macy's Thanksgiving Day Parade, including the first in 1924.

He never wanted to work at the family store. A skilled pianist and songwriter, Straus told his father that after he graduated from Harvard in 1921 he intended to make his living as a professional musician. Jesse Straus heard him out. Then he said, "The hell with that. You're coming to Macy's."

Jack Straus did as he was told. But for much of his adult life, he kept two pianos in his New York apartment on East 72nd Street, and two more at his twenty-five-acre country estate in Jericho, out on Long Island. He also studied jazz piano with Teddy Wilson and Eddy Duchin. "If you had a company party and didn't have a piano, it was a terrible mistake," says David Yunich, the former Macy's vice chairman. "That was how Jack expressed himself." Later, Jack wrote a song called "Hearts Are Trumps," even though he knew better.

In 1931, Jack's father walked into his office, gestured toward the front door, and said, "It's all yours." Governor Franklin D. Roosevelt had chosen Jesse Straus to head New York's Temporary Emergency Relief Administration. Two years later, President Roosevelt named him ambassador to France, and Jesse Straus immediately steamed off to his new post, leaving a brother in charge.

While Jesse was drinking champagne with Morgans and Vanderbilts in Paris, Jack Straus struggled to adjust to his new responsibilities as one of Macy's most senior executives. "My brother told me he felt overwhelmed," says Robert Straus, a private investor who lives in southern California. "Jack thought he had been asked to do too much at too young an age. It must have affected his relationship with his own son, because I know he didn't want Ken indulged on any level."

Although Macy's employees were encouraged to call him Mister Jack, sales clerks found him cold and haughty, and guffawed when he had the Macy's underwear buyer come downstairs and choose his shorts for him. Straus hired only beautiful women as his secretaries, and named Robert Montgomery, one of his favorite actors, to the Macy's board. (When preparing for upcoming board meetings, Macy's executives sometimes dismissed mundane topics by saying, "Do you think Robert Montgomery cares about that?") Straus was a dapper but quirky dresser who only wore striped narrow ties manufactured by Comfort & Co., a distinguished British silk firm. This obsession was so well-known within the company that when word came down that he was about to visit an outlying store, branch managers hid their paisley ties and replaced them with versions of the striped ties Straus preferred. Straus would always tour the tie department before leaving, nodding his head in approval, and muttering, "That's how it should look."

He was also obsessive about his health. When Jack Straus traveled, say associates, he carried two suitcases at all times: one for his clothing, the other for his pills and remedies. He once rushed off to see Dr. Arthur Antinucci, his physician, after noticing that his hands had turned bright red, only to be told that the color was dye from his new red briefcase. Wonderfully, this story never embarrassed him.

Dr. Antinucci, however, told other patients that Jack Straus was a pain in the ass.

Under Jack Straus's watch, Macy's in 1945 acquired O'Connor, Moffat and Co., a San Francisco department store, establishing Macy's as a national department store company. To his credit, he was also the driving force behind Macy's push into suburban markets. However, he was an uninspired merchant with little insight into his customers, a shortcoming that would cost the company dearly. In May 1952, the Schwegmann Brothers discount chain of New Orleans won a precedent-setting decision that significantly weakened the rights of manufacturers to set retail prices on the goods they made. The ruling, which was handed down just before Memorial Day, caused much debate inside Macy's. For decades the department store company had offered its shoppers a 6 percent discount on their cash purchases—with the exception of fixed-price merchandise. Now Macy's had to decide whether to reduce prices on those goods as well.

Richard Weil Jr., Macy's president as well as Jack Straus's cousin, was in favor of extending that 6 percent discount to everything in the store. In a neighborhood already overcrowded with retailers, he said, that promise was the foundation of Macy's franchise. And to his ever-lasting regret, Jack Straus agreed with him.

Over the Memorial Day weekend, Macy's sales clerks repriced thou-sands of items whose prices had formerly been set by their manufac-turers. The following Tuesday morning, newspaper readers were greeted with full-page ads listing all of the items which had now been discounted by 6 percent.

For New Yorkers, it was the start of one of the funniest price wars the city had ever seen. "Every one of our competitors, from Stern's to Gimbel Brothers to Bloomingdale's, took us on," says David Yunich, a senior Macy's merchant at the time. "One of them went after us in books, another in drugs, another in small electrics, and so on." Within weeks Macy's was selling Monopoly board games for six cents each and copies of Margaret Mitchell's *Gone With the Wind* for 89 cents.

Soon the company was racking up such losses that it had to sell WOR, a radio station it had owned since buying Bamberger's in 1929. "We were losing our shirt, and getting publicity that made us look ridiculous," says Yunich. "Jack fired Weil over that issue." Straus sub-sequently named himself president and relinquished his chairman-ship until 1956.

Like many wealthy men, Jack Straus was concerned with his place in New York society, and it bothered him that none of the Waspy coun-try clubs where he occasionally played golf ever invited him to join, presumably because their members thought he was Jewish. This hurt because it was only partly true.

Although Jack Straus was born into the Jewish faith, his first wife, Margaret Hollister, was an Episcopalian, and she raised their three children—Kenneth, Patricia, and Pamela—in her faith. When the Strauses were mistakenly informed in December 1944 that their son's division was cut off during the Battle of the Bulge, Mrs. Straus became so upset that she asked her husband to convert and join her in church.

Jack did so on Christmas Day, effectively ending the family's ties to Judaism.

Shortly after the war ended, Ken Straus went to his father and told him that he wanted to join Macy's. If he thought his decision would please his father, he immediately learned otherwise. Crisply, Jack said that before Ken went ahead with his plans, he should understand the ground rules. Macy's had been publicly traded since 1922, and it was no longer a family business. If Ken wanted a job, he would have to use the 35th Street entrance of the store and apply for work like everybody else. If Ken was hired, Jack continued, he would never discuss Macy's with Ken again, either at home or at work. He would also do his best to avoid Ken in the store, and at various company functions.

Jack said he was telling Ken this because he couldn't allow himself to be influenced by his son's judgment. It was as much for his own peace of mind as Ken's, he added. Neither of them would be happy if others at Macy's believed Ken had his father's ear.

When Ken said he understood and got up to leave, Jack Straus reached for his arm and said he had one last thought he wanted him to remember. If Ken didn't do his job, his father would fire him on the spot—if no one else did it first.

And for the next twenty-three years, until Ken Straus was elected to the board of Macy's in 1970, his father was as good as his word. He never visited a department where Ken worked, or toured a branch store that Ken managed. And he never asked Ken his views about business or the company. Twice each year, however, they shared lunch together in a private dining room, where they were joined by the family financial adviser.

Much as his own father had done for him, Jack Straus would see that his son was trained to manage the family fortune.

In the years that followed Jack Straus's retirement in 1968, he did much as he pleased. There were long games of golf, endless sessions on the piano, and the company of grandchildren. When he was in the mood to reminisce, he ate in the Macy's corporate dining room, where executives studiously did their best to avoid him.

But that came to an end when Ed Finkelstein said he wanted to buy Macy's and take the company private. In the time it takes to park a car, the world Jack Straus had devoted a lifetime to constructing was in pieces.

A week or two after the meeting, Ken Straus received a phone call at home from his father's physician, Dr. Arthur Antinucci. "I've made it a practice of only talking to the spouses of the patients I treat, but I feel that I must discuss this with you," said Dr. Antinucci. "Something has happened at Macy's that is having a serious effect on your father's health."

The doctor then told Ken something his father had concealed from him: for the past year, Jack Straus had been battling lymphoma. Although his medical team thought that they had the disease in remission, the cancer had suddenly returned. Dr. Antinucci said he believed it had been triggered by an event that had put Straus's life in emotional turmoil.

"Doctor, I'm well aware of what's going on at Macy's," replied Ken, "but I'm powerless to do anything about it."

The physician waited for an explanation. When it wasn't forthcoming, he ended the conversation. "I just wanted you to know it is having a serious impact on your father's health."

Ken Straus thanked him and began to plan how he would tell the rest of his family.

Chapter 5

"There was a sense of frenzy in the air."

Despite the hostility his proposal created among his fellow directors, Ed Finkelstein didn't flinch. In early July, he succeeded in calling together the entire board and sitting them down. In the meeting that followed, his lawyers and bankers explained how debt financing worked and why Macy's employees would benefit if the company went private.

For Martha Peterson, it was an awkward, difficult situation. "Most of us were taken by complete surprise when Ed made his announcement," she says. "Earlier in the year he mentioned that the retail business was entering a new phase and said that Macy's needed to reexamine how it did things. Christmas hadn't been good, and he wasn't pleased with our immediate prospects, either. So we expected him to make changes. But we didn't have a clue as to what those changes would be." Despite her doubts, however, Peterson listened carefully as Ira Millstein, Finkelstein's lawyer, outlined the board's obligations. Regardless of their personal views, Millstein said, they were there to represent the company's shareholders. "I didn't view him as the enemy," says Peterson. "It was straightforward and helpful."

In the weeks that followed, the Macy's board tried to chart a course, with each director setting his or her own agenda. Jack and Ken Straus talked about the long traditions of the company. Larry Fouraker, the retired dean of the Harvard Business School, spoke about business ethics. Met Life chairman Robert Schwartz reviewed the financial issues and suggested that if Finkelstein felt it was hard working for his present board, he would learn otherwise when he worked for the banks.

Other directors, including Martha Peterson, tried to remain neutral. As a college president, Peterson had been trained to distance herself from her emotions. Students were allowed to get angry; administrators could not. "We all wanted more information," says Peterson. "If this was a great idea, we wanted to be knowledgeable enough to support it. If it was a bad idea, we had to be knowledgeable as to why. But one thing was certain: we didn't want to make a decision about the buyout based on the advice of the people proposing it." In late July, the company's outside directors decided to form a special committee to study Finkelstein's proposal. They named themselves as members and appointed Harold Shaub as chairman.

Shaub, an ardent fly fisherman with a polite, folksy manner, became president of Campbell Soup in 1972, three decades after he joined the company. Shaub grew up in rural Lancaster County, Pennsylvania and matured into a patient listener who placed a premium on common sense. As the head of one of the country's best-known food companies, he understood the implications of debt and how it could affect a business's future. Not surprisingly, then, Shaub didn't approve of selling Macy's to a group of private investors led by Finkelstein.

"Frankly, I was concerned about a great organization sliding into oblivion," says Shaub. "I didn't think they had the financial resources to do a deal that big. And even if they pulled it off, they were going to have serious problems if the economy weakened. But we were getting these highly confident letters from Goldman, Sachs, and we had to go forward."

What concerned Shaub most was the effect a leveraged buyout would have on Macy's balance sheet. Since 1982, the department store company had succeeded in reducing its debt load while adding new assets. Although Macy's had enjoyed superb growth throughout the early 1980s, it had only $144 million in debt compared to $1.48 billion in shareholder equity, a ratio of one dollar of debt for every eleven dollars in equity. If Finkelstein succeeded in buying the business, however, the company would lose that sturdy foundation. (After the buyout was completed, Macy's had $3.15 billion in debt and only

$290 million in equity, or ten dollars in debt for every dollar of equity.)

Shaub knew that Finkelstein and Handler were aware of this. Yet in a series of meetings with the special committee, both men, as well as other inside directors, were invariably poised and upbeat. They were long-range planners and thinkers at a time when Wall Street was fixated on quarterly performance, they insisted. Taking Macy's private would reward its public shareholders while guaranteeing a better future.

When Mark Handler said that management should be given the opportunity to move forward because the entire organization favored it, Shaub's opposition began to waver. "I began to see our job as getting the best price for shareholders while doing the best to protect employees," he says.

The convincing show of unity reflected the iron fist of Ira Millstein, a bicycle-riding antitrust lawyer at Weil, Gotshal & Manges who was Finkelstein's closest adviser. A powerful, fast-growing firm, Weil, Gotshal & Manges was then on the verge of achieving national prominence. Orchestrating the Macy's buyout promised to widen Ira Millstein's personal horizons while adding luster to the law firm he had helped manage for the last nineteen years.

Millstein, a tightly packaged bundle of nerve and menace who could silence a room with a single look, had known Finkelstein casually for years. Yet when Marvin Fenster, Macy's in-house counsel, brought them together in early May, "sparks flew," as Fenster later put it. That summer, Fenster took his son on a long-promised trip to Italy as a college graduation gift. By the time Fenster returned, he was no longer Finkelstein's top legal adviser. "To put it simply, Ira wanted to call the shots," says Fenster. "There was nothing I could do."

Inside Macy's, Millstein was sometimes called "The Cardinal" behind his back, an unfavorable reference to Cardinal Richelieu, the scheming chief minister to Louis XIII who dominated the French government. "Many people felt that Millstein completely dominated Macy's and was the power behind the throne during the leveraged buyout," says one former senior Macy's manager. Some of this might have been jealousy: Millstein and Finkelstein quickly became inseparable, speaking once or twice a day, going out for dinner, finishing each other's sentences. Blood brothers.

Meanwhile, investment banker Stephen DuBrul Jr. wrote memos

to other directors explaining how leveraged buyouts worked. He also outlined what other boards had done when faced with similar situations. There was nothing illegal about Finkelstein's offer, he acknowledged, but that didn't mean it was in the best interests of the corporation.

In some cases, he said, companies were raided only after there was blood in the water. The potential buyers wanted the business because they believed they would do a better job managing it. In other cases, as with some of the recently raided big oil companies, their assets were worth more than the entire company. When Chevron acquired Gulf for $13.4 billion in 1984, Chevron's executives explained it was cheaper to buy Gulf's oil reserves on Wall Street than to drill for new gushers of their own.

But Macy's, DuBrul insisted, didn't fit into either category. It was a well-managed business whose stock was trading at a fair price, despite the recent decline in value. Yes, the recent Christmas season had been disappointing. But DuBrul had worked with retailers most of his professional life, and his instincts told him that Macy's had an exciting future. The company had already committed itself to building twenty-six new stores and spending $1 billion on remodeling its older stores. At the same time, a new, aggressive generation of buyers were working their way up the ranks and appeared ready to assume additional responsibilities. When those new stores opened, DuBrul said, Macy's would have the necessary talent to manage them.

At the heart of Finkelstein's proposal was a deeply moral question, DuBrul continued: did a small group of men who had access to all of the corporation's secrets have the ethical right to buy the business for themselves, or were they obligated by their position to put the long-term interests of shareholders above their own?

"I told them that Ed's proposal was sheer greed and megalomania," says DuBrul. "This was one more tragic figure of his type who had begun to believe his own press clippings. What we had was an internal cancer, and we had to decide how to deal with it."

In August, the outside directors hired the law firm of Shearman & Sterling. Shareholders were eventually going to review everything they had done, and the committee wanted the record to show that they had behaved properly.

Meanwhile, Finkelstein was fuming over the delays. He was also disappointed when Fred Eckert, his investment banker at Goldman,

Sachs, cryptically mentioned in late August that he wouldn't be able to spend much time working on the buyout. His wife was seriously ill at the time, but Eckert, intensely private, didn't feel comfortable discussing it.

Instead, he briskly told Finkelstein that he had picked a new point man. Jim Lane was a hardworking, engaging thirty-three-year-old vice president of private finance, Eckert said, and he would now oversee day-to-day developments.

Perhaps predictably, Finkelstein blew up. "Ed was nuts in this period," says Eckert. "He's a cuddly human being with a great heart. But you have to understand his personality. One minute he believes that the only thing that people respond to are beatings. So he screams and threatens. Thirty minutes later, he believes that the only motivation is cajoling. So then he's your uncle. But Jim had a lot riding on this, I had a lot riding on this, and Ed had a lot riding on this. So we made do."

A month later, Eckert received a note from Finkelstein. He was thinking about Eckert's problems, Finkelstein wrote, and he hoped that everything would turn out well.

When Labor Day passed without a word from the Macy's special committee, Finkelstein and his advisers decided to act. On September 9, they sent a letter to Harold Shaub that Jim Lane later smugly described as "a bear hug." In it, they wrote that each of Macy's management directors believed their fiduciary responsibilities obligated them to vote in favor of going forward with an all-cash offer. They also stated that they were sure that Macy's shareholders would welcome an opportunity to vote yes or no on just such a bid.

The letter did exactly what it was intended to do: it forced Macy's outside directors to begin making decisions.

Four days later, on the advice of Dick Dilworth, the special committee hired an investment banker: James Wolfensohn, an Australian-born former Olympic fencer, a concert cellist, lawyer, and the consummate Wall Street insider. Following a superb career at the Shroders banking group in England, Wolfensohn quit in 1977 when the board refused to appoint him chairman. Although he would never say so, some suspected that Wolfensohn was passed over for the top spot because he was Jewish. In the weeks that followed, job offers poured in from some of the world's great financiers: Sigmund War-burg, Andre Meyer, and David Rockefeller.

Wolfensohn stunned them all by joining Salomon Brothers in New York, then regarded as a second-tier firm. "They were nothing but a bunch of bond traders," sniffs Dilworth. Despite his disappointment with Wolfensohn's decision, he later became close to Wolfensohn while working to save Chrysler from collapse. Dilworth was a senior director of the auto company; Wolfensohn served as a leading finan-cial adviser.

In 1981, shortly after Salomon Brothers was acquired by the Phi-bro Corporation, Wolfensohn resigned, taking with him an estimated $10 million. "Allegedly he was going to spend his time improving his musical talents, but of course it didn't turn out that way," says Dil-worth. "I had no idea whether he would be available to work with us at Macy's, but I told Don Smiley and Steve DuBrul that I would call him. I felt it was essential that whomever we hired not have any prior Macy's relationship."

There was pressure on Wolfensohn from the day he started. Finkel-stein, Millstein, and Goldman, Sachs had an offer on the board, a timetable, and a plan. "You have to remember the climate of the times," says Wolfensohn, silver-haired and slightly disheveled. "There was a sense of frenzy in the air. Everybody felt they could borrow ninety-five percent of what they needed to make an acquisition, and in most cases they were right.

"Also, once such a bid is made, the damage to the company is sub-stantial if it isn't successful. If the insider group feels that their meri-torious attempt to buy the company is rejected by the slave owners for whom they had been working, you have a very different business. The very act of making an offer always changes a company."

What he wanted to do was slow the process down. And a few days after being hired, he had his chance. Finkelstein sent Shaub a second letter on September 17 offering $68 a share for Macy's common stock. The price, the first that Finkelstein had formally offered, rep-resented a 30 percent premium over the market value of Macy's shares.

Instead of sitting down with him, however, the special committee approved a resolution describing the buyout as "inappropriate" and not in the "best interests of the company." They also agreed that they were obligated to maximize shareholder values, which indicated they might begin searching for additional bidders.

A few hours later, on the same day, the full board, including Finkelstein and Handler, met to vote on the special committee's resolution. Since the special committee outnumbered the Macy's directors by a margin of eleven to six, the stinging rebuke was overwhelmingly approved.

The animosity between Finkelstein and some of his former directors was finally out in the open.

"This was our chance to let the management know that the special committee wasn't going to move any faster than was appropriate," says Wolfensohn. "We weren't going forward with a gun to our heads." And the Macy's outside directors weren't obligated to accept Finkelstein's offer, regardless of the price. If they believed that shareholders would earn greater returns by keeping their shares, the special committee could vote accordingly.

They now turned to Donald Smiley. If the former Macy's chairman was willing to return to the company and run the business, they could oust Finkelstein and take control. Smiley, however, rejected the offer, leaving the special committee with few options. It would now be very difficult to turn down Finkelstein's bid—and convince shareholders that Macy's had enough management to grow the company in the near future.

"I had no enthusiasm for what was being done, but I thought it was going to happen," says Dick Dilworth. "At that point, my only interest was seeing that shareholders got a reasonable return."

When others acknowledged that they felt the same, Wolfensohn met with Goldman, Sachs in mid-October. Accompanied by Dilworth, Shaub, and Barbara Preiskel, he told Ira Millstein that the special committee would be willing to sell Macy's if Finkelstein raised his price to $72 a share. Millstein refused. A few days later, however, on Friday, October 18, the two sides met at Wolfensohn's offices and reached a compromise. Finkelstein would pay $70 a share, or about $100 million more than he originally offered.

Terms called for Finkelstein to make a formal bid by December 1, 1985, with the bidding to remain open for the following forty-five days, until January 15, 1986. In the interim, members of the special committee, as well as Jim Wolfensohn, would solicit outside bids for the company. Moreover, Finkelstein pledged to cooperate with any third-party bidders who emerged.

The next morning, Jim Lane of Goldman, Sachs drove to Rhode Island to attend his youngest brother's wedding. Early Monday morning, heading south on Interstate 95 back to the city, he turned on the radio and heard that Macy's was going to go private in a leveraged buyout valued at $3.5 billion.

Lane was stunned. Before he left Wolfensohn's office late Friday night, both sides promised to keep the buyout secret until Goldman, Sachs firmed up support with potential investors. This was critical, since some inside the investment banking firm questioned whether Macy's business was strong enough to support a $70 price. Rather than make a bid and then have to reduce it, Lane wanted to first test the market. Goldman, Sachs had never before managed such a huge buyout. If it failed, the firm would be embarrassed, and his own hopes of making partner would be finished.

Lane later learned that there had been a leak. First, a Wall Street analyst had called Macy's asking if the retailer was going private. Then one of the company's public relations executives was asked the same question by an acquaintance. When this was relayed to Finkelstein, who was in Texas for a store opening, he immediately issued a press release.

For Jim Lane, it would be the first in a litany of unpleasant surprises.

Macy's stock, which opened on October 21, 1985, at $47 a share, jumped $16.125 to close at $63.125. Macy's chairman Edward Finkelstein intended to pay $70 a share for Macy's 51.2 million shares of common stock, the nation's radio and television stations reported that day, with the transaction to be presented formally when the financing was in place.

Finkelstein proudly told interviewers that he was offering a price that was "the maximum price anyone would pay." He added that Macy's stock had risen more than $4 in the previous week, apparently on rumors, and that the run-up in shares had forced him to make his announcement before he had obtained his financing. More than one hundred fellow Macy's executives would be investing with him, he added, a level of participation unheard of in management-led buyouts.

By day's end, two million shares of Macy's stock had traded hands, making it the third most active issue traded. The news also drove up the price of other retail stocks, including those of Federated Department Stores, Allied Stores, May Department Stores, and Associated Dry Goods.

Some, though, were concerned that Finkelstein was promising to pay more than he could afford. "It's a hell of a big price," said the late Edward Johnson, a veteran analyst at Johnson's Redbook Service. "What happens if there's a recession? How can they pay the interest on all that borrowed money?"

Some skeptics also questioned whether Finkelstein could raise the money. Macy's common stock had sold for as low as $40.75 earlier that month, and there was speculation that the company's assets weren't worth more than $55 or $60 a share.

A small group of observers, including Walter Loeb, a former Macy's executive who worked at the investment bank Morgan Stanley, insisted that Finkelstein's offer wasn't surprising. Finkelstein, Loeb noted, doesn't "like anyone looking over his shoulder, and going private will allow him to run the company without a lot of second-guessers."

When the news of the proposed leveraged buyout flashed across computer screens that afternoon, no one felt worse than Peter Solomon, the investment banker in charge of the Macy's account at Lehman Brothers Kuhn Loeb.

Solomon was good-looking in a casual, athletic way with closely cropped hair and a Wall Streeter's breezy self-confidence. His grandfather, Joseph Rabinowitz, had founded the Economy Grocery Store in Boston, later known as Stop & Shop, and his father, Sidney Solomon, was the former chairman of the Abraham & Straus department store chain.

The relationship between Lehman Brothers and Macy's, like the ties between Macy's and Goldman, Sachs, stretched over decades. Both investment banking firms had worked well together, helping Macy's raise money when needed, and providing it with financial advice.

Now that partnership was finished. For Solomon, the break-up couldn't have come at a worse time. In the early 1980s, Lehman Brothers Kuhn Loeb was ripped apart by a feud involving Lewis Glucksman and Peter G. Peterson, a former secretary of commerce.

Peterson eventually left the firm in 1983, but less than a year later, the 134-year-old investment banking house was merged into Shearson/American Express. A new firm was then created in April of 1985: Shearson Lehman Brothers Inc., a wholly owned subsidiary of American Express. Peter Solomon survived the merger and was even made co-head of investment banking. Still, many of the firm's most valued clients were leaving in droves, creating concern and fear.

Macy's was Solomon's largest remaining account. It was also his client of longest standing. To learn from the wires that it was now up for sale—and that Goldman, Sachs was handling the sale—was a devastating blow. A few weeks later, he went to Macy's Herald Square to meet with Finkelstein and discuss why it had happened.

He was hurt, Solomon said. Lehman Brothers had an honorable history with Macy's that extended back for decades. Why were they being cast aside now, especially for Goldman, Sachs, which didn't know a thing about the buyout business?

Finkelstein stared at Solomon and paused. Then he replied, "Your firm is finished, and everybody knows it. I never gave any thought to using you." Furthermore, he added, he was no longer interested in anything Solomon had to say to him.

"You're wrong," Solomon said angrily. "You don't have any idea of what's going on. Lehman Brothers is alive, it's well, and it has a future. I'm sorry you don't see that."

Solomon then reminded Finkelstein that he had put himself at great personal risk five years earlier, when he had served as Deputy Mayor for Economic Policy and Development for New York City under Mayor Edward Koch. Legionnaire's Disease had broken out in New York and, as Finkelstein knew, city inspectors identified an empty water tower atop the Macy's building as the likely source. Despite pressure from the media and from other city officials, however, Solomon refused to identify Macy's as the cause of the problem. He knew how the outbreak of the disease destroyed the reputation of the Bellevue Stratford Hotel in July 1976 in Philadelphia, and he didn't want the same thing to happen to the world's largest department store. Solomon held his ground, and eventually the crisis passed. Many months later, when a reporter for *The New York Times* accused him of concealing the truth, Solomon agreed he was right. Macy's employed thousands of people, generated millions of tax dollars, and was a major tourist destination, Solomon replied. He had no intentions of endangering it, especially when the problem was remedied as soon as it was discovered.

Finkelstein hadn't been chairman of Macy's at that time, but he was president of Macy's New York, and he had staked his career on the revitalization of the Herald Square store. Now this was how he was paying Solomon back.

"I'm very disappointed in you, Ed," said Solomon finally, getting up from his chair, "very disappointed." Then, as he began to open the door to leave, he turned back and said, "I wish you good luck."

Finkelstein did a double take. "You wish me good luck?" he asked.

"I do, because you're going to need it," said Solomon. "I've been around for a long time. And to be very trite, what goes around, comes around." The entire meeting only lasted twenty minutes.

On September 19, Jack Straus, the former chairman of Macy's, died at Roosevelt Hospital at the age of eighty-five. A small jazz ensemble played at his funeral, putting smiles on the faces of mourners with their rendition of "When the Saints Go Marching In."

"I don't think that anybody can prove that the leveraged buyout killed my father," says Ken Straus. "But Macy's was number one, number two, and number three with him."

Chapter 6

"It looked good."

Ed Finkelstein never knew it would be like this, that in the end, his dream of buying Macy's would depend on a group of kids working at Goldman, Sachs. Sometimes, when they gathered together at Macy's to discuss strategy, he would begin by saying, "I respect young people." Then, as he gazed into the sea of eager faces, gears would grind and he would erupt into mesmerizing, earsplitting temper tantrums. It didn't help that he barely knew Jim Lane, although the two would grow more comfortable after Finkelstein learned that Lane once tried out for the Philadelphia Atoms, a now defunct professional soccer team.

Lane liked to joke that the first thing he ever read was a Chicago Cubs box score. The second was the price of IBM stock. James M. Lane, his father, had worked at Chase Manhattan for twenty-five years, a money manager at a time when money managers were the kings of Wall Street. Jim, né James N. Lane, inherited his father's fascination with business. After graduating from Wheaton College, a small Christian liberal arts school based in Wheaton, Illinois, he followed his father into banking and took a job at Manufacturers Hanover Trust. Later he earned an MBA from Columbia University, and then, through a fellow Wheaton graduate, he received an invitation to join Goldman, Sachs.

Jim Lane was the firm's only banker who always carried a pocket-sized edition of the King James Bible. Since he now had fewer than ninety days to raise $5 billion, including $1.5 billion to refinance Macy's credit card operations, prayer seemed appropriate.

And the financing plan was unusually complicated. Rather than tapping one or two markets, Goldman, Sachs would sell a combination of mortgage-backed securities, bank loans, notes, management equity, and three junk bond issues: senior subordinated debentures due in 1998, junior subordinated debentures due in 2001, and zero coupon bonds due in 2006. It was a highly elaborate structure, a virtual Eiffel Tower of debt.

Goldman, Sachs's Fred Eckert simply referred to it as a "brilliant nightmare."

Jim Lane was not superstitious. But sometimes he wondered if this deal was cursed. First, Fred Eckert's wife took sick, forcing Eckert to pull back from the biggest deal of his career. Then, only eight days after Macy's announced the buyout to the press, Rita Reid sat herself down in Lane's office and said they had a problem.

Unlike many of her colleagues, Reid graduated from Hofstra University on Long Island rather than an Ivy League school or a small New England college. She began her career in research, and then worked her way up by doing the hard number-crunching scut work everyone else avoided. She had now devoted an entire week to reviewing Macy's credit card operations, tearing it apart, deciphering its mysteries. Her conclusion: the cash flow projections Goldman, Sachs was using for the next ten years, projections that the firm would use to sell Macy's debt to bankers and other investors, were off by about $1 billion.

Although the Macy's credit card facility was not widely understood, it played a vital role at the company, so much so that some analysts viewed Macy's as a bank that used clothing to draw customers. Like many department store companies, Macy's advanced customers credit to make their purchases and then charged 18 percent annual interest, creating a mountain of valuable consumer IOUs. Shoppers valued the credit as a convenience, and Macy's used it as a sales tool, offering reduced or delayed payments to new or favored shoppers. The big three auto makers operated finance units for much the same reasons, as did General Electric, which started its General Electric Credit Corp. to spur sales of the refrigerators and washing machines it once made.

What Reid's discovery meant was that Goldman, Sachs would have to begin again. Without the additional $1 billion in revenues, Macy's

couldn't support a debt repayment schedule based on paying $70 a
share. Reid's projections instead indicated the retailer would struggle at $60. The $10 difference represented about $500 million in the
total purchase price, and $70 million a year in interest charges.

Goldman, Sachs would now have to rejigger its projections. Jim
Lane didn't want the job. Neither did Reid. Finally, the firm assigned
the task to Thomas Delavan, an analyst fresh from Middlebury College and the most junior member of the staff's leveraged buyout
team. As estimates flew back and forth between Goldman, Sachs,
Macy's, the banks, and other would-be investors, it would be Delavan's
job to collate and enter them into Goldman, Sachs's computers. Each
time a bank challenged a Goldman, Sachs assumption, Delavan would
have to address it as well, as in: what happens if net income in 1987
is only X instcad of Y?

Soon Delavan was turning out a steady stream of projected ten-year
income statements, cash flows, and balance sheets. Then, to Delavan's
shock, the banks started asking for fifteen- and twenty-year projections. As Delavan knew, nobody could accurately predict what business would be like in ten years, let alone twenty. (These projections
also raised questions inside Macy's. At one point, one senior merchant
turned to Finkelstein and said, "We can't predict what business we are
going to do tomorrow. How can we base this deal on ten-year projections?" Finkelstein's reply: "You're not the chairman yet.")

Toward the end of each day, Lane, Reid, and Robert Kaplan, an associate in private finance, often huddled together in a funk, deeply
depressed, trying to wade through the latest batch of data. Inevitably,
before they went home, they would ask Delavan for one more computer run. As the weeks went by, the loyal Delavan was forced to work
longer and longer hours, sometimes until nearly dawn. The following morning, he would drag himself back to the office and start again.

Much of what he churned out was then sent out to potential investors, heavy missives that became known as Delagrams.

Soon Lane and the others realized that Delavan wasn't looking so
well. His face was pale, his hands trembled. Concerned that he might
crack, they hired another analyst to help, a South American playboy
with a degree from Harvard. It was too late, however. The computer
model Delavan had constructed was ten pages wide and forty pages
long. No one else could understood it.

Tom Delavan never complained. But after a month or so, he began to wilt during morning conferences, his head drifting down toward the table, his eyes glazing over, until finally, without ceremony, he drifted off. Delavan was falling asleep so often that the bankers visiting Goldman, Sachs to discuss terms began to notice. At first, this caused great merriment. Then, because they were bankers and enjoyed a good bet, they formed pools and began to wager on the exact moment Delavan would doze off.

This was hard work. Goldman, Sachs made house calls at fifteen banks and six different financial institutions, starting with Chase Manhattan Bank, where Ed Finkelstein was a director. Although Chase had shunned leveraged buyouts in the past, Finkelstein was confident that the bank would make an exception. They knew him personally, and they were familiar with Macy's.

And yet Chase passed. The bank said it wanted to invest, but the price looked too rich. There were coverage ratios that had to be met, so much in assets for every dollar loaned by the bank, and at $70 a share, Macy's didn't fit within the boundaries of those ratios. Besides, the terms called for the banks to be repaid after ten years; they preferred six. Come back if the deal changes, they said. Really.

Metropolitan Life Insurance passed too. In early meetings with Goldman, Sachs, Finkelstein sounded certain that Met Life would invest. After all, Robert Schwartz, the company's chairman, served on Macy's board. But Schwartz's friends say that even if Schwartz had supported the buyout—which he didn't—he would have opposed any investment because of the appearance of a conflict of interest. Schwartz wouldn't have wanted anyone to suggest that his Macy's vote as a director was influenced by his desire to create an attractive investment opportunity for Met Life.

It was yet one more example of Finkelstein's failure to read his board correctly.

Citibank N.A. and Manufacturers Hanover Trust, however, were interested. In exchange for $10 million fees, they were willing to act as co-agents, buying $200 million worth of Macy's debt each and trying to sell another $800 million between them. There were no guarantees, though. It would be a "best effort" only.

Jim Lane's second bit of good news was as unexpected as it was welcome. Sheldon Seevak, the Goldman, Sachs partner in charge of real estate financing, had intended to divvy up the eighty-four stores Macy's owned or leased into four different groups, and raise about $200 million in mortgage financing from each package.

What he didn't count on were the empire-building instincts of Donald Knab, a senior real estate executive at Prudential Insurance Company of America. Knab, who was once described by *Institutional Investor* as the "single most powerful player in American real estate," stood six feet six inches tall, literally towering over everyone else.

Knab was intrigued by the Macy's buyout because he thought that most of the retailer's department stores were in prime centers, malls so strong that other retailers would jump at the chance to take over the sites if Macy's defaulted. He also knew that Goldman, Sachs was trying to interest Prudential's corporate finance department in investing in new Macy's debt or equity.

Knab now took the single biggest gamble in his life. A few days after talking to Seevak, he made a powerful presentation to Prudential's board of directors, arguing that Prudential should make only one investment in the Macy's buyout—and that it should be in real estate. No matter who later invested in Macy's, he assured the board, everyone would have to stand and salute each time Prudential walked in the room. After all, without its stores, Macy's didn't have a business.

The board, which included David Yunich, the former Macy's vice chairman, liked what it heard, especially after Knab suggested that Prudential stood to earn 12 percent or more a year on its investment. Knab then got on the phone and called Seevak back.

"Shelly," he said without any preliminaries. "We're not going to participate in your mortgage financing."

In the silence that followed, Knab barked, "We're going to take it all, or we aren't going to take any of it."

"Are you serious?" asked Seevak.

"Absolutely. We're going to take the entire mortgage issue," replied Knab. "And I want cross defaults on everything." Cross defaults meant that a single missed mortgage payment would constitute a default on the entire package. And if Macy's didn't cure that default within an agreed-upon time frame, Prudential could begin foreclosure proceedings.

There was something else, Knab continued. In consideration for providing the entire real estate facility, Prudential wanted a kicker en-titling it to share in revenues at the stores it was financing once sales passed a certain level.

Seevak, thrilled, indicated that he thought this could be arranged.

As soon as they finished, Knab picked up the phone again. This time he called Frank MacDougal, the president of Prudential Mort-gage Capital. "Frank, I've just worked out a deal with Goldman, Sachs," he said. "Take care of the details, won't you?"

It was virtually the last thing Knab had to do with the largest single transaction in Prudential's history: an $811 million mortgage loan se-cured by first or second mortgages on seventy-one stores. But it would take MacDougal until May 1986 to nail down a final agreement.

Others, too, were studying the Macy's proposal, including General Electric. Jack Welch, chairman of GE, and John Weinberg, the senior partner at Goldman, Sachs, were good friends, a relationship that re-flected decades of trust between the investment banking company and the giant technology company. Sidney Weinberg, John's father, had also served GE as a director for many years.

As soon as Finkelstein announced his bid to buy Macy's, Welch and John Weinberg began discussing a role for General Electric Credit Corp., a diversified financial services subsidiary. Easing the way was the fact that Macy's and GE shared two board members: Lawrence Fouraker and Barbara Preiskel. In addition, Gertrude Michelson, a Macy's senior vice president, sat on the GE board. Michelson and Finkelstein had joined Macy's at the same time, and were part of the same training squad. By one account, they were ranked one and two in that group—with Michelson finishing first.

One former executive at GE Credit says the finance company's ini-tial interest was so strong that it weighed an ownership stake well in excess of 20 percent. But when GE Credit's analysts reviewed the sup-porting documents, they realized that Goldman, Sachs had failed to factor in certain accounting provisions mandated by GAAP—gener-ally accepted accounting principles—for companies involved in lever-aged buyouts.

Instead of showing net profits over the next five years, Macy's in-stead would suffer substantial paper losses. And if GE Credit owned more than 20 percent, it would have to consolidate those losses on its books.

"Once we found that out, we decided not to take more than a nineteen-point-nine percent stake," says this former executive. "That allowed us to treat our Macy's stock as an investment. What also struck us as amazing was that Goldman, Sachs had geared the entire deal to a level of profitability we thought was impossible for Macy's to maintain: annual earnings before interest, taxes, depreciation, and amortization of nearly fifteen percent.

"There was no way Macy's was going to do that well. So we challenged it in a meeting with Ed Finkelstein. We said, 'Where do these numbers come from?' And Ed said, 'These are the numbers we're going to produce, I'm going to get them. Don't question it.'"

GE Credit was crucial to Goldman, Sachs because its support would likely convince other potential investors. What Goldman, Sachs wanted was for GE Credit to commit itself to a $400 million junk bond issue of senior subordinated debentures.

Another meeting was then arranged, this time at the GE Credit office in Stamford, Connecticut. "We told them that we were willing to go ahead, but that they would have to lower the price," says the former GE executive. "It was embarrassing for them. But the very next day, that's what they did."

They had to. Despite their best efforts, Citibank and Manufacturers Hanover Trust weren't able to find buyers for $800 million in new Macy's bank debt. The Prudential talks were moving ahead, but mortgage financing requires reams of documentation, and the deal wasn't close to being finished. And though GE continued to express interest in investing, the two sides were still far apart.

Every day that passed brought them closer to the January 15 deadline.

At the end of the first week of December, Lane decided to tell Finkelstein they would either have to reduce the bid or lose the deal. Blessed with common sense, Lane insisted on being accompanied by others from Goldman, Sachs, including John and Jimmy Weinberg.

Sure enough, Finkelstein was beside himself. "You told me you could do this," he screamed at Lane. "You've failed. It's an embarrassment to you as well as myself. This is terrible. We promised seventy dollars a share and we're going to pay seventy dollars a share."

When he finally quieted down, Lane shook his head no. "You've made your point," he said. "But the numbers don't work. Now, what are we going to do about it?"

Several days later, on December 11, Goldman, Sachs sent a thick package of documents to Jim Wolfensohn's offices. Inside were letters from Citibank, Manufacturers Hanover Trust, and GE Credit, indicating that they were willing to participate in Finkelstein's buyout—but at $68 a share, or about $100 million less than Finkelstein had offered.

A week later, Macy's outside directors agreed to accept the lower offer. As Jim Wolfensohn pointed out, the lower price still represented a 30 percent premium over what the stock had been selling for when the buyout was announced. Besides, there weren't any other bidders.

But in exchange for approving the lower offer, the special committee demanded that if Finkelstein was unable to complete his financing package by January 15, he would have to promise not to participate in a hostile acquisition proposal for the following eighteen months. Finkelstein agreed, and two days later, he sheepishly announced that he was reducing his offer to $68 per share.

Wall Street remained skeptical. Macy's shares fell only 25 cents to $63.375, which meant that the stock was still selling well below the $68 that Finkelstein was now promising to pay. Apparently many doubted that Finkelstein would be able to raise even that much.

The next four weeks were the worst in Jim Lane's life.

The banks demanded some of the same security that Goldman, Sachs had pledged to Prudential. Citibank claimed the right to remedy any subsequent mortgage defaults, a strategy designed to prevent Prudential from foreclosing in case the Macy's buyout floundered. Two insurance companies, Equitable and Teachers, wanted the senior notes they were negotiating to buy to be treated as equal to the senior bank debt, even though their notes matured later. GE Credit, dickering over $400 million worth of senior subordinated debentures due in 1998, also wanted certain mortgage rights on some stores.

Two days before the January 15 deadline set by the special committee, Lane called Fred Eckert in Chicago and said, "Fred, it's all blowing up. I can't get any lenders to agree. We're going to have to get them all in one room and fight it out."

"I'll catch a plane," Eckert replied. "Set it up."

Lane then phoned GE Credit, the banks, the insurance companies, and Prudential. Either they would all meet that evening at Goldman, Sachs at 8 P.M., he said, or the deal was dead.

Everyone came, of course. Huge fees were at stake.

At exactly 8 P.M., Eckert and Lane walked into the conference room. Without saying a word of greeting, Lane suddenly reached into a bag he was carrying and whipped out seven sticks of faux dynamite attached to a digital timer. He then tossed the bomblike device onto the center of the table.

People leaped back. Then, when they realized the bomb was a fake, everyone burst into gales of nervous laughter.

"Any one of you can blow this deal up," said Lane. "That's where we are right now. You're each fighting for issues you think are important. And you're right, they are. But there comes a time when you have to decide whether you want to do a deal or not." The meeting would last nearly all night.

Like a giant Thanksgiving Day turkey, Macy's was carved into many large and bite-sized pieces. Prudential took all the nonrecourse senior real estate debt. Citibank and Manufacturers Hanover Trust agreed to provide the senior bank debt. Behind them would be senior notes held by Equitable and Teachers, notes that the banks agreed would be equal in standing with their own. Underneath all that would be a package of subordinated debt, including $400 million of senior subordinate bonds that GE Credit agreed to buy.

Late the next day, Jim Wolfensohn went to New York Hospital to see Ed Finkelstein, who was about to undergo minor surgery. Dressed in his hospital gown and prepped for his operation, Finkelstein signed off.

Kekst and Co., a New York public relations firm hired by Finkelstein to help with the buyout, subsequently issued a release announcing that Macy's Acquiring Corp., a holding company, and R. H. Macy & Co. had agreed to merge. With the possible exception of weary Tom Delavan, no one was more jubilant—or exhausted—than Jim Lane.

Shortly afterward, Lane left New York and checked himself into Our Lady of the Mississippi, a Trappist monastery in Dubuque, Iowa, where he stayed for nearly two weeks.

One of the strangest chapters in Harold Shaub's comfortable life now began to unfold. When it was finished, American retailing would be forever changed.

Intent on finding a buyer to outbid Ed Finkelstein, Shaub conscientiously worked his way through his Rolodex, reaching out to friends at Brascan Ltd., a Canadian holding company controlled by Peter and Edward Bronfman, and later, to William Andres, the former chairman of Dayton Hudson Corp. in Minneapolis.

No go.

Then he received a call from a young man who introduced himself as Tom Randall. Randall, a would-be deal broker, had graduated from Franklin & Marshall College in Lancaster, Pennsylvania, in 1974, earned a graduate business degree, and joined Paine Webber Inc. Eleven years later, he opened Tribco Partners, an investment boutique. All he had to show for his efforts, however, were two clients and a joint venture relationship with the investment banking firm of McLeod Young Weir in Toronto. Canadians were investing south of the border, and McLeod Young Weir hoped Randall could find companies for their clients.

One such client was Robert Campeau, one of fourteen children born into a poor French Canadian family. An eccentric but successful real estate developer, Campeau, sixty-two years old, began his career building single-family homes before graduating to office towers, shopping centers, and commercial centers. Although his strange, sometimes garish behavior was the grist of local Toronto gossip columns, the Campeau Corp. was highly regarded by fellow builders and home owners.

What he wanted to buy, he told Austin Taylor and Daniel Sullivan of McLeod Young Weir, was an American savings and loan association or an insurance company. A few weeks later, Shearson Lehman Brothers, which owned a small stake in McLeod Young Weir, identified a savings and loan institution that met Campeau's requirements. Instead of hurrying off to see it, however, Campeau jetted away to Europe, where he remained incommunicado for weeks. Even after he returned to Toronto, he showed no interest in the American bank. Discouraged, but unwilling to abandon a wealthy client, Taylor and Sullivan invited Morgan Stanley to Toronto for a meeting with Campeau.

The Morgan Stanley team was unimpressed. Robert Campeau, they said, lacked seriousness.

On the verge of giving up, Taylor and Sullivan remembered their firm had an arrangement with someone in New York who did merger and acquisition work. Since Tom Randall was desperate for work, the timing was perfect. As it happened, Randall remembered Campeau's name from a bid that the developer had once made for Royal Trustco, an influential Canadian trust company and real estate brokerage business. Campeau's takeover had failed, but only because the Canadian business establishment slammed the door in his face, buying back Royal Trustco shares and preventing him from borrowing additional capital. It was partly because of that fiasco that Campeau now wanted to invest in the United States.

Randall knew that Campeau had a reputation for being difficult and unpredictable. Still, he found himself much impressed at their first meeting. Campeau, dressed in a dark, hand-tailored suit, had dazzling blue eyes and a high-voltage smile. He also had the demanding manner of someone accustomed to making decisions and getting things done.

Randall now began hunting for a financial company Campeau could acquire. Since Campeau had earned his fortune in real estate, however, Randall thought it made sense to also interest him in American shopping centers. A friend at Allied Stores had whispered that five of Allied's regional shopping centers would soon be put up for sale, and Randall decided to mention them to Campeau.

Allied was then one of the biggest department store companies in the country with $4.1 billion a year in sales. It operated such chains as Bonwit Teller, Ann Taylor, Brooks Brothers, Bon Marché in Seattle, Jordan Marsh in Boston and Florida, Maas Brothers on the west coast of Florida, and Garfinckel's in Washington, D.C. Randall knew Campeau couldn't afford to bid for Allied itself, but he thought that the $300 million to $500 million that the five centers would likely command was within the developer's range.

Campeau, however, said no thanks, he already had enough real estate. When Randall then suggested that it might be possible to open a Brooks Brothers store or two in some of Campeau's Canadian centers, the developer perked up and said yes, he might be interested after all.

At about the same time, Randall read about the Macy's buyout. Reasoning that Ed Finkelstein would almost certainly have to sell some of Macy's shopping centers, he called a partner at Goldman, Sachs, explaining that a client might be interested in making a bid if there was an auction. The response was so tepid, however, that Randall decided Goldman, Sachs had already lined up a buyer.

Still, he mentioned the idea to Campeau. To his astonishment, Campeau became highly agitated, so much so that he instructed him to forget everything else.

In the weeks that followed, Campeau called every day, demanding that Randall set up a meeting at Macy's and expressing irritation that it hadn't already been done. Finally Randall reached a retired partner at McLeod Young Weir, who in turn put him in touch with Harold Shaub. A few conversations later, Shaub agreed to meet with Randall and Campeau at the Pierre Hotel in New York.

It was an experience Shaub says he will never forget. After they were introduced, Shaub carefully explained that the Macy's board wasn't interested in selling off the company in piecemeal fashion. Why not make a run at the entire company, Shaub urged, stores, centers, and all?

Campeau, though, was not interested in this idea. "He was intense, very intense," recalls Shaub. "All he wanted to talk about was shopping centers. I finally said he should speak to Jim York, who headed up our real estate holdings."

When the meeting ended, Shaub left believing he had wasted his time. Instead, he had firmly planted the idea of acquiring an American department store company in Campeau's mind.

Two days later, Campeau told Randall that they should be thinking on a larger scale. "Why can't I participate in Finkelstein's deal?" Campeau asked. "I'd like to meet him. Set it up."

Eventually, Finkelstein gave Randall sixty seconds on the telephone, explaining that he had already put together his deal and that he didn't want to see a Mr. Campeau. If Randall's client was still interested in real estate, however, Finkelstein would arrange a meeting with Jim York. And if he had time, Finkelstein added, he would stop by and say hello.

The week before Christmas, Campeau and Randall, together with Ronald Tysoe, Campeau's personal assistant, went to Macy's Herald Square to chat with Jim York, who oversaw the company's real estate holdings.

York, a gentlemanly figure in a hard-edged business, was quickly turned off by Campeau's negotiating tactics. Instead of asking how Macy's planned to sell its properties, Campeau immediately made a lowball offer and insisted that Macy's end any negotiations with other potential buyers. "Frankly, when I saw that was his approach, the meeting was over as far as I was concerned," says York.

According to Tom Randall, Campeau fidgeted throughout the talks. Worse, he frequently interrupted to ask, "When are we going to meet Finkelstein?" York was soon so embarrassed that he finally picked up the phone and asked Finkelstein if they could make a short visit. Finkelstein, only a few doors away, said no.

Jim York says he doesn't recall phoning Finkelstein during his meeting with Campeau. Still, Campeau didn't see Finkelstein that day, and he left Macy's believing he had been personally snubbed. "Bob got very angry at me," says Randall. "I tried to explain that he had to dance with these people, and that they needed time to size him up. Finally he cooled down, and before he stepped into his car, he asked me to focus all of my attention on Allied Stores. You could see what was happening. He had been dissed, but after he got over being angry, he changed gears."

Months later, Campeau announced that since he was in the mall building business, it made sense to own retail companies whose stores could rent space in his centers. Other real estate developers would come to similar conclusions, including George Herscu, an Australian developer who would buy two New York institutions, B. Altman & Co. and Bonwit Teller, and A. Alfred Taubman, who acquired the Wanamaker's chain in Philadelphia and Woodward & Lothrop in Washington, D.C. All would lose millions.

Tom Randall's relationship with Robert Campeau ended in a dispute over fees. Not too much later, Campeau was sitting in the crowded offices of McLeod Young Weir when he turned to banker Daniel Sullivan and said, "What do you think about buying all of Allied? Not just the shopping centers, everything."

Everyone in the room burst out laughing. "Bob, you're a real card," replied Sullivan.

Less than a year later, in November 1986, Campeau was celebrating his acquisition of Allied Stores for $4.1 billion.

Tom Randall, to his disappointment, wasn't invited to any of the victory parties.

While Harold Shaub met with Robert Campeau, Jim Wolfensohn was contacting everybody he knew in the buyout business. Only two potential buyers requested a meeting with the special committee.

The first was Jerome Kohlberg Jr. of Kohlberg Kravis Roberts & Co., the buyout firm. Kohlberg, however, said he wasn't interested in a hostile bid. Unless Finkelstein and his fellow managers were willing to stay in place and let KKR take a majority position in Macy's, KKR would have to pass.

The second callers were the Hafts of Washington, D.C., the family of discount store operators. In December, Herbert Haft and his son Robert, together with assorted lawyers and investment bankers, flew up to New York to learn more.

Robert Haft wasn't sure what to expect. He thought that the Macy's board was supporting Finkelstein's buyout bid and that its directors were now doing what they had to do to appease shareholders. An hour later, he realized he was mistaken. "Instead of protecting management, they were actively marketing the company," he says.

Donald Smiley, the former chairman, sounded rhapsodic about the company's future. Macy's was already the greatest department store retailer in the world, he said, and if certain changes were made in its merchandising presentation, the company should do even better.

The Hafts were impressed. These were people who obviously understood how Macy's worked and knew where the company was heading. Wolfensohn was still putting together a complete package of Macy's financials, however, which meant that the Hafts didn't have access to as much information as they needed. Still, they were intrigued enough to ask for a chat with Finkelstein.

They soon got one. And to Robert Haft's surprise, Finkelstein actually seemed pleased to see them. He took the Hafts from floor to floor, pointing out which departments were doing better than others and explaining why. "We weren't controlling the meeting, he was," Haft says. "After we saw the store he took us up to his office on the thirteenth floor to look at his pictures on the wall and talk about the history of the company. At some point it got to be lunch, and we went to their dining room, where they presented us with more financial information. We ended up talking for hours about what they were doing and where they were going. Ed was funny, he was charming, and he explained the business in detail. I guess he had lived with it for so long he felt he owned it anyway. We were all relaxed, and there was a lot of kidding through the whole thing. Mark Handler was also there, although he seemed to be dominated by Finkelstein."

When the meeting finally broke up, Robert Haft stood outside on the sidewalk and marveled at the events of the day. It was like visiting a magic kingdom, he finally decided. You stepped into an important world on the thirteenth floor, and then you left via a special elevator that opened into an incredible emporium. The Christmas holiday season was under way, it was a busy day, and the main floor was filled with thousands of shoppers talking and carrying bags. Finkelstein had said that the Herald Square store itself was worth hundreds of millions of dollars, and now Haft could see why. (For his part, after the Hafts left, all Ed Finkelstein wanted to talk about was their hairstyles.)

Weeks later, father Haft and son began to have doubts. Early on in their discussion, Finkelstein mentioned the importance of improving Macy's service, and of meeting the standards set by their West Coast rival, Nordstrom. But as the day progressed, Finkelstein frequently referred to the need for better products and the good relationships Macy's had with its suppliers. Macy's, Haft decided, reflected Finkelstein's own major interest: merchandising. But if Finkelstein was the merchant, what did Handler do?

Finkelstein didn't show much interest in the company's actual buyout proposal, either, hurrying past the numbers in order to better concentrate on the business itself. Finkelstein, Haft decided, already viewed himself as an owner. The plan was only a confirmation.

There were other concerns, too. After the buyout was complete, Finkelstein intended to continue to open new stores in such states as Louisiana. To the Hafts, however, it made more sense to open stores in areas where Macy's already had a following, and where its distribution and advertising costs would be lower. Instead, the Hafts were told that everyone knew Macy's, and that entering new markets wouldn't be a problem.

"The presentation was exciting, but we didn't see them facing up to the issues of new debt," says Robert Haft. "Ed's thinking was the numbers worked because somebody set the values and created a model, and that later, nothing was going to change. When you listened to him talk about knocking off polo shirts and he said it worked, you believed him. But when he talked about the financial model, you weren't as assured."

At the end, the Hafts decided against making a bid of their own. And when friends later called and asked whether they should invest in Macy's equity or debt, the Hafts recommended against it.

In the four months that followed, many things would happen: Citibank and Manufacturers Hanover Trust would again fail to syndicate enough bank debt. Instead, Mark Solow, the head of the leveraged buyout department, was forced to ask Bankers Trust to bail them out. Bankers Trust finally agreed to sell $500 million worth of Macy's debt, but insisted on co-billing as a lead banker, and a $10 million fee.

By mid-February, Macy's filed plans with the Securities and Exchange Commission to sell $450 million in subordinated debentures due in 2001 and $770 million in junior subordinated discount debentures, commonly known as zero coupon bonds, due in 2006. Nearly three months later, at the insistence of the banks, Macy's agreed to offer $650 million in subordinated debentures, and $910 million in zero coupon bonds. Because the zeros were so risky, they sold at such a steep discount that Macy's pocketed only $300 million for paper it would later have to redeem at three times that amount.

Macy's also reduced the length of the bank debt from ten years to six, reducing the risk for its bankers.

In exchange for $59.6 million, GE Credit acquired preferred shares in Macy's equivalent to a 19.9 percent stake on a fully diluted basis. The financial services company also bought $400 million worth of Macy's 14.5 percent senior subordinated debentures payable in 1998. Five days after that purchase, Goldman, Sachs sold the entire offering on the public market, providing GE Credit with an immediate profit of $25 million. The reason: Interest rates had fallen so sharply that the Macy's notes had now become highly desirable.

Finally, in early May, Prudential and Macy's reached an agreement regarding the real estate financing. The documentation was so complex and cumbersome that the ensuing paperwork filled three bookcase shelves. Proxy statements were then readied and mailed. Although the buyout was assured, Macy's small shareholders would finally have a chance to have their say.

Everyone was happy, even Peter Solomon, the co-head of investment banking at Shearson Lehman Brothers. A few weeks after his emotional meeting with Finkelstein, Solomon had met with Goldman, Sachs and walked out with a piece of the buyout that would earn his firm a small but pride-saving fee. He even invested some of his own family money in the new Macy's shares. "It looked good," he says. "This was a company I knew."

Chapter 7

"Maybe you will go bats doing this deal."

On June 19, 1986, Macy's public shareholders met for the last time at the New York Penta Hotel at 33rd Street and Seventh Avenue.

A month earlier, Macy's distributed proxy materials to shareholders of record as of May 15, soliciting their votes on the proposed buyout. This special meeting was being held to tally those proxies and bring to a close Macy's sixty-four year history as a publicly traded company.

Finkelstein opened the gathering by introducing himself and three others who shared the dais: Mark Handler, Macy's president and chief operating officer; Harold Shaub, the chairman of the special committee; and Marvin Fenster, secretary of the corporation.

After looking down at the sea of faces before him, he also introduced the company's board of directors, most of whom were in attendance. Then Finkelstein, as a transcript of the meeting shows, began to talk about Macy's, its history, and its future.

Not ten minutes into the meeting, Evelyn Davis, a pesty, outspoken shareholder rights activist who often asked embarrassing questions, interrupted Finkelstein's speech. Announcing that she was wearing black because she was "in mourning" for Macy's, Davis promptly questioned the legality of the meeting itself, noting that it hadn't been approved by the Securities and Exchange Commission.

Marvin Fenster replied that the company had received oral permission from the SEC, an answer that momentarily silenced her. Once she sat down, though, John Gilbert, a second shareholder rights advocate, stood to say he was dressed for two funerals, one for Macy's, and one for Gimbel's, which was about to close. Commenting on the crowds that were swarming through Gimbel's in search of bargains, Gilbert said, "They went bats with it. I never wish anybody bad, but maybe you will go bats doing this deal."

"Thank you, Mr. Gilbert," responded Finkelstein. "You are your usual gracious self."

Marvin Fenster now proposed that Macy's be sold for $68 a share. Finkelstein seconded the motion. To be approved, the merger needed the votes of two thirds of all stock outstanding. The common and the preferred were voted together as a single class.

While the proxies were being tallied, Finkelstein once again began to review the company's history. "One hundred and twenty-eight years ago, Rowland H. Macy started an innovative dry-goods store on Fourteenth Street," Finkelstein said. "He refused to haggle on price, which is what made Macy's different, and the customers liked it. R. H. Macy became a company known for its formidable undertakings and impressive successes. Though the company has had its ups and downs, during the last decade Macy's has emerged as the nation's premier retailer, an innovator, and a leader in financial performance. Our emergence as an industry leader has been marked by our ability to predict and respond to retailing trends, coupled with our willingness to blaze new paths, and to reach out in new directions."

He then thanked shareholders for supporting the growth of the company since 1922, when the business went public. In the current climate, however, when Wall Street was fixated on quarterly results, Macy's would now find it easier to "implement long-term strategies" and to react to "current trends in this fast-moving economic environment" as a private company.

"I need hardly remind you that two major New York stores have just announced that they will close," he said. "They join the long list of retail failures in the New York community. You can take it as fact that the pace of retail competition is no less hectic every place where Macy's operates."

For Ken Straus, the former director, the gathering was a humiliating spectacle. His family had been associated with Macy's for more than a century; in Manhattan, an elementary school, a public park, and a housing project all carried their name, a testimony to their skills at balancing public interest with managing a business.

Yet on Macy's last day as a public company, Ken Straus sat among a row of dejected directors, feeling like an errant schoolchild as Finkelstein preened on stage. "Ed launched into a history of the company, starting with Roland H. Macy, and then jumped straight to Finkelstein," says Straus. "Nobody else was mentioned."

Finkelstein then opened the meeting to questions from shareholders. Once again, Evelyn Davis spoke up. Macy's was one of the first companies in which she invested, she said, and she still remembered attending her first Macy's stockholders meeting in 1959.

"I like you personally," she told Finkelstein. "But I find it very sad that you are doing this to us, and I am voting against the merger. I want to point out something. Just about forty years ago, when I first came to the United States—the first thing my father and I did after seeing the Statue of Liberty, the first thing, on the first day, was to go shopping at Macy's. I was only a teenager. So this is very sad indeed. In all due respect, if Jack Straus was alive, he wouldn't have approved of this. And I am sure right now he is turning over in his grave."

She then wanted to know if Finkelstein had received promises of financial help from real estate developer A. Alfred Taubman, or from retailer Leslie Wexner, chairman of The Limited. When Finkelstein replied that he had not, Davis waggled her finger and said, "Watch out for those two. They are going to get the best of you. That would really be the end of everything."

To Finkelstein's relief, the next speaker, Donald Rahman, a shareholder from Farmingdale, Long Island, was more enthusiastic. Rahman purchased his Macy's shares in 1935, during the Depression, and his investment had proven "as good, if not better, than gold," he said. Although he didn't look forward to paying capital gains on his profits, Rahman wanted to congratulate Finkelstein on a "Herculean accomplishment in scraping together three and a half billion smackeroos to buy out this great company. I frankly didn't think there was that much money left in the country after everybody paid their taxes. And I want to say to you, R. H. Macy and Company, a few words that have been on my mind for the past fifteen years. Sweetheart, I love you. Believe me. It all goes back to 1935. A quiet table for two with candlelight in a quiet corner of my stockbroker's office. I love you, baby. I am going to miss you."

Finkelstein grinned and gave his thanks.

He was not, however, finished. Charles Tanenbaum, an attorney and investor, announced he was very upset. He was there, he said, to represent the interests of his wife, who owned 2,572 shares, some of which had been purchased by her family prior to 1943.

First he questioned Finkelstein's projections for the company. The proxy indicated that Finkelstein believed Macy's earnings would grow from $4.05 a share to $8.44 a share, an increase of 108 percent. Yet during the prior five years, the best in Macy's long history, the company's earnings per share had increased only 72 percent, from $2.14 to $3.69. What he found confusing, Tanenbaum remarked, was that when Finkelstein first proposed the buyout to the full board a year earlier, on June 25, 1985, he warned that future sales and earnings would likely be less impressive than in the early 1980s. What Tanenbaum wanted to understand was why Finkelstein had been pessimistic when he was trying to buy the company but was so upbeat when he was trying to finance his purchase.

Finkelstein replied that he didn't see any contradiction. Macy's earnings had grown an average of 25 percent annually during the years he was chairman, while the estimates contained in the proxy projected only a 10 percent annual growth.

Tanenbaum then began to question Finkelstein's integrity. He had just finished reading an article by Michael Thomas that described how leveraged buyouts were often financed on the basis of cash flow projections, estimates that shareholders were never shown. The fact that Finkelstein had raised $3.7 billion to take over the company suggested that Finkelstein and other Macy's insiders had done the same to their shareholders.

Now Finkelstein began to lose his temper. Tanenbaum was wrong about that, he said. The only projections anyone had seen were the ones presented in the most recent proxy, which Tanenbaum had before him.

Perhaps Finkelstein thought Tanenbaum would now go away. Instead, the shareholder was only warming up.

After reviewing the history of the negotiations with the board, Tanenbaum began, it was apparent that Harold Shaub and the special committee had rejected $68 a share on September 18. Yet they accepted a $70 offer a month later. As a result, more than half of all Macy's shares changed hands, effectively putting the company in the control of arbitrageurs who were only interested in the highest possible price.

What confused him, Tanenbaum continued, was the board's decision to later accept the very $68-dollar-per-share price that they had once rejected. He would now like to know why.

Finkelstein didn't answer. Instead, Harold Shaub explained that the special committee had worked hard to get the highest possible price for the company, which he was confident they had done. He also reminded Tanenbaum that the special committee wasn't selling the company. Rather, that decision would be made by the company's shareholders. And they apparently approved, because of the 39.6 million proxies Macy's had so far received, 38 million had voted in favor of the sale.

Tanenbaum, though, refused to back off. Directing yet another question at Finkelstein, he noted that in 1981, 2.25 million shares of Macy's stock had been allocated to the company's executives to be used as options and performance bonuses. If Finkelstein was so interested in providing more incentive to his managers, why didn't he ask Macy's board to make a second allotment? Such a decision would have been more fair than buying the company outright, he continued. In the new Macy's corporation, there would be only 1.75 million shares of stock available to management, of which Finkelstein had allotted 932,000 shares, or more than half, to the company's top nine executives. That left only 818,000 common shares for everyone else.

Before he could continue, Finkelstein interrupted.

"Do you want a response to that, or are you just interested in making a speech?" he asked, visibly angry.

"I simply want . . ."

"We have talked to three hundred and forty management executives in the last few months," Finkelstein interrupted. "Mr. Handler and myself have talked personally to about eighty of them. The readings I get from David Brown [Macy's senior vice president of personnel] and other personnel people is that they are extraordinarily excited about their forthcoming opportunity. They see the potential benefit far in excess of anything we could have offered them as a public company. There is risk involved, of course, but the reaction has been very, very positive. In the last few months we have had almost no defections. And the few people we have lost have gone to other leveraged buyout opportunities.

"Let me remind you of one thing, if I may. In 1974, when I returned to Macy's New York, the corporation had very middling earnings, and the Macy's New York division was losing money. If you owned your stock in 1984, or acquired it about that time, the value of the corporation was about $100 million. If you had invested $1,000 in Macy's at that point, your investment would have been worth twenty-two times that much at the time of our buyout announcement. And we are buying you out at thirty-five times that original investment. The management team that is going to be involved in this effort—and the one we wish to hold together—is the one that created that progress. James Wolfensohn thought our price was fair. And from what I am told, almost ninety-seven percent of shareholders have agreed. Clearly you represent a small minority point of view."

After a momentary pause, however, Tanenbaum continued to attack. Under the terms of the buyout, he said, Finkelstein would in effect become "a czar" because he would retain sole voting rights for all of management's shares. "This deal turns over the control of Macy's completely to one man who will have the authority to sell the chain or do anything else," Tanenbaum barked. "Is this in the company's best interests?"

Finkelstein was unmoved. The company's new investors were sophisticated, he said, and they would see to it that the necessary covenants and issues of corporate governance were in place. "The chief executive is not allowed willy-nilly to make decisions to sell off divisions or buy divisions," he said.

Finally weakening, Tanenbaum agreed there was little point talking about the future of the company since present shareholders weren't going to participate. Besides, he didn't want to extend the meeting too far, because if he did, shareholders wouldn't be given the free lunch that Macy's traditionally served them once a year.

That wasn't an issue, Finkelstein replied. There would be no box lunch today.

Tanenbaum was losing, but he refused to go quietly. Instead, he said it bothered him that Finkelstein's stock options were being accelerated, and that as a result, Finkelstein would own 143,000 shares of common stock. At $68 a share, Tanenbaum continued, Macy's chairman would pocket $9,724,000, of which he would then use $4.4 million to buy his 25 percent stake in the new company.

"You are walking away with twenty-five percent of the new stock, and

$5.3 million in cash before taxes," said Tanenbaum. "Moreover, the exchange of your old shares for the new shares is tax-free—whereas the rest of us are paying taxes. Did you ever consider being a little more generous, in putting a little more of your own money into this deal instead of taking control for nothing and walking away?"

"I don't consider my investment nothing," countered Finkelstein. "You have made your points, and I will be ready to entertain another question."

Tanenbaum declined. "I just wonder if there are any fellow stockholders who would welcome going to court and presenting the facts," he finished. "Perhaps you would permit us pause to give us an opportunity to litigate the question of propriety of a president who has been a fiduciary officer for five years and is now taking over the company for nothing because Wall Street is willing to buy the paper." (A subsequent suit went nowhere.)

"Your comments are now well out of line, and your facts are incorrect, but we won't get into that at the moment," snapped Finkelstein.

The remaining ballots were then collected. When all of the proxies were counted, there were 40,463,773 in favor of Finkelstein's proposal, and only 863,315 against. It was a landslide.

One shareholder then rose and asked if Beverly Sills would sing a chorus of "Auld Lang Syne," creating laughter and applause, but no song.

At 12:30 P.M., Finkelstein entertained a motion to adjourn. The company was his.

Chapter 8

"Ed was a man on a mission."

It began with shoppers swarming into the stores, squabbling good-naturedly with their kids over back-to-school clothes, and reaching for summer markdowns still on the racks.

This was Macy's at its best, bustling with big crowds, humming with promise. The quarter that ended October 1986, Macy's first as a privately held company in more than half a century, was a smash. Sales at stores open at least a year improved more than 12 percent. Cash flow, or earnings before interest, taxes, and depreciation, rose sharply, sending the message that the debt-laden retailer would pay its bills. "The people who lent us the money are all very pleased," said Ed Finkelstein, elated. "The buyout is working." Later he told *Business Week* that when Macy's went public again "at least seventy people in the organization will be multimillionaires."

This was how it was going to be. Finkelstein's team would work, trust their instincts, and then reap the rewards. And Finkelstein would do more reaping than anyone. As owner of 4.8 percent of Macy's stock, including all shares and options, he hoped to one day be worth nearly $400 million, assuring his place as one of the country's richest men.

It was the stuff of fairy tales. But years later, one senior executive who owed tens of thousands of dollars when Macy's went bust, muttered that the early success had been the worst thing that had ever happened.

To analysts following the three classes of Macy's junk bond debt issued when the retailer went private, the results reflected the retailer's renewed strength and purpose now that Finkelstein was focusing on business instead of his deal.

And yet Macy's needed fine-tuning. The Gap, Wal-Mart Stores, and Dillard Department Stores had invested in state-of-the-art distribution systems, enabling them to cut costs and advertise prices Macy's struggled to match. It was all part of a bigger riddle. Department stores had always measured value by breadth of selection, or their exclusive designer lines, or even the quality of their service. But as Ralph Lauren, Liz Claiborne, and other suppliers opened cheap factory stores, value increasingly meant only the lowest possible price.

Macy's, which needed to pack in the crowds, would have to reduce overhead.

It wouldn't be as easy as firing two dozen junior buyers, either. Department stores, created in the nineteenth century, were intended for customers who had long, leisurely hours to shop, and who would pay extra in exchange for being spritzed with perfumes and given free umbrellas. In turn, Saturday afternoons at Macy's meant French chefs hawking enameled cookware; Mutant Ninja Turtles strutting their stuff for future Generation X-ers, and high school choirs singing Bach. It was as much a spectacle as the shows on Broadway. Philadelphia retailer John Wanamaker once said that he knew that half of his advertising dollars were wasted; he just never knew which half. Tampering with Macy's original formula of too much and too loud would be just as dangerous. Still, only a year or so earlier, Finkelstein removed the Davison's logo from his Atlanta stores and hoisted up the Macy's flag, explaining it made more sense to promote one name. The move was expected to save millions of dollars in advertising costs and make it easier to introduce private label brands.

Finkelstein looked across the Hudson River at the company's twenty-four Bamberger's stores, and decided to do it again. The division was re-christened Macy's New Jersey, severing Macy's remaining ties to the Straus era.

It was good business, but customers and Bamberger's employees also found it a melancholy reminder of how tradition can be erased by executive decree. Macy's relationship with Bamberger's dated back to October 1929, when the Strauses bought L. Bamberger & Co. The retailer's ten-story flagship store on Market Street in downtown Newark was one of the country's largest, with 1,245,000 square feet of space, including four floors below ground. Its assortments of Hickey Freeman men's suits and pricey women's cosmetics drew comparisons to Chicago-based Marshall Field & Co., and its collections of sheets, comforters, and housewares lured customers from the most remote corners of the state. Joseph Nagy, a former Bamberger's executive and its unofficial historian, says 1929 sales of about $38 million were among the highest of any department store in the country that year.

Like Macy's, Bamberger's boasted a colorful history. Louis Bamberger, who cofounded the business in December 1892, was a nononsense entrepreneur who valued his employees and gambled on new technology. By the time he sold out, the department store company's assets included the pioneer radio station WOR, known as the Bamberger Broadcasting Service, and *Charm*, an in-house fashion publication with a circulation of 85,000. At his insistence, Bamberger's was also one of the first to provide a low-cost, quality cafeteria.

After the Strauses took over, Louis Bamberger and his sister, Caroline Fuld, helped fund The Institute for Advanced Study in Princeton, New Jersey. The fledgling think tank then hired Albert Einstein as its first full-time professor, causing French physicist Paul Langevin to compare its importance to "the transfer of the Vatican to America."

So was the world of science turned upside down by an aging bachelor who'd mastered the equally mysterious art of buying and selling.

Macy's later sold *Charm* magazine and the radio station at a fraction of their real worth. Bamberger's, though, became an integral part of the empire. Dozens of senior executives invested years in New Jersey, proving themselves before being transferred to New York. One of the best among them was David Yunich, a square-shouldered, former professional baseball player who oversaw Bamberger's statewide expansion during the 1950s. Yunich was blessed with plenty of common sense and the natural grace of a gifted athlete, and in 1962, Charles Revson, the founder of Revlon Inc., tried to hire him away. Revson's offer included 500,000 shares of stock and an apartment in New York City.

When Yunich replied that he was satisfied at Bamberger's, the lipstick king ignored him.

"Everybody has a price," Revson said. "Name yours."

Yunich paused. A minute later, he countered with the most outrageous sum he could think of: $1 million cash, net after taxes.

"You've got it," replied Revson, standing up to end their meeting. "Call my lawyer and he'll arrange it."

But Yunich never got his money. When he went home and told his wife, she threatened him with divorce. "She didn't like Charlie," says Yunich, who later served as chairman of New York's Metropolitan Transportation Authority. "He was a very crude guy. You'd go to his place for lunch, and he'd serve you on a gold service. But then you'd go into the living room and have to sit on a pillow that said, 'Put Your Ass Here,' or 'Fuck You.' I'm not a prudish guy, but I could understand my wife's reaction. Yet how many times do you get to say no to a million bucks? So I told a friend of Jack Straus's, and within five days I was made president of Macy's New York. It was good-bye to Bamberger's."

After Yunich transferred to Herald Square, he was succeeded at Bamberger's by Herbert Seegal. Seegal, in turn, brought in Ed Finkelstein as his chief merchant. And when both were promoted to bigger jobs in 1969, Mark Handler, Finkelstein's protégé, succeeded Seegal. A bon vivant who enjoyed an early martini, Handler was always ready with a joke or a pat on the back. And his eagerness to delegate responsibility was legendary. "Mark held the reins lightly," says one former Bamberger's manager. "One day, Ab Gomberg, our sales promotion executive, walked in with a make-up of a new spring catalog, seeking a signature. Handler simply looked at him and waved him off, saying, 'If you like it, I'll like it.' " Yet Handler's touch worked wonders. During his tenure, Bamberger's expanded gracefully into Pennsylvania, and then south, tailoring its assortments to local tastes.

And during the 1970s, when the floundering Macy's New York division was losing money, the profits from Bamberger's kept the corporation afloat. Bamberger's enjoyed its own corporate culture, its own board of directors, its own buyers, and its own computer system. The retailer even had a newsletter, "Around the Clock," which published such stories as "High fashion in fabrics," and "Glove sale on!"

For its employees, who relished outperforming the Macy's staff, sacrificing the Bamberger's name was like abandoning a favorite relative.

What most didn't know was that American Express had made Finkelstein's decision a lot easier. The financial services and travel giant, eager to gain access to the tens of thousands of Bamberger's customers, offered $1 million in promotional funds if the suburban chain would accept its green charge card.

Its timing was exquisite. "We knew it would cost about that much to change our signs and promote our new name, so Bobby Friedman, who was running the business, decided to go ahead," recalls Dan Bergman, a former Bamberger's executive. "He also felt it would make Eddie happy to change our name. As Bobby explained many times, Eddie was chief executive of Macy's. Anything not named Macy's diminished his feelings of being in charge. So Bobby, in order to curry favor with Eddie, offered to change the name on his own."

Bergman thought it was a bad idea because Bamberger's own charge card business was a key profit center. It also provided customer names for the retailer's valuable mailing lists. But after suggesting the idea to Finkelstein, Friedman returned to Newark, hunted down Bergman, and bragged, "Eddie said he was proud of me."

Soon afterward, Friedman was asked if the suburban stores would merge with Macy's New York division. It was a delicate issue, since a marriage would create layoffs, including many staffers who had invested in Finkelstein's buyout of Macy's. Friedman dismissed the idea outright.

"Why tinker with a good thing?" he replied. "We have twenty-four stores to take care of. We need an organization."

His remarks were greeted with relief. Although Bamberger's had lost its name, the hundreds of jobs that would otherwise have been jeopardized by a merger were safe. At least temporarily. (Mr. Friedman declined to be interviewed.)

For Ed Finkelstein, eliminating the Davison's and Bamberger's names enabled him to accelerate Macy's commitment to its house brands. Finkelstein had grown increasingly passionate about Macy's private label collection of more than sixty names, among them Jennifer Moore and Morgan Taylor. Soon he began shipping huge quantities of these faux designer labels into the former Bamberger's stores, pushing out longtime vendors in the process.

He knew the customers were complaining about finding the same designer names in all the stores. Besides, when one store advertised a sale, all the others had to follow, crimping the profits. But if Macy's created its own designer brands, Finkelstein would decide what went on sale, at what price, and when.

The daring strategy was already a big hit at The Limited, a clever, resourceful chain Finkelstein admired and envied. The Limited had hit the fashion jackpot twice, first with Outback Red, a line of bush-country wear that included jodhpurs, wide-brimmed straw hats, and cable-knit sweaters, and which debuted just before the release of Robert Redford's movie *Out of Africa*. The second line was Forenza, a collection of bold sweaters and stirrup pants. When teenage girls embraced both, record profits followed. "If you own the real estate, and then design and produce your own clothes, it's analogous to drilling the oil, refining the oil, and owning the gas station," says Tom Puls, president of Donna Ricco Inc., a New York dress house. When Macy's paid $20 for a private label dress, its buyers added the traditional manufacturer markup of $20, and then doubled the price at retail. The profit spread was $60, or a third more than Macy's made on a dress that it bought in the garment center a few blocks west of Herald Square.

Finkelstein loved this business. Every month, Macy's merchants were encouraged to buy ever-larger quantities of in-house brands, be they sheets, women's sportswear, or shoes. "We never said we didn't want it," says Jay Friedman, a former Macy's group vice president. "It was a question of how much, and at the expense of which brands domestically. But they rarely let me cut back. Ed was a man on a mission."

But it was a risky, sometimes expensive business. Orders were placed as much as nine months in advance, with letters of credit that meant Macy's had to tie up big amounts of cash. At the same time, some styles were out of fashion by the time they were delivered. Or they didn't fit. Or only size seven blouses were shipped. And if the clothes didn't sell, Macy's alone shouldered the loss. Department store buyers had grown accustomed to calling vendors and demanding markdown money, or co-op dollars when a season's clothes didn't sell. Some manufacturers were even told to write five-figure checks, a form of extortion disguised as relationship building.

But when its in-house brands didn't sell, Macy's carried the full burden itself.

Macy's top merchants were too scared to argue, largely because Finkelstein's oldest son, Mitchell, was the managing director of Macy's buying office in Hong Kong.

A gifted tennis player, Mitch attended elite local tournaments as a teenager, playing against several future high-ranking Macy's merchants. After high school he enrolled at the University of Redlands,

Above: Retailer Rowland H. Macy's store on the corner of Sixth Avenue and 14th Street in New York City in 1885, wrapped in mourning bunting because of the death of President Ulysses S. Grant.

CORBIS-BETTMANN

Rowland H. Macy went broke four times, built one of the greatest department stores in the world, but feared leaving his fortune to his only son.

CORBIS-BETTMANN

Above: Edward S. Finkelstein in his office on the thirteenth floor of Macy's Herald Square; it was the only company for which he ever worked. AP/WIDE WORLD PHOTOS *Below:* The Straus family moved Macy's north to Herald Square, laying the foundation in 1902, with an elevated subway line only a few steps away. CORBIS-BETTMANN

Three years later, in 1905, the store was bustling with crowds;
note the horse-drawn carriage midway between the two sets of trolleys.

Macy's Herald Square store on June 19, 1986, the day that shareholders overwhelmingly approved Ed Finkelstein's $3.7 billion leveraged buyout.

After outbidding Ed Finkelstein, Canadian real estate developer Robert Campeau merged Federated Department Stores with Allied Stores, creating one of the biggest department store companies in the world. If Finkelstein had won Federated, Macy's would have emerged as a publicly traded company, and might never have filed for Chapter 11 bankruptcy protection. KEN SAWCHUK/*NEWSDAY*

After Mike Ullman joined Macy's, Ed Finkelstein described him as one of the hardest workers he'd ever met, but after Macy's collapsed in Chapter 11 bankruptcy, he believed Ullman had conspired behind his back.

COURTESY OF MYRON (MIKE) ULLMAN III

In September 1990, Macy's top trio of managers were still smiling:
Mark Handler (*left*), Ed Finkelstein (*center*), and Mike Ullman.

Laurence Tisch went from
being one of Ed Finkelstein's
biggest supporters to launching his own bid to buy the
company. Later, his bulldog
approach to the negotiations
with Federated Department
Stores likely resulted in an
additional $500 million for
creditors.

With Ed Finkelstein gone, Macy's two new cochairmen, Mike Ullman, *left*, and Mark Handler, formed an uneasy alliance that never created the revenues gains Macy's so badly needed. *NEWSDAY*

Ace department store merchant Allen Questrom wouldn't work for Robert Campeau; he instead led Federated Department Stores out of Chapter 11 bankruptcy protection and then stunned the country by buying Macy's. *NEWSDAY*

A few months after Macy's agreed to Federated's takeover, Barney floated
serenely at Macy's sixty-eighth Thanksgiving Day Parade in November 1994.

a progressive liberal arts school in Redlands, California, about sixty-five miles east of Los Angeles. Friends say he briefly attempted to earn his living as a professional tennis player. When that didn't work out, Ed Finkelstein asked Mark Handler to help find Mitch a job.

Handler immediately turned the problem over to Dan Bergman. Says Bergman: "Mark and I were in California at the Beverly Hills Hotel when Mark said to me, 'Eddie's son, Mitch, is in town. Would you talk to him? Maybe we could use him. Or maybe something else will occur to you, and you can give the kid some advice.' "

Bergman met Mitchell in the hotel's lounge. "Mitch was sulky, laid-back, and totally devoid of any interest whatsoever," says Bergman. "He wasn't unpleasant. He was boring." A few hours later, Bergman left without having offered Mitch Finkelstein advice or a job, mostly because Finkelstein didn't appear to want either.

Instead Mitch was hired as a fact checker at *New West* magazine. After deciding that he didn't want a career in journalism, he enrolled at the University of Southern California intending to earn his MBA.

After a year he dropped out and went to work for Walter Schoenfeld, whose Seattle-based apparel company, Schoenfeld Industries, did about $10 million a year in sales with Macy's. Although several former Macy's executives say that Walter Schoenfeld was forced into giving the younger man a job, he says it was his idea.

"I hired Mitch as a friend of the family," insists Schoenfeld. "I've known his parents, Ed and Myra, since the early days."

Schoenfeld first sent Mitch to El Paso, where he worked for four months in a factory, learning about production. Mitch was then transferred to Hong Kong, where he stayed for a year. He traveled twice to Korea, twice to Taiwan, while overseeing quality control issues.

Although Mitch briefly returned to Los Angeles in hopes of launching his own business, he eventually joined R. H. Macy Corporate Buying in September 1981 as executive administrative assistant to the managing director in Hong Kong.

Soon afterward, he met Hui Ling, a beautiful actress who had starred in twenty-five dramas and comedies produced by entertainment kingpin Sir Run Run Shaw, a kung fu practitioner and one of the wealthiest men in Asia. Mitch and Hui Ling married in 1986 and had two children: Joshua and Sara. By then Mitch had been promoted five times to senior vice president.

"If there was a dominant partner in that marriage, it was Hui Ling," says John Shepardson, a former Macy's group vice president who on occasion visited Mitch at his Hong Kong townhouse. "She was very tough, very smart, and very attractive. When they first met, in the early 1980s, she spoke little English. By the time they were married, she was fluent—she taught herself." What most impressed Shepardson was that Hui Ling spoke to her daughter in Chinese, while the girl's father spoke in English. "It was amazing to watch," says Shepardson. "Sara would say a sentence to her father in English, and then turn around and say a sentence to her mother in Chinese. And she would do it without hesitation."

When asked how Mitch and Hui Ling were able to get along before they spoke the same language, Shepardson replied, "Chemistry."

One executive who frequently worked in Hong Kong describes Mitch's primary responsibilities as insuring good vendor relations. And while Mitch's salary may have been higher than it would have been for a non-Finkelstein, he says Mitch "contributed" in a significant way.

Still, Mitch would sometimes disappear to play tennis, returning late in the afternoon. (In interviews, Ed Finkelstein always defended Mitch's work habits, emphasizing that Mitch went to the office six days a week at 7 A.M. Even if Mitch played tennis, his father said, he always put in a full day. And often entertained at night.)

But as Mitch rose inside the company, his impressive salary created jealousy. By 1988, he was earning $260,000 a year as a senior vice president, plus another $91,000 housing allowance that covered some of the costs of a three-level townhouse. The mortgage on his townhouse was also guaranteed by Macy's, say those familiar with the situation.

This wasn't atypical in the Far East, where American companies often paid extra to keep top people in place. And yet Mitch was widely disliked, not only because some found him lazy, but because he goaded Macy's merchants into buying more private goods than they wanted. "Mitch would hover over them if they didn't write enough orders," says one executive who worked with him. "If Ed said that twenty-seven percent of all sportswear was to be private label, Mitch would do what he had to do in order to make sure merchants took it to that level. This would include calling his father, or calling people that the individuals worked for."

The turning point came in 1987, when The Limited promoted a Shaker sweater that turned into the year's hottest fashion item. Macy's had its own version, but when its stores sold out early in the season, The Limited cornered the market.

Furious that Macy's had missed an opportunity to exploit a profitable trend, Finkelstein berated his buyers for letting the company down. Determined not to make the same mistake, Macy's buyers now began placing larger orders for private label goods. If they were sure they could sell 10,000 sweaters, for example, they bought 40,000. Macy's private label goods soon monopolized key selling areas, including moderate-priced women's sportswear, where they topped 30 percent of all goods on the floor, compared to an average of 20 percent or less at other department stores.

Macy's vendors considered it a dumb mistake. Bud Konheim, president of Nicole Miller Ltd., a top women's apparel house, recalls that when he joined his father's children's clothing business in 1955, Macy's had buying offices at Herald Square that were open to manufacturers large or small. "They had certain days where buyers were required to see us," says Konheim. "If ten thousand vendors showed up, you'd get a number, sit in the waiting room, and the buyer would take everybody, without favoritism, without passing anybody.

"Test and reorder was the Macy's game, and it forced the ready-to-wear manufacturers to be fast and sharp. Macy's didn't write big orders, they wrote test orders. My father was just starting out again, and we got an order to test. And it sold like crazy. So they gave us a reorder, and suddenly we were off and running. Bloomingdale's wasn't sharp yet; it was still a cheap bra and girdle store, the first stop in from Queens, where they'd sling it out on the counter. Macy's was the quality department store for the middle class. After we began to sell them, we sold everyone else. But it all started at Macy's, where the doors were open to everyone."

One by one, however, those doors were closing.

Midway through President Ronald Reagan's second term in office, the economy exploded. Jobs were plentiful, housing prices were on the climb. On weekends, families crowded regional shopping centers on both coasts, transforming them into the equivalent of concrete village greens. Television camera crews trailed behind senior citizens taking their early morning constitutionals; hours later, those leisurely strolls became feature stories on the evening news. Some shopping addicts even wore T-shirts that read: "He who dies with the most toys wins."

It was a scene. And few paid keener attention than a trio of mall czars: Edward J. DeBartolo of Youngstown, Ohio; A. Alfred Taubman of Woodland Hills, Michigan; and George Herscu of Sydney, Australia. Long accustomed to getting their way in a rough-and-tumble business, they were growing increasingly upset over the lucrative terms dictated by department store companies in exchange for their pledge to open stores in proposed new malls. And without those guarantees, the big banks wouldn't provide loans for new projects.

Eventually the mall men decided they wouldn't take it any longer. In an astonishing show of financial clout, they bought some of the country's best-known department store companies, intending to use them as captive anchor stores.

It was the proverbial big idea, as irresistible as a new pink Cadillac. In 1985, mall developers owned only 3 percent of all department store companies in the United States. Three years later, they controlled 40 percent.

George Herscu was the zaniest of the bunch. A Romanian-born survivor of the Nazi death camps, Herscu entered Australia penniless in 1950, found work as a laborer, and then sold milk shakes. Nearly four decades later, he was the boss of one of that country's largest development companies, the Hooker Corp. A flashy, outspoken personality who rubbed the local business establishment the wrong way, Herscu's empire eventually collapsed during an extended recession. And in December 1990, he was convicted of bribing a Queensland state cabinet minister and packed off to jail for five years. Before his demise, however, Herscu collected an odd assortment of American name-brand retailers that included Bonwit Teller, the specialty store company; B. Altman & Co., the carriage trade Fifth Avenue department store chain; 80 percent of the Merksamer Jewelry chain based in Sacramento, California; a majority joint-venture interest in Parisian, a highly-regarded specialty store business based in Birmingham, Alabama; and 80 percent of the troubled Sakowitz women's specialty store company in Houston that he rescued from Chapter 11 bankruptcy protection.

Operating in the United States as the L. J. Hooker Corp., Herscu invested more than $750 million in America starting in 1987. In addition to his retail properties—most of which proved to be losers—

Herscu also bankrolled several regional shopping centers, including the mammoth 1.8 million-square-foot Forest Fair Mall in Cincinnati, Ohio, where Marie Osmond sang at the ribbon cutting ceremony. "I know what to build, I know what I want, and I know the vision," he said by telephone shortly before his business collapsed.

Herscu, a proud but vain personality, became a parody of the American immigrant: He jetted into the country a wealthy man and departed busted and brokenhearted. He even lost the suburban mansion that he'd modeled after Tara in the novel *Gone with the Wind*.

George Herscu, at least, had an excuse: He was an out-of-towner.

Others should have known better, including Macy's investor A. Alfred Taubman. This mastermind builder erected some of the country's poshest shopping centers, including the Short Hills Mall in New Jersey, and then won the respect of retailers everywhere by meticulously maintaining them. Not satisfied, Taubman bought the troubled Woodward & Lothrop department store company in 1984 for $230 million. Two years later, he paid out another $183 million and acquired the sixteen-store John Wanamaker chain. It was a bold move, especially since the Philadelphia retailer's downtown flagship store needed a complete renovation. Taubman merged the two chains under the banner of Woodward & Lothrop Inc., and hired former Saks Fifth Avenue merchant Arnold H. Aronson, to run them. The brainy Aronson had some good ideas, but not enough to keep the stores from later filing for bankruptcy and being sold off.

Both Herscu and Taubman bought broken businesses and lost fortunes trying to fix them. Canadian developer Robert Campeau had a grander vision: he wanted to be the king of all the department store retailers. A former factory worker who left school when he was only fourteen, Campeau electrified Wall Street in the fall of 1986 by offering $2.7 billion for Allied Stores Corp.

A sprawling, underachieving conglomerate, Allied was then the nation's sixth largest department store operator. Its properties included seventeen department store businesses and seven specialty store divisions, among them Brooks Brothers, the men's retailer whose customers once numbered Marlene Dietrich and presidents Theodore Roosevelt, Woodrow Wilson, and Abraham Lincoln; and Ann Taylor, a snappy women's business whose growth reflected the emerging role of professional women in the workforce. Among Allied's various department store groups were Maas Brothers in Florida; Jordan

Marsh of Florida and Boston; Stern's in New Jersey; and Bon Marché in Seattle.

Despite those glittering names, Allied earned only $159 million on $4.1 billion in sales for the fiscal year ended February 1, 1986, or less than a 4 percent return on sales. In a new age of consolidation, Allied operated divisions as small as Heer's, a two-store department store company based in Springfield, Missouri, and Deys, a chain of four department stores based in Syracuse, New York.

Robert Campeau was viewed inside Canada as a flamboyant renegade who should have stuck to the construction business. Frustrated at being excluded by that country's inner circle, he decided to make a new start in the United States. A first-class builder and real estate man with a nose for value, Campeau had been negotiating with retailers for much of his adult life. Now he set his sights on owning Allied. Since Campeau Corp. earned less than $10 million (U.S.) in profits, and had a market value of $200 million, it should have been impossible, since Allied had a market value of about $2 billion.

But self-interest and greed made the plan work. Citibank N.A., First Boston Inc., and Paine Webber Group Inc. all loaned Campeau millions and raised billions more in exchange for huge fees. By early October, Allied was close to surrender.

Then, real estate developer Edward J. DeBartolo teamed up with financier Paul Bilzerian and offered to buy Allied for $3.5 billion in cash. It was only $1 per share more than Campeau's bid, but Allied's senior management accepted within nanoseconds. "Having worked closely with Edward DeBartolo for a number of years, I know that he brings to our organization a deep knowledge of Allied's operations, keen insight into retailing, and a unique comprehension of the interplay between retailing and real estate," said Thomas Macioce, Allied's chairman. "It will be an outstanding partnership." DeBartolo, a secretive, resilient figure, had built more than two hundred shopping malls, and owned the San Francisco 49ers football team.

Others might now have accepted defeat. Robert Campeau instead began buying large blocks of Allied's stock on the open market. By the time Macioce and his new partners realized what was happening, it was too late. Although they filed suit, a federal judge ruled that the purchases were lawful. Bowing to the inevitable, Allied agreed to Campeau's offer on Halloween, 1986, less than two months after the developer's public bid.

A subdued Macioce gamely described the sale as "the best of all deals."

Campeau's new department store business cost him $4.1 billion, including $612 million paid in fees to his lawyers, bankers, and other advisers. Most of the money was borrowed from banks, pension funds, and others. The most surprising lender was Edward DeBartolo, who also bought a half-interest in Allied's five centers.

Less than a month later, Macioce resigned.

Campeau gleefully took the helm and immediately went about selling sixteen of Allied's twenty-four divisions to pay down the debt. Mixing late night pleas with showy temper tantrums, Campeau browbeat his investment bankers into raising about $1 billion in asset sales by the end of 1987. It was simply brilliant, and if he had stopped there, says one former investment banker who worked closely with him, his gamble might have succeeded.

"Allied was an excellent deal," insists M. Jeffrey Branman, a former First Boston investment banker. "We sold off sixteen doggie divisions that accounted for forty percent of sales but only twelve percent of earnings and reduced our debt by one billion dollars. If you properly allocated central corporate expenses, those divisions had no earnings. And we still had Ann Taylor, Brooks Brothers, and four department store divisions. Bob created about one billion dollars in value in the first year."

Riding high, Campeau asked First Boston for a list of other potential takeover targets in the retailing field. The name that finally emerged was Federated Department Stores, based in Cincinnati. In honor of Cincinnati Reds baseball player Pete Rose, Branman suggested calling their takeover plan "Project Rose."

A pioneer holding company, Federated was formed in 1929 when Simon F. Rothschild, the head of Brooklyn-based Abraham & Straus, asked the presidents of Bloomingdale's, based in New York, Filene's, based in Boston, and F. & R. Lazarus & Co. of Columbus, Ohio, to cruise the Long Island Sound on his yacht. Sixteen years later, Fred Lazarus Jr., a founding father of Federated, took charge and launched an aggressive expansion plan. In the years that followed, he purchased Foley's in Houston in 1945; Burdines in Miami in 1957; and Bullock's in Los Angeles in 1964.

It was a superb collection of businesses, with each division operating as an independent entity complete with its own buyers and promotion schedules. Federated owned about 650 stores, generated more than $10 billion in sales, and produced more than $500 million a year in cash flow. It also owned real estate assets valued in excess of $3 billion. In Florida, Federated operated the Burdines chain, dominating the country's fastest-growing state with a savvy blend of middle and upscale prices. In New York, Bloomingdale's helped define sophisticated taste with annual extravaganzas that featured wares from India, Israel, and Italy. Federated's moderate-priced Abraham & Straus unit, based in Brooklyn, had been metropolitan New York's best-managed retail business in the early 1970s and still gave fits to rival Macy's. In Georgia, the Rich's chain was as much a part of local culture as football and Ty Cobb. Federated also owned the Lazarus department store group in Ohio, Ralphs Grocery in southern California, and several fledgling specialty store businesses.

"This was a company built to withstand any hurricane," says one former director. "It was rock solid, and it provided employment to tens of thousands of people."

Yet Federated was slipping, in part because of an ill-timed diversification strategy into specialty store retailing. Howard Goldfeder, its chairman since 1981, liked to boast, "Our size and diversity is our strength," but the strategy only created confusion about Federated's direction, especially since the specialty stores proved costly failures.

Goldfeder also lacked the muscle to rein in the strong-willed merchants who ran Federated's department store units, preventing the parent company from combining its financial, advertising, and buying functions. Unable to compete with discount stores and manufacturer outlet stores on price, Federated's pretax profit margins declined steadily after the 1970s.

Federated's directors realized that the company was vulnerable and installed various antitakeover measures. But there was little defense against a depressed stock price. And when the market crashed on October 19, 1987—driving Federated's shares from the mid-50s to the mid-30s—Campeau began buying, convinced that he could achieve huge savings by merging back-office and buying operations of the two department store giants. "Basically throughout the fall we did analysis on Federated," says Branman, the investment banker. "Our big mistake was that we launched against Federated without buying a big block of stock."

The problem was that Robert Campeau wasn't the only bargain

hunter. Donald Trump, the flashy New York developer with a flair for self-promotion, began purchasing Federated stock in early December. The following month, he filed notice with the Securities and Exchange Commission indicating he might buy up to 15 percent of Federated's shares.

It was the Wall Street equivalent of nailing a "for sale" sign on Federated's front door. Fearing a bidding war was about to break out, Campeau offered on January 25, 1988, to buy Federated's ninety million shares for $47 each, or about $4.2 billion. He also set a February 22 deadline, putting pressure on Federated's board.

Caught by surprise, Federated's lawyers immediately sought legal and legislative relief, warning that a Campeau takeover would destroy the company and cost the state of Ohio millions of dollars in lost taxes. Federated's employees, fearing the loss of their jobs, wrote to Washington, asking for help.

Many of Howard Goldfeder's friends and colleagues called to offer support, including Ed Finkelstein. By now, the Macy's buyout was widely regarded as a triumph. Not only was the business humming, but in the fall of 1987, Macy's launched Aeropostale, the first of three distinct specialty store chains designed to compete with The Limited and The Gap. Aeropostale, whose stores were decorated with airplane propellers and shipping crates, specialized in weekend wear, such as rugged corduroy trousers. A second specialty store chain, Charter Club, sold preppy women's clothes for a fraction of the prices charged by Ralph Lauren. The third, Fantasies by Morgan Taylor, specialized in sexy lingerie. Wall Street generally applauded the moves. And in early January, Finkelstein reported that Macy's had turned a small profit during the trailing fifty-two weeks. Buoyed by the results, he also predicted that Macy's would end fiscal 1988 solidly in the black.

For Howard Goldfeder, Finkelstein's phone call represented a ray of hope, especially because Campeau soon raised his own bid to $61 per share. Although Federated's board rejected the offer as inadequate, many longtime shareholders now sold their shares to Wall Street arbitrageurs whose only interest was getting the highest possible price for their stock.

With tensions mounting, a senior Federated adviser approached Laurence Tisch and confided that Federated might be interested in a merger. Intrigued, Finkelstein signed a confidentiality agreement and asked his investment bankers—Drexel Burnham Lambert Inc. and Kidder, Peabody & Co.—to review Federated's books. A week later, Finkelstein told his own board that this might be a unique opportunity. Without committing themselves, the directors formed a special committee whose members included Finkelstein, Mark Handler, mutual funds operator Michael Price, A. Alfred Taubman, and Laurence Tisch.

Finkelstein privately confided that he was skeptical that a deal could be worked out. "I'd just spilled my guts borrowing $3.5 billion, and I didn't think anybody would lend me two more cents," he later said. "But the Federated people wanted to create an auction, and rightly so."

The plan Finkelstein drew up called for Macy's to pay for the merger by simultaneously selling some of Federated's most valuable divisions. He would keep Bloomingdale's, Burdines, and two businesses in California—Bullock's/Bullocks Wilshire and the I. Magnin specialty store chain. Macy's had long dominated retailing in northern California, but its efforts to expand into the southern portion of the state had been stymied by other retailers. Although I. Magnin barely turned a profit, it too would fill a key strategic need. Many top tier fashion houses, cosmetics companies, and luxury brand tabletop firms, including Baccarat and Steuben, refused to do business with Macy's because of its blue-collar image. Owning an exclusive specialty store company would change that attitude in an instant.

While Finkelstein was working on his plan, Campeau was fretting. Aware that delay would increase the likelihood of a new bidder, he sold Brooks Brothers to Marks & Spencer, the English retailers, for $770 million. Famed for its well-made clothing, particularly its underwear, Marks & Spencer had decided to use Brooks Brothers as its vehicle to expand into the United States.

Blessed with this huge cash commitment, Campeau hiked his Federated offer to $66 a share on February 25, or 40 percent higher than his original bid. He also revealed that Edward DeBartolo and the Reichmann family, a powerful clan of Toronto-based developers, were also backing him.

Sensing victory, the following day Campeau raised his bid to $68 a share, or about $6.1 billion.

It was a fabulous offer, and the Federated board had to accept. Rather than signing the deal immediately, however, Howard Goldfeder pleaded exhaustion. Turning to J. Tomilson Hill, director of mergers and acquisitions at Shearson Lehman Hutton, and his lead investment banker, Goldfeder said, "We've got a plane waiting to take us to Cincinnati. We'll sign on Monday."

While Robert Campeau spent the weekend vacationing in Europe, Ed Finkelstein met with his board, urging them to make their own bid. By now, Federated's lawyers had drawn up a contract completing the sale to Robert Campeau. But when they were informed of Finkelstein's interest late Sunday night, they promptly invited him to address Federated's board the following morning.

It was one of Finkelstein's finest moments. Flanked by Mark Handler, his lawyers, and his investment bankers, he eloquently explained that a combined Macy's/Federated company would dominate retailing for years to come. Merging the back-office and distribution operations would save at least $100 million in expenses, he said. Finkelstein also planned to increase Federated's use of private label brands, bolstering profit margins and providing better value to the customers.

He even had a sensible and appealing financial strategy. Macy's would buy four fifths of Federated's stock, he explained, with the remainder to be paid in new Federated/Macy's shares. This would enable Macy's to go public again, allowing Federated's shareholders to share in the combined company if they chose. Finkelstein also promised Federated would be fairly represented on the combined board.

Late the next day, March 1, Macy's board held a special meeting at the Fifth Avenue office of its law firm, Weil, Gotshal & Manges, to discuss Federated's warm response. During the meeting Howard Goldfeder called to say that if there was going to be a deal, Macy's— or Campeau—would now have to move fast. In a brazen attempt to encourage a higher price, Goldfeder said that the two would be allowed to revise their offers.

Minutes later, the Macy's board voted to buy 70.4 million shares of Federated at $74.50, a cash outlay of almost $5.3 billion. The money would be raised by Drexel and Kidder, Peabody. Macy's also planned to issue equity in the combined Macy's/Federated to redeem the remainder of Federated shares.

The blended offer of stock and cash was valued at about $6.1 billion. Although Robert Campeau's all-cash offer was more desirable, it appeared likely that Federated would back the Macy's offer on the grounds that joining with Macy's would create a stronger company.

"Federated's directors didn't like the idea of being merged with Allied," says James Freund, a senior partner at Skadden, Arps, Slate, Meagher & Flom, and one of Federated's key legal advisers. "Then Ed came along. The board saw him as the premier merchant in the country, which meant that Federated's employees would be in good hands. He also offered a proposal that would allow everyone to go forward with a piece of the business."

The following day, the boards of both companies signed a definitive merger agreement. Once again, it seemed that Robert Campeau had been outmaneuvered. "After the Federated board agreed to the Macy's offer, I went over to the offices of Weil, Gotshal to work on some final details," says Freund, the Federated lawyer. "There was Ed Finkelstein, sitting by himself. It was the moment of his greatest triumph, but he had no one to share it with. So I introduced myself, said congratulations, and told him it was a great deal for everyone. Then he perked up. Finally, somebody, albeit a lowly lawyer, was paying attention. It was an odd moment. We were in a room filled with empty pizza boxes, a mess, and he was there, waiting for somebody to shake his hand."

And to his surprise, Finkelstein discovered that borrowing more money wouldn't be a problem. By now he had such a stellar reputation in the investment community that Macy's bankers were able to raise $6 billion in commitments in only a few weeks, with some lenders literally faxing in their offers. They had reason to be enthusiastic, too, since projections called for the new Macy's/Federated to turn a profit within twelve months. Macy's also anticipated selling off various Federated divisions valued at nearly $3 billion.

But it wasn't over. Robert Campeau raised his offer. This in turn prompted a new bid from Finkelstein. Which in turn . . . Back and forth they went for days, creating an intense but exhausting drama. Finally Federated's directors announced they would make a final decision on March 30.

Meanwhile, some Macy's directors were growing unhappy. Laurence Tisch, the chairman of Loews Corp., initially supported the first offer for Federated because he thought it represented a good value. But as Finkelstein put more money on the table, Tisch had misgivings. "The higher the price went, the more financing we would need,"

Tisch recalls. "And the more financing required, the higher the interest rate would be that we would have to pay. The fact that you may be able to borrow $4 billion at ten percent doesn't mean you will be able to borrow $6 billion at the same rate," adds Tisch. "Instead, you may be looking at thirteen percent. The difference in terms of dollars is enormous. Ed, though, said he could do it, and that he would generate eight percent compound sales gains every year."

At one board meeting called to discuss buying Federated, Tisch became so emotional that he shouted, "I will not vote for this. I don't intend to be part of the largest bankruptcy in retail history."

And he had reason to be upset. His own estimates suggested that the first 12.5 cents of each sales dollar generated by the combined company would go to pay interest costs. If the economy slowed, Macy's would be hard-pressed to repay its debts.

Finkelstein, though, insisted on bulling ahead. Addressing Federated's board on March 30, he offered $78.92 a share for 80 percent of Federated's stock. But he left without an endorsement.

Finally one of Federated's lawyers suggested that Campeau meet privately with Finkelstein at Finkelstein's Upper East Side carriage house. The two would settle it man to man.

The April Fool's Day meeting began crisply at 7:30 P.M. Finkelstein was flanked by Ira Millstein of Weil, Gotshal & Manges, and several others, while Campeau was accompanied by lawyer Alan Finkelson of Cravath, Swaine & Moore, and investment bankers from First Boston.

Five hours later, Campeau walked out a winner.

The compromise called for Campeau to buy Federated's stock at $73.50 in cash. In turn, Macy's would purchase the Bullock's/Bullocks Wilshire unit in Southern California and the San Francisco–based I. Magnin chain, for $1.1 billion. Macy's would also receive about $60 million to cover expenses related to its failed bid.

"We believe we made a prudent decision," Finkelstein said the next day. "It had gotten ridiculous . . . Twenty months ago, we went private. We have since opened three specialty store businesses and just added two great franchises. We have a controllable debt. We are running our business. It's terrific."

But the deal wasn't quite as rosy as Finkelstein contended. Before Macy's could borrow more money to buy the two West Coast businesses, it had to repurchase its 13.5 percent senior notes that would otherwise have come due in 1996—long after Macy's was expected to go public through a stock offering. (The issuers of those notes had written covenants designed to prevent Macy's from adding more debt.) The net cost of buying back the notes was $54 million. There were also additional expenses associated with bidding for Federated that weren't covered by the payment provided by Robert Campeau. Those costs, plus various restructuring charges, amounted to $62 million net.

All told, Macy's spent $116 million in after-tax dollars. Some recalled that in 1985, Finkelstein agreed to pay $70 a share for all of Macy's common stock, only to be forced to reduce his price to $68. The two dollar difference per share represented an extra $100 million, a sum Finkelstein's own investment bankers advised couldn't be repaid based on Macy's projected cash flow.

Now, less than two years later, Finkelstein had placed a huge bet that the smart money crowd was wrong.

Chapter 9

"I don't think there is anything anybody could tell you about anything."

With the backing of institutional investors and the support of new friends such as Edward J. DeBartolo, Robert Campeau again raised the money he needed.

This time, DeBartolo anted up $480 million in exchange for a 7.5 percent block of Federated stock. The two developers also announced ambitious plans to build five to ten new malls a year for the next five years, using their new Federated stores as anchors. By now DeBartolo had also invested in retailing, having purchased Higbee Co., a scuffed-up department store chain based in Cleveland, in partnership with Dillard Department Stores Inc., a moderate-priced retailer based in Little Rock.

Robert Campeau, a predator who never unloaded trucks in July like Sam Walton, or managed a textiles department like Ed Finkelstein, now oversaw the largest group of department stores ever assembled. "We're kind of proud that we were able to do two hostile takeovers in a period of fifteen months," he exulted during a news conference at the Waldorf-Astoria Hotel, pounding the podium to emphasize his excitement. "I think it's a helluva deal."

In the days following Campeau's improbable victory, Blooming-dale's chairman Marvin Traub shamelessly declared that he had "a great deal of respect" for his new boss and that he was looking forward to working with him. But Traub was the exception. Allen Questrom, Federated's lanky vice chairman, and the merchant once considered most likely to succeed Howard Goldfeder as Federated's chairman, confessed that he felt as though a loved one had died. "I grew up in Federated, and this is certainly not in my best interests," he said. Although Robert Campeau offered to make him head of Federated/Allied, Questrom insisted on resigning. "It wasn't that I didn't like Bob," recalled Questrom a few years later, his voice colored by a Boston accent. "But I looked at the numbers, I saw the debt, and I knew the deal was not going to work. It wasn't magic. I just knew the business."

What surprised Questrom was that so many lenders readily accepted Campeau's rosy projections. There were two kinds of investors, Questrom decided. Some were like Warren Buffet. They met with management, and saw for themselves if the company had a clear strategy and a product customers wanted. Then there were the investors who concentrated only on revenues, cash flow forecasts, and profit margins. As Questrom knew, however, numbers didn't always tell the whole story.

His departure was a serious setback. The son of a machine shop operator, Questrom graduated from Boston University in 1964 with a degree in finance before joining the training squad at Federated's Abraham & Straus division in Brooklyn. While he was there, he met his future wife, Kelli, whose penchant for wearing her husband's clothes later caught designer Ralph Lauren's eye. Intrigued by the rail-thin woman dressed in Oxford button-down shirts and men's pleated pants, Lauren hired her as his public relations director in the early 1970s. Later Kelli would become well-known for the houses she remodeled as her husband moved from city to city.

Allen Questrom's own good looks and energetic management style made him a corporate favorite, and by 1975 he was executive vice president of the Bullock's/Bullocks Wilshire unit in Los Angeles. Three years later, he was named president of the Rich's department store group in Atlanta, which Federated had acquired in 1976. Eager to turn around the flagging business, Questrom introduced Rich's customers to designer clothes and encouraged his sales staff to make shoppers feel welcome. When Rich's performance sharply improved, Questrom's stock rose inside Federated, and in 1980 he was named Rich's chairman and chief executive. Simultaneously, James Zimmerman, an operations executive vice president at the Sanger Harris department store company in Dallas, was transferred to Rich's as president. It was an intriguing partnership. Questrom, like many merchants, was impatient, demanding, and given to brooding. Zimmerman, a Rice University graduate with a degree in business administration, was disciplined, understated, and preferred working behind the scenes. Like Questrom, however, he had worked his entire professional career at Federated.

The two men formed a close friendship during the next four years. And when Questrom surprised his bosses by asking for an open-ended leave in 1984, he recommended Zimmerman as his successor. Uncertain whether he wanted to stay in retailing, Questrom devoted much of that year to traveling the world with his wife, skiing, and weighing a possible new career as a movie producer.

Instead, Howard Goldfeder lured Questrom home by offering him the chairmanship of the ailing Bullock's/Bullocks Wilshire division. Founded by a Canadian named John Gillespie Bullock, the Bullock's Department Store opened in downtown Los Angeles in 1907. In the decades that followed, it matured into a local institution, catering the birthday parties of the children of such celebrities as Bing Crosby, and offering bridge lessons and puppet shows. By the mid-1980s, however, Bullock's had been nudged into partial obscurity by Neiman Marcus and J. W. Robinson's, both of which were attracting Los Angeles's hip, wealthy West Siders.

In the following months, Questrom introduced such top designer collections as Escada and Giorgio Armani in a bid to attract the women who normally shopped Rodeo Drive. He also courted members of the nascent Los Angeles fashion scene by promoting their work, a decision that appealed to many proud city loyalists. He also motivated his salespeople with a lucrative commission program.

By 1988, the Bullock's department store group was one of Federated's most profitable, with pretax profits of 9 percent on $695 million in sales. Meanwhile, the Bullocks Wilshire specialty stores were producing respectable pretax profits of 5 percent on $110 million in sales.

And then came the sale of both to Macy's.

"I was very unhappy about the whole thing," says Questrom. "All the people who contributed to the Bullock's success were out of a job, and I didn't want to work any more, either. It was like sitting shiva. None of it made any sense. I was sort of out of my head."

Questrom didn't return to work until August, when he was named chief executive of Neiman Marcus Group Inc., the Dallas-based luxury retailer. Before leaving Los Angeles, however, he and his wife made headlines one last time: Madonna, the pop star, bought their home in the Hollywood Hills for $3 million.

Years later, when his leveraged buyout had gone bad, critics called it Ed Finkelstein's Folly.

Finkelstein's initial bid for Federated called for Macy's to emerge as a publicly traded company, a step that would have meant immediate profits for his fellow investors. Instead, he'd settled for the two California divisions while saddling Macy's with $1.1 billion in new debt.

The biggest lender was the Swiss Bank Corp., one of Switzerland's three largest commercial banks. Swiss Bank had been a minor player in Macy's original buyout. But when the Prudential Insurance Company of America refused to help finance the two Federated divisions—it rightly doubted the long-term value of the I. Magnin leases—Swiss Bank's emissaries rushed to Herald Square.

Before leaving, they'd agreed to lend $560 million against the value of those same I. Magnin stores. "We thought it was an attractive piece of business, so we competed to get it," says one former top-ranking Swiss Bank executive. "It was probably our largest real estate speculation."

The Swiss were betting on a twenty-six-store specialty group that turned a tiny operating profit of about 2 percent on $302 million in revenue. Originally founded by immigrant Mary Ann Magnin in 1876, the classy store on Union Square tempted San Francisco's wealthiest shoppers with the latest from Chanel, Giorgio Armani, and others. When new shipments arrived, a disciplined sales staff reached for their lists of loyal, big spenders. Still, it was a borderline business. During the late 1970s and 1980s, I. Magnin expanded into Chicago, Phoenix, and Rockville, Maryland, often with stores that were either too small or in the wrong locations.

At home in San Francisco, I. Magnin was losing customers to Neiman Marcus and Saks Fifth Avenue, two specialty store chains with a knack for opening elegant, exciting stores that appealed to women who could afford Chanel's eggshell-colored blouses.

In desperation, Federated began fiddling with the retailer's luxury image by introducing dozens of low and mid-priced vendors. This only annoyed I. Magnin's remaining customers, since the aspiring middle class rarely set foot in the store. Finally, in February 1987, Federated named feisty Barbara Bass as I. Magnin's new chief executive. Bass, a Smith College graduate, began her career in retailing at Burdines in 1972, moved to Macy's California three years later, and then accepted a bigger job at Bloomingdale's in 1980, where she matured into one of Marvin Traub's top merchants.

It didn't take Bass long to realize her shoppers were more interested in fashion than bargains, and she promptly eliminated the moderate-priced merchandise. Instead, she trumpeted I. Magnin's commitment to European designers and top-line American names like James Galanos. "I. Magnin Takes Off the Velvet Gloves," praised the *San Francisco Business Times* in January 1988, in an article that credited Bass with sparking a revival at a business that once seemed lost.

Ed Finkelstein, however, fired Bass as soon as he took over the business. Earlier in her career, Bass had rejected a generous offer to return to Macy's, mostly because she believed her chances of becoming a chief executive were greater at Federated. Ed Finkelstein didn't forget, and he didn't forgive.

Within days of his negotiations with Campeau, Finkelstein flew to San Francisco and said he had a successor for her job. Bass nodded, and said that she knew who it was: Rose Marie Bravo, a Macy's merchant from New York. Finkelstein then asked Bass if there was anything she wanted to tell him about running the business.

"I don't think there is anything anybody could tell you about anything," she replied frostily.

A moment later, Bass's phone rang. She rose, walked over to the open door, and said, "Unless you have anything else, I'm busy."

As soon as Macy's took control, I. Magnin's buyers were instructed to add huge quantities of goods on the theory that the business had been operating too leanly. But the upper end of the fashion business isn't like the moderate-priced world, where shoppers relish huge selections. Luxury retailing demands at least the appearance of scarcity. And as Macy's learned, the limited number of customers who could afford top designer lines were already shopping at I. Magnin. Within months, huge piles of expensive goods were sitting in the stores, unsold.

The markdowns that followed transformed I. Magnin's slim operating profits into losses.

Other changes also hurt morale. I. Magnin's cosmetics buyers learned that the chain was now expected to share exclusive launches with Macy's, eroding one of I. Magnin's fundamental promises: that its elite customers would be the first to sample the newest skin care lines.

Twice a year, California designer James Galanos came to I. Magnin and hosted a trunk show. And every season, the same elite customers spent $150,000 each on his clothes. But after the store changed hands, Finkelstein decided to celebrate Galanos's appearance by hosting a black-tie event complete with caviar. The same six people came, and spent their $150,000. Afterward, however, I. Magnin was saddled with tens of thousands of dollars in expenses.

Eighteen months after leaving I. Magnin's, Barbara Bass was named chief executive of The Emporium, a moderate-priced San Francisco-based department store chain owned by Carter Hawley Hale Stores, Inc. Its biggest competitor, of course, was Macy's.

Managing Bullock's/Bullocks Wilshire and I. Magnin would be about tactics, organization, and administration, areas in which Ed Finkelstein considered himself an expert.

The simplest strategy would have been the most effective. He could have followed the dictates of geography and merged the former Federated businesses into Macy's California, a well-managed business headed by Harold Kahn, whose dominating personality caused some to call him Genghis Khan behind his back. Not that he cared. Kahn was a gifted merchant whose skills had made him one of Finkelstein's favorites. He was a producer, and so highly regarded that he was allowed to purchase 492,000 shares in Finkelstein's buyout, making him the company's fourth-largest management shareholder.

Marrying the California stores would have created major savings in distribution, advertising, finance, buying, and back-office operations. And since Kahn expected to eventually succeed Finkelstein as Macy's chairman, he was looking forward to the challenge.

Instead Finkelstein restructured the corporation, creating fear and anger among many of his top executives, including Hal Kahn. Finkelstein first merged the Macy's New York stores with Macy's New Jersey. He named Arthur Reiner as chairman, appointed Herbert Yalof as president, and dubbed the $3 billion (sales) division Macy's Northeast.

Finkelstein then transferred Robert Friedman and Rudolph Borneo, the former chairman and president of Macy's New Jersey, to Macy's Atlanta, where they were given similar titles. In their new posts, the two were also made responsible for the Atlanta stores; five stores in Texas; twenty-two Bullock's department stores; and seven Bullocks Wilshire specialty stores. The new Macy's South unit had about $1.5 billion in annual revenues.

Meanwhile, Rose Marie Bravo, the chief executive of I. Magnin, was told she would report directly to Mark Handler, Macy's corporate president, who was based in New York.

Only Macy's California, whose twenty-five department stores generated $1.6 billion in revenues, was unaffected.

When later asked why he insisted on putting together the Los Angeles and Atlanta stores, Finkelstein offered an explanation that made little sense. The two divisions had similar climates, he said. Buyers in San Francisco, where Macy's California was based, wouldn't understand the needs of customers in sultry Los Angeles. Instead, that job would be more aptly handled by merchants in sunny Atlanta.

Nobody with firsthand knowledge of the conservative Atlanta market thought this made sense, particularly the top team at Bullock's/Bullocks Wilshire. All promptly resigned, including James Gray, Bullock's chairman; Frank Doroff, president; and Terry Lundgren, president of the Bullocks Wilshire specialty stores.

For Gray, the parting was particularly bitter. Even before Finkelstein officially took control of Bullock's/Bullocks Wilshire, say former colleagues, Gray sought Finkelstein out and asked him to keep his hands off. The request annoyed Finkelstein, who rebuked Gray by insisting that any business could be improved, including Bullock's.

Tempers cooled. But after Finkelstein said he intended to merge Bullock's/Bullocks Wilshire with Macy's Atlanta, Gray warned the Macy's chief he was making a big mistake. "It's my money and I'll run it how I choose," Finkelstein snapped.

Despite their run-ins, Finkelstein admired talent, and he offered Gray a top job in San Francisco, working closely with Harold Kahn.

Kahn and Gray met and felt they could get along, but Gray finally rejected the offer, half-jokingly explaining that he didn't want to "work for such an autocratic personality." In June, Gray was named president of Burdines, a Federated division.

To some longtime Macy's hands, the most surprising departure was that of Frank Doroff. A Wharton School graduate, Doroff had earlier worked at Macy's New York for eleven years. Widely admired inside the company for his easy, compassionate management style, Doroff was also a terrific tennis player who was frequently invited to join Finkelstein at the Wall Street Racket Club. Still, Doroff's star faded when his business hit a rough patch, and after Howard Goldfeder, then chairman of Federated Department Stores, offered him a more senior job as general merchandise manager at Bullock's, Doroff accepted.

Although Finkelstein sometimes showed contempt for those leaving the Macy's family, he wrote Doroff a warm letter of congratulations and wished him luck.

Now, having bought Bullock's, Finkelstein wanted Doroff to stay on in a less important role as director of stores. And Doroff was tempted. His family loved the active, outdoor California lifestyle, and he had always admired Finkelstein personally. But he was also convinced that Bullock's couldn't be managed from Atlanta, and he finally decided to quit.

This time Finkelstein didn't write him a note.

After Finkelstein put his own Macy's team in place, the Bullock's stores underwent major changes. Many of the California vendors were dropped, a commission program intended to motivate lowly paid sales clerks was abandoned, and the sketches that Bullock's used in its advertising were dropped in favor of photographs. Even the sparse, understated appeal of the stores was changed in favor of racks and tables loaded with goods. "It was tumultuous," says one former Bullock's manager. "Ed was flying high, his business was unbelievable, and he figured he could do no wrong. But we had a feel for more upscale kinds of things, for what made Bullock's different from the other stores in town. I think they thought we never had enough inventory, so they piled it on. Later, somebody told me that Macy's never earned the money that Bullock's made when we were owned by Federated. Never."

.   .   .

Three thousand miles away, the merger of Macy's New Jersey with the Macy's New York stores created immediate chaos.

Under Donald Smiley, Macy's former chairman, the retailer's divisions were encouraged to view each other as competitors. While this may have helped build sales, it also meant that nobody objected when the twenty-four Bamberger's stores installed IBM cash registers to capture sales and inventory information while the twenty-one Macy's New York stores relied on NCR registers for the same tasks. The two divisions were unable to share sales or inventory information, since the two systems were incompatible.

Other issues were just as maddening. Not only were many of the two hundred major departments at each chain identified by different numbers, but so were the subsets known as classifications. The tie buyer, for example, differentiated between silks and wools, or solids, checks, and stripes. He also needed to know how many ties were in stock at each store, and how many were on order. These subsets were tracked by computer. But since the identification numbers of the two chains weren't identical, managing the combined stores became nearly impossible until a conversion table linking the two was created.

"It was a nightmare," says one former Macy's executive. "They had different procedures for receiving new merchandise, different pay policies, and even different vacation systems. The merger cut across every element. Nobody escaped. And the people part was lousy. There were redundant jobs, so people were laid off. It was very rough."

Jay Friedman was one of many employees discouraged by the merger. When Friedman joined Bamberger's in 1980, the department store company ranked as one of the best in the country. "We had a terrific business run by people who knew what they were doing," says Friedman. "Everyone was open to new ideas. The esprit was tremendous."

Although Friedman rarely had an opportunity to speak with Finkelstein, he was familiar with Finkelstein's successes in San Francisco and New York. So when Friedman was invited to invest $17,500 in the Macy's buyout, he immediately agreed. "I knew there were risks," says Friedman. "But my loyalty and devotion to the company was at a very high level. I was going to die there. When they offered up a piece of the pie, my concern wasn't that I had to write a check. It was: is that all I can have?"

After Macy's went private, Friedman began putting in eleven- and twelve-hour days because he wanted the buyout to succeed. And when Macy's common shares were valued at more than twenty times their original cost during the battle for Federated, Friedman felt his faith was justified. Still, he was growing increasingly concerned about the steady push to buy more private label shoes. Although the Jennifer Moore line sold well, a second collection, marketed under the Morgan Taylor label, was a disappointment. "We had a good private label product," says Friedman. "It was a question of how much, and at the expense of what brands domestically. But Ed was enamored of Leslie Wexner's private label program at The Limited."

Friedman was a group vice president with two divisional merchandise managers reporting to him at the time of the merger. Although his job was secure, his morale fell as longtime friends were forced out. Two years later, he resigned. "I was expensive, I was bored, and I decided it was silly," says Friedman. "They offered to buy my stock back, but I'd already paid for it by then, and I thought it would be worth something when my kids went to college." Of the estimated thirty-four senior Bamberger's executives who were divisional merchandise managers or higher at the time of the merger, only six still had their jobs when Friedman left.

If the move had created major savings, the disruption to the lives of hundreds of employees might have been justified. Instead, there was so little planning that operating expenses for the combined companies were higher in fiscal 1989 than the combined expenses of Bamberger's and Macy's New York in 1988. "Part of it had to do with severance packages, but the real problem was that everything was so rushed that nobody knew what to do," says John Shepardson, a former Macy's group vice president. "It was a fiasco."

As Jay Friedman and his coworkers later realized, however, Ed Finkelstein had good reason for trying to slash expenses. Although the buyout had started brilliantly, Macy's was now struggling. In early November, the retailer disclosed that it had lost $188 million for the fiscal year ended July 1988, or more than thirteen times that year-earlier loss of $13.8 million.

The dreadful results largely reflected costs associated with the failed bid for Federated Department Stores. Yet even when those expenses were excluded, Macy's lost about $29 million. Perhaps more ominously, sales at stores open at least one year had increased only 1.5 percent—or less than the inflation rate. "This wasn't supposed to happen," said one junk bond investor. "Macy's was supposed to be a growth story."

Footnotes in the annual filing that year also disclosed that Macy's had revised its agreement with Ed Finkelstein regarding the purchase of his carriage house on East 77th Street. When Macy's was still publicly traded, it bought the property for $2.6 million, with Finkelstein contributing $700,000. But Macy's had now returned his original stake. Although the retailer was now sole owner, Finkelstein and his heirs retained the right to purchase the property at the original cost for up to six months after he left the company.

For Ed Finkelstein, other perks included a handsome $1.1 million salary and liberal use of the corporate jet. He was also able to reward family members, including Mitch, who earned $351,000 in salary that year plus a generous housing allowance for working in Hong Kong. Daniel Finkelstein, Mitchell's younger brother, was paid $200,000 plus a $50,000 incentive bonus.

Others closely associated with Finkelstein also did handsomely. Mark Handler, Macy's president, earned $851,000 in salary. Macy's also spent $397,500 with The Basket Handler, a gift item business operated by his wife, Barbara. In addition, Mark Handler's sister-in-law, Jane R. Justin, was on the payroll as a fashion designer, working on Macy's private label lines and earning $265,000 annually.

Macy's, long dominated by the Straus clan, was once again a family affair.

Recognizing that he needed help, Finkelstein hired Myron (Mike) Ullman III as Macy's new executive vice president and chief financial officer. A blue-eyed, square-jawed Midwesterner from Canfield, Ohio, Ullman was an unlikely choice. Although the Macy's culture was heavily Jewish, Ullman was a deeply committed churchgoer. Ullman, soft-spoken, reserved, and unfailingly polite, also exhibited little of the bravado that the top Macy's men exuded.

The two met when Finkelstein was searching for investors to buy the various divisions of Federated Department Stores he intended to sell if his bid succeeded. Ullman was then managing director of Wharf (Holdings) Ltd., a Hong Kong–based holding company with significant retail, hotel, and shipping interests. From 1982 to 1986, Ullman worked at Sanger Harris in Dallas, and he was now representing Wharf in its negotiations to purchase Foley's, a department store chain in Houston.

They were an unlikely pair. Finkelstein, dressed in handsome pin-striped suits, was outgoing and energetic, while Ullman, a conservative dresser, was intensely reserved, a quality he concealed by focusing entirely on work. The oldest of seven children, Ullman was accustomed to accepting responsibility, as well as dealing with older men in serious business situations. In an interview with *Horizons* magazine, his sister Chris Stubbins described him this way: "Mike's always been very centered. When he was in junior high, he was saving his allowance in a big jar that he sealed shut so he wouldn't be tempted to remove any of the money. He was always so focused and very conservative. I think he was born wearing wingtips." As an undergraduate student at the University of Cincinnati, he used a physician's billing system to manage his fraternity's finances. "I treated the brothers as patients, and made everything a procedure," he joked years later. "Every month, they got a bill from the doctor."

After graduating in 1969 with a degree in industrial management, he joined IBM, where he worked for seven years, including a stint as the international account manager for Procter & Gamble. But rather than accept a transfer to New York City, he resigned from Big Blue and returned to the University of Cincinnati as vice president of business affairs. "Mike was only twenty-nine years old when he arrived, and I was fifty and feeling passed over," said Robert Deubell, a university official. "But after several weeks, I realized he was probably the most astute young man I had ever met. I learned something from him every day. And it wasn't unusual for Mike to work until midnight on a special project."

Ullman's reward came in 1981, when he was selected by President Ronald Reagan to serve as one of fourteen White House Fellows. He spent the next year working as executive assistant to U.S. Trade Representative William Brock III. When the fellowship ended, Ullman had six job opportunities, including offers from a broadcaster, a real estate firm, and a retailer. After sketching out a grid that measured the pros and cons of each offer, he joined Federated's Sanger Harris chain in Texas in 1982, where he worked as an executive vice president much as James Zimmerman had before him. (Sanger Harris was eventually merged into Foley's.)

Four years later, his former college roommate, Peter Woo, offered him a new job in Hong Kong. Peter Woo's father-in-law, Y. K. Pao, had retired as Wharf's chairman, and Woo was succeeding him. In the fall of 1986, Ullman, his wife, Cathy Emmons, and their four sons moved to Hong Kong.

A year later, Ullman and his wife adopted a three-year-old Chinese girl. Then Macy's and Federated announced they were going to merge, and he became Wharf's point man in talks to acquire Foley's. "By the time we finished, we had a fully executed contract to buy that business for $870 million in cash," says Ullman. "I met Ed four or five times, but most of my negotiations were with his advisers." After the Macy's/Federated merger collapsed, Robert Campeau sold Foley's to May Department Stores.

This did not, however, end all talks between Macy's and Wharf. Instead, toward the end of April 1988, Macy's approached Ullman with a different plan. Since Wharf had been willing to pay $870 million to buy Foley's, maybe it would make a similar investment in Macy's.

Wharf was interested, and six weeks later, the company said it would invest $1.5 billion if Macy's would use the funds to pay down its huge debt.

The Macy's board, however, rejected the offer. "They wanted to use some of the proceeds to cover their original investment," says Ullman. "We liked the company, but we thought it was overleveraged." For the second time that year, Macy's had missed a critical opportunity to slash its debt and interest payments.

A few months later, Ullman received a phone call from Ed Finkelstein. The Macy's chief explained he was in town, visiting his son Mitch. What he wanted to know, he continued, was whether Ullman would meet him for breakfast.

Ullman agreed, expecting that Finkelstein wanted to review Wharf's decision not to invest in Macy's. To his surprise, Finkelstein began by telling him that he'd been greatly impressed by his negotiating skills and wanted him to join Macy's as chief financial officer. Although Finkelstein didn't say so, Macy's board was pressuring him to hire a top-level operations executive. Finkelstein and Handler were both merchants, and they knew little about the support side of the business, including computer systems.

Although flattered, Ullman explained that he and his family expected to live in Hong Kong for at least five years. Besides, he said, if he did leave Hong Kong before that, it would have to be for a broader assignment.

Finkelstein said he understood. But in the weeks that followed he continued to call and talk about Macy's terrific future and the part Ullman could play there. Finally, Ullman visited him for a day in New York, and when Finkelstein then agreed to widen his responsibilities, Ullman resigned from Wharf and moved his family to Greenwich, Connecticut. In addition to his role as chief financial officer, he would also serve as executive vice president, responsible for accounting, credit operations, and all non-merchandising areas.

Mike Ullman returned to the United States nearly broke. Still, when Finkelstein asked him to buy five thousand shares of Macy's stock as a sign of faith in the company, Ullman felt obligated to agree. Later, he bought another ten thousand shares. Both purchases were made with borrowed money. Although anxious about that commitment, Ullman was forty-two years old, his office was directly next to Finkelstein's, and his future had never looked brighter.

Within a few weeks of Ullman's arrival, Macy's reported more discouraging news. For the quarter ended October 29, 1988, the company lost $19 million compared with a $6.4 million profit in the same quarter a year earlier.

Macy's attributed the poor results to expenses related to its recent acquisitions and other financing issues. However, outsiders like Walter Loeb, a respected analyst at Morgan Stanley and a former Macy's executive, suggested that one of Macy's biggest problems was its dependency on private label goods. By some accounts, Macy's own brands now accounted for more than 30 percent of Macy's total inventory, at least 10 percent higher than any other major department store company. "I've known for a while that they're overstocked in private brands, which have not been selling well," Loeb said.

Although Macy's sales climbed 20 percent to $1.6 billion, the increase came primarily from the new Federated units. Same store sales, which excluded revenues from the Bullock's/Bullocks Wilshire and I. Magnin stores, were down 5.2 percent.

During the past decade, Macy's shareholders had grown accustomed to the fabled retailer dominating each and every market in which it did business. Now, a little more than two years after Ed Finkelstein had bought the company, Macy's was stumbling badly.

Chapter 10

"What happened was that Ed was turning Macy's into Finkelstein's."

Even as Ed Finkelstein tried to stanch the losses, he was brooding over The Limited, the specialty store business whose gee-whiz private label manufacturing and distribution set-up were giving Macy's fits.

The creation of eccentric retailing guru Leslie Wexner, The Limited had now blossomed into more than 3,300 stores, including its signature Limited shops that mostly appealed to teenagers and working women in their twenties; the Victoria's Secret division, whose sexy lingerie catalogs made underwear fun again; Lane Bryant, which sold apparel for large-size women; the Lerner lower-priced women's chain; Abercrombie & Fitch, which mixed blue oxford shirts, cardigans, and trout fishing books; Henri Bendel, the sputtering high-fashion retailer; and Express, a brilliant offshoot of the original Limited division that had grown from two stores in 1980 to more than four hundred.

Still, Leslie Wexner was the Rodney Dangerfield of retailing. Nobody respected him, partly because he attended trade shows with bodyguards in tow. A moody, introverted cipher who lived by himself in enormous houses, Wexner envisioned a major acquisition that would have provided him with national stature. In November 1986, for example, after establishing a $1.4 billion line of credit, he expressed interest in buying the Ann Taylor and Garfinckel's specialty store business from Allied Stores Corp., then under attack from

144

Robert Campeau. Nothing happened. When Federated was being raided, he met with Federated's chairman Howard Goldfeder to offer his help. Goldfeder, too, rejected him.

Frustrated, in late 1988 Wexner dusted off an earlier takeover plan. Joining forces with shopping mall magnate Edward DeBartolo, he launched his second bid to buy Los Angeles–based Carter Hawley Hale Stores. Although he offered $1.8 billion cash, Carter Hawley Hale's management shunned him by restructuring into two publicly traded companies.

It was shortly after this humiliation that Gilbert Harrison, an investment banker at Shearson Lehman Brothers, whispered the name Macy's in Wexner's ear.

Harrison was a handsome, impeccably dressed workaholic with an encyclopedic knowledge of the retail business. Not all of his deals were home runs; earlier, he'd helped Australian George Herscu assemble a ragged collection of retailers that eventually went bust. But Harrison understood retailing, and he enjoyed a wide circle of friends in the United States and Europe.

Harrison had all the right credentials, including an undergraduate degree from the Wharton School of Business and a law degree from the University of Pennsylvania. After graduating from law school in 1965, Harrison moved to New York, where his first two clients were both retailers: Alexander's, the discount chain, and Shoetown Inc., which he later sold on three separate occasions, each time for more money. At a time when he was earning $25,000 a year, he knew that bankers his own age were earning three and four times that. Realizing that he was fed up with practicing law, and that what he really enjoyed was negotiating, Harrison opened Financo Inc. in Philadelphia, specializing in retailing. By 1985, it was one of the country's largest unaffiliated mergers and acquisitions firms. About that time, Michael Milken, the junk bond specialist and an old friend from Philadelphia, encouraged Harrison to move to Los Angeles to work for him. Instead, Harrison sold his business to Shearson Lehman and joined the investment banking firm as a managing director. Four years later, about the same time he was speaking with Leslie Wexner about Macy's, Harrison decided he was weary of the politics in a big firm. He bought the Financo name back and opened for business, but not before agreeing to split any Macy's fee with Shearson Lehman.

By now Harrison and Wexner had spent long hours together exploring a possible move to trump Robert Campeau's bid for Federated Department Stores. Nothing came of it. But recognizing how eager Wexner was to make a big acquisition, Harrison brought up Macy's. Although it was having trouble, Harrison suggested that it would be a perfect fit with The Limited.

Wexner quickly agreed. For years, he had attempted to convince a department store company to lease him space and allow him to open various Limited retail concepts in their stores, much the way department store chains leased out space to jewelry merchants. What he wanted to do, Wexner said, was bring "specialty stores into the tent."

But nobody wanted him there. If he owned Macy's, of course, he could do what he wanted. "Wexner became intrigued and said he wanted to pursue it," says Harrison. "The question was how."

Harrison called Macy's director Laurence Tisch and sounded him out. His timing was good. Although Harrison had no way of knowing it, Tisch had grown increasingly disenchanted with Finkelstein ever since the Macy's chief pushed through the purchase of the two Federated divisions for $1.1 billion.

Over lunch, Tisch confided that a merger with The Limited might be a pretty good idea. But Tisch emphasized that it wouldn't be smart to approach Finkelstein directly, since Finkelstein might find it insulting.

Harrison, familiar with the need to coddle chief executives, said he understood. Soon after, Leslie Wexner called the Macy's chief directly, one merchant to another. The talks slowly heated up, with Finkelstein eventually jetting off to Columbus for an all-day Saturday meeting. Ever the good host, Wexner met the Macy's chief at the airport in his BMW. He then wowed Finkelstein with a tour of The Limited's huge receiving facility, which handled the specialty chain's private label shipments from the Far East.

Meanwhile, Wexner couldn't decide whether he wanted to buy Macy's outright, or make a smaller investment with an option to acquire the rest at a later date. The price was a problem, too. Finkelstein's investment bankers, Goldman, Sachs & Co., valued Macy's at $1.5 billion, or five dollars for every $1 dollar that Finkelstein and his fellow investors had anted up in 1986. Wexner thought $900 million sounded right. Moreover Felix Rohatyn, the Lazard Freres banker who was advising Wexner, thought even that price was too high, given Macy's huge debt.

The most heated discussions centered on who would lead bined companies, Wexner or Finkelstein. And Wexner di matters by bluntly advising that Macy's close its money-losing postale, Fantasies by Morgan Taylor, and Charter Club specialty stores. "To say they disagreed is putting it mildly," says one former senior Macy's executive. "It was like being in a room with two people who didn't know how to listen to each other."

Then the business press got wind of the talks, and the talks were over. Macy's was portrayed as concerned about its ability to pay down its debt, with The Limited seen as providing financial stability. Ed Finkelstein, infuriated, penned a letter to fellow shareholders stating Macy's was in solid financial shape. Outsiders had approached the company on several occasions, he added, but "none have been appropriate." Macy's, he made clear, wasn't for sale.

Thus ended Gilbert Harrison's hopes of making millions by brokering a Limited/Macy's marriage. "Ed told someone that the only reason Wexner was interested in Macy's was because he was afraid Macy's was a threat to him in the specialty store business," sniffed Harrison. "Can you imagine that?"

A year later, Leslie Wexner was mired in his own problems. Sales were down, The Limited's stock had tumbled, and a new private label line, Paul et Duffier, was a bomb.

Talks between the two companies never resumed.

What was significant, however, was that for the third time in less than a year—first with Federated, later with Wharf—Macy's had missed a chance to go public or sell its equity for a big profit. It would be the last such chance Macy's employee owners, many of whom had borrowed heavily to invest in the buyout, would have.

There was nothing in Ed Finkelstein's demeanor that hinted Macy's was struggling. In his spacious, mahogany-walled offices, surrounded by photos of his children and grandchildren, Finkelstein, peering over his glasses, radiated absolute confidence in his own abilities and Macy's. And with four decades of experience to call on, and a showman's grasp of markets stretching from New York to California, he was a formidable presence.

He was also becoming increasingly grand. For years, Macy's rented a boat to view the annual Fourth of July fireworks that it sponsored, inviting staffers and their families to enjoy an evening's sail. Once on board, the guests wandered wherever they chose. But in the late 1980s, Macy's executives were issued tickets assigning them to specific sections, a move that strongly conjured up first class, second class, and steerage ratings. "No one wanted to go because it was insulting," says one former Macy's hand. "But if you didn't go, you risked the wrath of Finkelstein."

Holidays didn't bring out his best. Soon after Finkelstein was elected Macy's chairman in 1980, he decided it would be a good idea to host a party for Macy's staffers following the Thanksgiving Day Parade. Everyone went up to the thirteenth floor, where they ate, drank, and took a minute to introduce their kids to Finkelstein in his office. It was a warm, endearing experience that set Macy's apart from colder, more rigid companies.

But following the buyout in 1986, this changed. First, Finkelstein decided that he would no longer sit in the grandstand, as had Jack Straus and Donald Smiley. Instead, he ordered a royal enclosure to be erected across from the grandstands, one complete with portable toilet. This infuriated the Macy's staffers sitting opposite him, many of whom were freezing in the cold November weather by the time the parade ended. But even more infuriating was Finkelstein's decision to limit access to his office during the Thanksgiving Day party that followed the Parade. Decreeing that the event was becoming too crowded, he issued all guests color-coded tickets and stationed a security executive in front of his door to check credentials. "What he did was create a party inside of a party," says one former executive. "Everybody noticed. All of the celebrities were inside, and all the rest of us were outside."

It was a far cry from the old days, when Jack Straus, the late Macy's chairman, insisted that the executive floor be the last to be air-conditioned. "My father knew who he was," says Ken Straus. "I'm not sure that Ed ever really did."

(Finkelstein later vigorously insisted that the enclosure was not heated, saying he "froze" alongside everyone else. He also pointed out that the party on Thanksgiving Day had ballooned to nearly five hundred people, including celebrities, and that he felt it was prudent to limit access to his office.)

Finkelstein's formidable presence, his schoolboy cockiness, and his sense of style and place convinced many that Macy's was well on its

way to achieving its goals. When *Forbes* magazine scrutiniz
tailer's performance in early May 1989, it focused on anni
obligations that topped $500 million. Still, *Forbes* concludeu ...
cash flow was more than enough to meet the retailer's needs, an optimistic assessment that Finkelstein instantly seconded. "The day we
started out we had completed a year where we did $4.7 billion in busi-
ness," explained the Macy's chief. "This year we'll do $7 billion. If you
set up your debt structure intelligently so your cost is fixed, and your
business grows, you begin to get the benefit of leverage in terms of
growth. That is the reason leveraged buyouts are attractive."

Impressed with one analyst's projections that valued Macy's at more
than $3 billion, the magazine opined: "This is precisely what well-done
leveraged buyouts are supposed to do: produce better business and
handsome rewards for the people who run them."

And there were bright spots. For the quarter ended April 29, 1989,
the retailer reported a $64.1 million loss on $1.48 billion in sales. Still,
as Finkelstein noted, that loss was far smaller than the $149.2 million
in losses the company had suffered in the same period a year earlier,
when it took a $55.5 million charge connected to its bid for Feder-
ated.

More important, he said, same store sales rose 7.2 percent. From
an operating standpoint, Macy's was firmly headed in the right direction.

The company had a plan, Finkelstein said, and the plan was working.

Elsewhere in the empire, though, some executives were starting to
show signs of strain. Bobby Friedman, the chairman of Macy's South,
missed New York, despite the fact that Macy's had loaned him $1 mil-
lion to buy a new house in Atlanta. In an August dinner meeting with
Finkelstein and Mark Handler, both of whom had flown in for their
customary monthly meetings, Friedman poured out his heart.

"Maybe I'm not cut out for this," Friedman worried aloud. "What
would happen to me if I said I shouldn't be here?"

Taken by surprise, Finkelstein didn't commit himself. "Let me talk
about it with Mark, and we'll get back to you tomorrow," he replied.

The next day, Finkelstein told Friedman that he had evaluated the
situation and decided to bring him back to New York as vice chairman for merchandising for Macy's Northeast. Friedman would report
to Art Reiner, chairman. Although it appeared to be a demotion,

Friedman later publicly insisted that the idea to return to New York was his, and that he had enjoyed a close relationship with Reiner since reporting to him in the late 1970s.

"Bobby Friedman wasn't moved because he was doing anything wrong, he was moved because he admitted he wasn't good enough," says Dan Bergman, the former Bamberger's executive. "Eddie was just thrilled, because this was his opportunity to move Hal Kahn out of California, and put Danny, his son, in Hal's job. It took Ed exactly one hour to decide this was the most wonderful idea."

A few days later, Finkelstein announced that Macy's was shifting some of its most senior managers. Hal Kahn, who was doing an excellent job as chairman of the Macy's California division, would return to Macy's Atlanta as chairman and chief executive, where he would also oversee Bullock's/Bullocks Wilshire from three thousand miles away.

Although Kahn, then forty-three years old, outwardly appeared satisfied with the decision, he was privately fuming. As everyone inside Macy's knew, he had already managed the Atlanta division, revived it, and been rewarded with his posting to San Francisco. He had believed that his next job would be chief executive of the corporation. That Dan Finkelstein, only thirty-four years old, was succeeding him made it even worse, since no one inside the organization—with the exception of Ed Finkelstein—believed that Dan was ready for such an important job. A nice guy, yes. A chief executive and skilled merchant, no. Although Dan was credited in the press for introducing the chic Anne Klein and DKNY lines to Macy's, many inside Macy's believed that he wouldn't have risen nearly as fast, or as high, if his father wasn't chairman. Indeed, Dan was named a senior vice president in late July 1986, less than two weeks after his father led the management buyout.

Former Macy's executives say that Dan Finkelstein sensed that Kahn was upset, and suggested Kahn should stay in San Francisco, while he went to Atlanta. His father said no.

Hal Kahn, Macy's fourth-largest management shareholder, had little choice. He would either move or he would lose his job. His wife and three children, however, stayed behind in Hillsborough, an upscale suburb of San Francisco. Later, he complained bitterly that he was only able to see them a few times each month.

"Hal arrived in Atlanta ready to kill, because he had been forced to move three thousand miles from home to make room for Eddie's son," says Bergman. "This was not a happy camper."

Hal Kahn wasn't the only Kahn furious over Dan's big promotion. Eugene Kahn, no relation to Hal and one of Macy's brightest young merchants, believed that he had earlier been promised the chairmanship of Macy's California when the post became vacant. Instead, he was transferred to Macy's South as a senior vice president, a job he almost refused. Furious at what he viewed as shameless nepotism, he later quit to accept the presidency of G. Fox in Hartford, Connecticut, a unit of May Department Stores. Inside Macy's, Eugene Kahn's defection was widely viewed as a sign that the buyout was in deep trouble. (Two years after Eugene Kahn joined G. Fox, that troubled company was merged with Boston-based Filene's department store unit. Kahn was named president and chief executive of the combined businesses, transforming him into one of the department store industry's most visible stars.)

Dan Finkelstein, a quiet, shy figure, had joined the San Francisco training squad in 1977. Now he was going to head one of Macy's key divisions.

"What happened was that Ed was turning Macy's into Finkelstein's," says one prominent retailer who asked not to be identified. "The people inside Macy's began to see that this was becoming a Finkelstein company and not a corporation. He put his own kids in big jobs, and what it meant was that there would no longer be any balanced criticism. Everybody has an Achilles heel, and this was Ed's: he was very loyal and supportive of his family. He had Mitchell in charge of private label in Hong Kong, and then he put Daniel in charge of California. What this meant was that nobody inside the company could deal with the topic objectively. The divisions couldn't criticize the private label product because of Mitchell. And it was all done to accommodate personal issues."

As summer now gave way to early autumn 1989, the retailing industry's other huge buyouts, Allied Stores and Federated Department Stores, began to experience serious financial problems. An earlier effort to sell high-interest junk bonds to finance the Federated transaction had failed, and a $400 million loan was coming due in mid-September.

In the early part of that month, Campeau Corp. announced plans to restructure the $10 billion debt of its two retail units. The bold plan included the possible sale of Bloomingdale's. When Robert Campeau had acquired Federated, he said he hoped to transform Bloomingdale's into a national chain. Now those dreams would have to be put on hold. In addition, Campeau Corp. said it was negotiating an emergency $250 million loan from Olympia & York Developments Ltd., the Toronto-based development company that owned 25 percent of Campeau's stock.

It was an open, bleak acknowledgment that Campeau's two retail businesses were faltering.

Taken by surprise, many apparel vendors promptly stopped shipping new goods to Allied and Federated in fear that the pair would file for Chapter 11 bankruptcy. A few days later, Olympia & York agreed to invest the $250 million, and it appeared that Campeau had once again avoided calamity. Still, there was no disguising the fact that Allied and Federated were both desperate for cash.

They weren't the only ones. Seemingly overnight, the entire retail industry was in turmoil. Marvin Traub, the chairman of Bloomingdale's, met with Drexel Burnham Lambert Inc. and the Blackstone Group about the possibility of raising enough money to buy the business. Melvin Jacobs, chairman of Saks Fifth Avenue, said he wanted to buy that business back from its parent, London-based B.A.T. Industries Plc, which was in the process of selling Saks, Marshall Field, the Breuners furniture chain, and the Southern department store chain Ivey's.

Not only were many of the country's most famous stores suddenly on the auction block, but half a dozen more appeared on the razor's edge of financial collapse. These included such household names as Seaman Furniture Co., Dart Drug Stores Inc., Miller & Rhoads Inc., and Jos. A. Bank Clothiers Inc. Once strong and vibrant businesses, each had been taken over by raiders or gone private in a management-led leveraged buyout. "It's the end of an era," said Kurt Barnard, publisher of *Barnard's Retail Marketing Report.* "Enormous changes are ahead in how these companies are owned and managed."

Macy's, too, was struggling. For the quarter ended October 29, 1989, its losses widened to $33.1 million, compared with a $19 million loss in the year earlier period.

Morgan Stanley's senior retail analyst, Walter Loeb, noted that the losses included costs associated with the purchases of Bullock's/Bullocks Wilshire and I. Magnin. But he warned that Macy's needed to reduce its staff and lower operating expenses.

Loeb, who had worked at Macy's in the 1950s, also zeroed in on Macy's private label program, which he said "has not been selling well."

Instead of jotting down a couple of lines to send to fellow shareholders, as had been their custom in prior quarters, this time Finkelstein and Mark Handler wrote a three-page letter. Attempting to put the best possible spin on Macy's performance, they wrote, "With all that is happening in department store retailing (and yes, it is chaotic out there), and all that is being discussed in the press, as well as by financial analysts, we decided that a more comprehensive letter from us was in order."

They then boasted how well they were doing with their Bullock's acquisition, explaining that they were now improving an "underexploited" business. Adding the West Coast division, they continued, would have significant long-term benefits, and create a stronger franchise than when the company went private.

"Our first quarter results . . . were somewhat disappointing, although essentially as expected," they added. "We had planned our EBITD [cash flow] down in the first quarter and did manage to just surpass our plan. We are now, however, satisfied with the results and feel they represent the continuing cost of our consolidation, which is not yet finalized. Nevertheless, we firmly believe that we are building a three division powerhouse!"

Although the two Macy's executives warned that the coming new year would be marked by a sluggish economy, they said they remained confident Macy's sales and profit margins would continue growing. They also noted that the company wouldn't open any new stores in 1990, and only one in 1991, a conservative strategy that would improve Macy's cash flow.

"Looking back, being a private, highly leveraged business has not interfered with the enhancement of our business," they concluded. "In fact, our entrepreneurial outlook has made the present Macy's an even stronger franchise than we contemplated and in which you invested in July of 1986."

But it wouldn't be that simple. The Christmas selling season generated as much as 40 percent of the year's total revenues, and the lion's share of the profits. Not only was the November–December–January selling period the busiest season, but retailers also had to pay down their short-term credit facilities. Typically, borrowings for new goods peaked in mid-November, with the chains required to repay those loans in full by December 31.

And while the 1989 Christmas season started on an encouraging note, with cool temperatures boosting gift sales of scarves, gloves, and sweaters, the customers didn't reach for their wallets with the same exuberance they had shown a year earlier. Some merchants warily blamed the economy, which was beginning to sputter, while others pointed to the record levels of debt consumers had already rung up on their credit cards.

What was clear was that retailers this Christmas would have to provide motivation. For the first time in recent memory, Santa Clauses and nifty window displays weren't going to get the job done.

The stores moved fast. On Thanksgiving, the day before the traditional kickoff to the Christmas holiday season, Macy's, Lord & Taylor, and Bloomingdale's each ran full-page newspaper ads offering reduced prices on nearly everything in their stores. In the suburbs, 50 percent-off signs were jammed into most mall store windows, creating the unmistakable whiff of panic. Even The Limited, which traditionally did less advertising and price promoting than everyone else in the mall, was offering "holiday bonuses" on every item.

It still wasn't enough. From coast to coast, the customers looked, dithered, and walked away. Those willing to spend demanded bargains. "The first question customers usually ask is 'How much?' " complained a manager at a Radio Shack in downtown Boston.

By early December, *The New York Times* was reporting that Dun & Bradstreet, the big credit rating company, had sent warning letters to its apparel industry clients urging them to stop shipping new merchandise to Federated Department Stores and Allied Stores, both of which were owned by Robert Campeau. Dun & Bradstreet was concerned about Campeau's faltering financial situation, especially since the proposed sale of Bloomingdale's, which was expected to produce at least $1 billion, was proceeding slowly.

Anxious Federated and Allied officials denounced Dun & Bradstreet's actions, and other credit companies continued to approve merchandise shipments. But the constant buzzing about Federated and Allied's fate deepened the sense that the Christmas season was dissolving into chaos. Then, a week later, Campeau Corp. disclosed that its third quarter losses for the period ended October 28 had widened to $186 million. Although Federated and Allied reported modest sales gains, their combined operating profit declined 9 percent to $174 million. One industry observer described the performance as "horrendous," while Alan Millstein, an acerbic-tongued retail consultant, said, "It looks like Campeau's position is deteriorating. I suspect it's giving some manufacturers which have extended them credit very nervous stomachs."

The timing couldn't have been worse. A year before, shoppers were filling their station wagons with gifts. This year, they were bragging publicly about their frugality.

As the business dragged, Federated and Allied slashed prices even further to keep the dollars flowing in. Meanwhile, the daily newspapers were filled with tales about hand-wringing consumers more concerned about paying their credit card bills than buying Johnny a new $200 bicycle.

If Finkelstein and his fellow merchants had sensed that the year would end this way, they could have kept their inventories low. But that wasn't the Macy's way. Every year Macy's buyers gambled on producing an even more profitable Christmas than the one that preceded it, and filled their stores to overflowing.

It had always worked in the past. But as everyone was learning, this was no longer a normal Christmas season. Between the growing national consensus that it was better to save than spend, and the Campeau-owned stores that were promoting eye-catching sales every few days, Macy's was being hammered.

Worse still, Macy's was loaded with private goods, merchandise it had designed and shipped in from the Far East. Unlike other retailers, Macy's couldn't turn to outside vendors for financial help in the form of markdown dollars or co-op advertising.

As the season drew to a crescendo, Campeau Corp. on December 13 acknowledged that its two retailers might have to file for Chapter 11 bankruptcy protection. Federated was on the verge of running out of money as early as January. Allied was in nearly as bad shape. And both chains were obligated to make daunting interest payments. For the quarter ended October 28, 1989, for example, Federated paid out $127.5 million in interest, while Allied handed over $74 million.

Within hours, many of the top credit companies in the apparel market issued instructions to their clients to halt shipments to Bloomingdale's, Rich's, Bon Marché, and the rest of the Allied/Federated stores. These credit businesses, known as factors, purchased vendor receivables at a discount and assumed the risks that the bills would be paid. Although out of the public spotlight, factors were now about to become the most powerful players on the retail scene, since a widespread call to halt shipments was tantamount to forcing a chain into Chapter 11 bankruptcy. Although small manufacturers could ignore such warnings, almost none did so. It was too risky.

For shoppers, Christmas shopping had become a bewildering and unsettling experience. Each morning they were assaulted with gloomy stories about the futures of stores they had frequented for years. It was so confusing that some consumers decided not to register for wedding gifts at certain department stores, since it wasn't clear if the companies would soon be in bankruptcy. For retailers, that uncertainty translated into lost sales and continued markdowns.

In early January, Robert Campeau bowed to the inevitable and gave up operating control of Federated and Allied, promising to involve himself only with Campeau's real estate operations.

It was too late. Within the week, Federated and Allied filed for Chapter 11 bankruptcy protection listing combined liabilities of $7.7 billion. More than 50,000 suppliers would file claims in excess of $6 billion, while hundreds of bondholders owed an estimated $3 billion faced the prospect of waiting years to discover whether they would receive any compensation for their investments.

Meanwhile, the 100,000 employees who worked at both chains were confused and angry, in part because very few retailers had successfully emerged from Chapter 11 bankruptcy. Although Federated and Allied arranged for $700 million in new financing, which meant they would soon begin receiving spring goods, the future for both businesses was cloudy.

Overlooked, however, was the fact that the two Campeau units had carefully been planning the filing for months. The same morning that Federated and Allied filed for protection, Federated's public relations office issued a press kit that explained how the two businesses would operate, their obligations under bankruptcy law, and definitions of various legal and bankruptcy terms. And when the two chains filed, they had plenty of cash on hand from their Christmas business. Although the bankruptcy process would almost certainly lead to the closing or sale of many stores, Federated and Allied were in fact in a strong position to move forward. The reason: the bankruptcy reflected the huge interest obligations that resulted from Robert Campeau's takeover. Each of the department stores Allied and Federated operated were making money—excluding the huge interest costs they had to bear. They would survive.

Moving quickly to allay the fears of Wall Street and the banking community, Campeau Corp. named G. William Miller, a former U.S. Treasury secretary and a director of Federated, to head up its U.S. retail stores.

At the same time, the U.S. retail operations announced that it was changing its name. Instead of operating as Campeau (U.S.), the holding company of Federated Department Stores, Allied Stores, and Ralphs Grocery Co. would now be known as Federated Stores Inc.

They were cutting their ties to Robert Campeau as fast as possible.

Even as Federated's employees were digesting that development, Allen Questrom, forty-nine years old, announced he was resigning as chief executive of the Neiman Marcus department store group to accept a new post as chairman and chief executive of Federated and Allied. He would be well paid, too: his new contract called for him to receive $12 million over the next five years. By contrast, he was reportedly earning $750,000 annually at Neiman Marcus, plus a guaranteed bonus of $150,000. Although some creditors grumbled that it was too costly a deal, Questrom was intimately familiar with Federated, and also had strong friendships in the manufacturing community at a time when many were angry and bewildered by the Chapter 11 filings. Considering the size of the bankruptcy, and the billions of dollars now at stake, the size of his contract was unimportant. If he succeeded, there would be enough for everyone.

Ironically, Questrom was not the first choice. Senior executives at Federated say that James Zimmerman, Federated's president and chief operating officer, was approached first but turned the offer aside, saying Questrom was better suited for the demands ahead. At Rich's, from 1980 to 1984, Questrom and Zimmerman had worked together as chairman and president, a period in which Rich's operations increased more than threefold. Now Zimmerman, a specialist in back-office operations, wanted to team up again.

Only the folks at the Neiman Marcus Group Inc. were unhappy. Less than two weeks after Questrom's appointment, the retailer filed a $19 million suit against Federated, Allied, and Olympia & York, the Reichmann family's development company that owned a significant chunk of Campeau Corp. In its filing, Neiman Marcus accused the defendants of improperly interfering with a contract that didn't expire until September 1991. As a result, Neiman Marcus was asking for $7 million in actual damages, and punative damages of $12 million.

"It was unfortunate," Questrom said several years later. "Yes, I had a contract, but I had a very long history at Federated, and when Federated approached me months before I joined, I went to Neiman Marcus and told them about it. Then, as time went on and the talks became more serious, I met with a senior executive at the Park Lane Hotel in New York and asked him to release me from my contract. I said, 'Look, I grew up in that company. I think I can help them. It's family.' He then said Neiman's wouldn't attempt to hold me. Also, I'd brought Terry Lundgren into Neiman Marcus with the idea that he would succeed me. And in fact he did do a great job. So it wasn't as if I'd left them in the lurch. But they later felt that their contract was interfered with, and while they didn't sue me personally, they sued the corporation."

(Federated eventually settled the suit for an estimated $2.5 million. In a twist of fate, Lundgren, who had earlier worked with Questrom as president of the Bullocks Wilshire chain before that business was sold to Macy's, rejoined Federated in early 1994 as the retailer's senior merchant.)

Soon after settling in to his new job, Questrom made his first major decision: Federated and Allied would eliminate three of their private label brands, a move that was expected to reduce annual private label sales by $100 million. The reason: Questrom didn't want to have to pay in advance for merchandise when he could order clothes in New York and not have to pay until thirty days after delivery. "We had to conserve our cash flow," said Questrom. "That's what you do in a tight situation."

A few months later, in May, the "for sale" sign was removed from Bloomingdale's. Allen Questrom hadn't returned to Federated to sell off one of the country's premier department store businesses.

But before he could pay back 300,000 creditors, businesses would have to be merged, including the three Florida chains: Maas Brothers, Jordan Marsh, and Burdines. Money-losing stores, like the Bloomingdale's branches in Stamford and Dallas, would be closed. All non–department store businesses would be sold. And more buying would be done centrally, enabling Federated/Allied to pare its payroll. But if everything worked as well as he hoped, and Federated/Allied emerged from Chapter 11 bankruptcy protection in good shape, he might even be able to make an acquisition at some point. You never knew.

Chapter 11

"Mismanagement, not debt, is almost always the culprit in the failure of a business."

I t read like any other Dear John letter, filled with apologies and re-grets.

"Dear Investor," wrote Ed Finkelstein, Mark Handler, and Mike Ullman on February 16, 1990. "Since it will be mid-March before our quarterly results are published, we felt it important to promptly share our thoughts about this past Christmas season and our plans for 1990."

Without providing details, the trio offered a discouraging preview of what would follow. While sales improved in December, they said, Macy's had been forced to take "substantial markdowns" to meet "competitive conditions."

Reading between the lines, Macy's had given away the store while waging a market share battle with Federated and Allied, both of which then filed for Chapter 11 bankruptcy protection. Still, nobody inside Macy's was blamed for having misread the season and overstocked the store. (For Christmas 1990, Macy's reduced its inventory by an astounding $650 million.)

"We don't expect that you will be pleased with the results of our most recent quarter; we certainly will not be," the Macy's men acknowledged. "We do, however, want to assure you that we are a strong force in the marketplace with our customers, suppliers, and real estate developers seeking our presence in new locations."

For Ed Finkelstein, the words came from the heart. On the heels of Macy's worst Christmas in memory, he bought an unspecified amount of Macy's junk bonds for his personal account, including the high risk 16.5 percent zero coupon debentures payable in the year 2006, when he would be eighty-one years old.

The move mostly reflected his desire to bolster morale; within days, he'd jotted off a note to fellow investors alerting them to his purchases and explaining that he would be buying more in the future. Concerned that his words might be interpreted as shilling for distressed junk bond debt, Macy's lawyers asked him to insert a disclaimer. "I am not, of course, encouraging anyone to purchase our debentures," he concluded.

On Macy's thirteenth floor, however, his handpicked senior executives understood the message. Within two weeks, at least a dozen followed Finkelstein's lead and bought Macy's junk bonds. "We were loyal people," says one former corporate official who wrote a check. "We had a lousy Christmas, but so what. We figured this is one of the great retail companies of all time, we're resilient, we've weathered bad Christmases before. Nobody thought it would be the end of the world. . . . Which it was."

Shortly afterward, everyone knew exactly how badly Macy's had performed. In what should have been the company's most profitable quarter, Macy's lost $39 million, compared with earnings of $72.6 million in the same period a year earlier. Same store sales increased 5.4 percent, but it was a hollow victory.

The size of the loss, coupled with the recent bankruptcy filings of Federated and Allied, prompted some on Wall Street to wonder whether Macy's was on the razor's edge of bankruptcy. Moody's Investors Service Inc., the credit agency, was threatening to downgrade Macy's debt, while the retailer's bonds had plummeted to only 60 percent of their original value. Even Macy's remaining admirers recognized that the company needed refinancing, most likely in the form of a big cash infusion.

Much as Laurence Tisch had warned during recent board meetings, the $1.1 billion that Finkelstein had insisted on paying to acquire Bullock's/Bullocks Wilshire and I. Magnin was beginning to loom large.

After joining Macy's in late 1988, Mike Ullman threw himself into doing what he knew how to do best: managing operations. He also tackled Macy's various computer systems. Although the retailer had once been a leader in information technology, it had fallen far behind Wal-Mart, The Gap, and others, reflecting the fact that neither Finkelstein nor Handler cared much about back-office operations.

Ullman, who had logged seven years at IBM, understood information systems. But very quickly, he realized that he would never succeed in aligning Macy's computer systems. Worse still, Macy's had invested more than $7 million in recent years in constructing its own data processing facility in Newark, with little to show for it. The Newark operation was a black hole into which money disappeared without consequence. Seemingly nobody understood what it was doing, or where it was headed.

Convinced that Macy's would never catch up, Ullman urged Finkelstein to put the business in the steady hands of the Sabre Group, a data processing unit owned by Federated Department Stores Inc. Sabre could supervise all of Macy's information systems needs in the Northeast, including sales, credit, and purchasing transactions, Ullman said. The system already worked, and while it was expensive, it could be installed in only a few months.

Although nobody said so, it was a tacit acknowledgment that the efforts to marry Bamberger's and Macy's New York had failed, calling into question why there had been such a hurried frenzy to merge the two businesses. Strikingly, it would also be the first time that a major department store retailer turned over its most intimate and sensitive financial information to a rival. Although Ullman quietly insisted that safeguards existed to prevent curious Federated chiefs from rifling through Macy's daily sales and reorders, some at Macy's were convinced that Federated would soon know their business as well as they did.

Initially, the Sabre pact didn't cover Macy's South and Macy's California. Instead, those two divisions continued using their own software. What this meant was that at a time when efficiency and cost-cutting were increasingly dependent on the speedy flow of information, Macy's still lacked a single, unified sales and inventory reporting system. It was a huge business, and one that still sometimes pulled in opposite directions. Yet in a real and powerful way, Federated had now established a beachhead inside Macy's, since its stores, and Macy's Northeast, would soon be completely compatible.

For Mike Ullman, the Sabre pact was a heady triumph. And indeed, by giving the pact his public blessing, Ed Finkelstein was anointing Ullman as Macy's fastest rising star, and a power to be reckoned with. It was an accomplishment largely earned by dedicated effort. Although Ullman suffered from an unexplained neurological disorder, he was a prodigious worker, leaving his home in Greenwich by 5:30 A.M. and arriving in the office an hour later. While he insisted on keeping Sundays free to attend services at the Bedford Community Church in Bedford, New York, where he was treasurer, Ullman was in the office almost every Saturday before Macy's Herald Square opened. He kept such a demanding schedule that one of his sons, Cayce, a college student at the University of Southern California in Los Angeles, sometimes resorted to communicating with him by fax.

Ullman allowed himself one indulgence: a vacation home near Montrose, Colorado, thirteen miles away from the nearest paved road. Before he left Hong Kong, his closest circle of friends agreed to subdivide several hundred acres on the remote Colorado mountain site. Ullman bought a lot and later built a modern log cabin house, complete with a Sub-Zero refrigerator. Perhaps because nobody at Macy's visited Ullman in Colorado, this property, so far from the crowded streets of Herald Square, created a sense of mystery about him.

Some found his zeal for fourteen-hour days absurd. "I can't say he pressured me to put in the same hours, but I was looked down upon because I wouldn't," says John Shepardson, a former Macy's group vice president who reported to Ullman. "Mike was very bright, very intense, very dedicated. But he created a culture inside the company that hadn't existed before. The question was: Do you work to live, or live to work? It was very much a philosophical issue."

Mark Handler, Macy's president, was also irked by Ullman's superman-like aura. Handler, who always had time for small talk, was appalled by Ullman's office hours. Soon after Ullman joined the company, Handler pulled Ed Finkelstein aside. Expressing his doubts, Handler reportedly warned his friend against trusting "the little prick."

Finkelstein shrugged off the criticism, attributing it to jealousy. (Handler denies making the remark.)

Besides, Ed Finkelstein had solid reasons for admiring Ullman's work habits. In recent months Macy's had reduced basic operating costs in maintenance, security, control/credit, merchandise processing, and several other back-office functions. In addition, there were

reductions in the selling staffs in many stores. Ullman also saved
Macy's $18 million a year by improving the rating of its credit card
receivables. Even the fact that Ullman lacked experience as a merchant worked to his advantage, since he never challenged Finkelstein
in the area that the Macy's chief viewed as most important.

The ties between the two were knitting strongly, with Finkelstein
assuming the role of teacher, and Ullman his student. With their offices side by side, the two spoke as often as fifteen to twenty times a
day. Finkelstein had enjoyed many protégés during his career. But he
had treated few with more interest, concern, and care than Mike Ullman. And that affection was returned by Ullman, who never once
voiced a doubt about Macy's future to outsiders. Convinced that Ed
knew what he was doing, Ullman insisted it was all going to work out.

Macy's wasn't the only retailer that would struggle in the spring of
1990. Thousands of retailers large and small were enveloped in a clash
that pitted a handful of professionally managed chains against older,
less dynamic businesses, some recently acquired by owners with no
feel for the customers.

The best were dominated by strong personalities who thrived on
buying and selling: Sam Walton at Wal-Mart; Leslie Wexner at The
Limited; Millard Drexler at The Gap; Ira Neimark at Bergdorf Goodman. But as such merchants became scarce, many proud names
slipped into obscurity. In early April, a bankruptcy judge approved the
closing of twelve Bonwit Teller stores, once one of New York's most
stylish specialty chains. More than two hundred potential buyers had
been approached to rescue the business; all passed, or offered less
than liquidation value. Further south, Garfinckel's, a genteel retailer
in Washington, D.C., whose shoppers included First Ladies Bess Tru-
man and Jacqueline Kennedy, was also near collapse. Its fate starkly
reflected the excesses of the 1980s, having passed through the hands
of five different corporate owners.

And in late April, in a move that would have ominous overtones
for Macy's, Ames Department Stores filed for Chapter 11 bankruptcy
protection while owing its suppliers $300 million. The filing caught
most factoring companies by surprise, which in turn created at atmosphere of anger and mistrust that spilled over into their dealings
with other retailers. Only a few years earlier, Ames had been an at-

tractive, well-managed business with a clever, low-cost strategy that appealed to shoppers in small Northeastern communities. Eager to expand its winning formula, Ames bought the troubled Zayre discount store business in 1989, intending to revive it. Instead, Zayre sapped Ames of energy, cash, and its bright future. At the time of the filing, nearly a third of Ames's stores were losing money.

As storm clouds swirled around Macy's in late May, Mike Ullman hired Diane Baker as Macy's new chief financial officer, adding a level of financial sophistication long missing in Macy's executive suite. Baker had worked at Salomon Brothers for twelve years, where she specialized in complicated financial issues, including the restructuring of Chrysler Corp. and International Harvester Co. She was also familiar with Macy's debt structure, having spent the prior ninety days at the company on a trial basis. This background in financial restructuring was so strong that some on Macy's thirteenth floor wondered if the company was in more trouble than Finkelstein was letting on.

Baker, too, was a workaholic. But unlike Ullman, who never raised his voice or showed signs of stress, Baker was sometimes demanding, short-tempered, and abrasive, qualities that may have contributed to her being passed over for partnership at Salomon Brothers. This didn't bother Ullman, who saw in her a financial whiz with extraordinary experience in guiding big companies through hard times. "I met her during negotiations to buy Foley's and was impressed," he says. "She understood restructuring, and she knew the bank side of the business. My own background was organization, systems, operations, not finance. I needed someone who knew that business and could talk to the pros."

And Macy's needed help. The values of Macy's three issues of junk bonds—$400 million worth of 14.5 percent senior subordinated debentures payable in 1998; $650 million worth of 14.5 percent junior subordinated debentures payable in 2001; and $910 million worth of 16.5 percent zero coupon bonds due in 2006—were in freefall, despite the enormous returns they now represented.

Worse still, several top factoring companies, including Heller Financial Inc. and Bank of New York, were so anxious about the retailer's finances that they were approving shipments of goods on an order by order basis. In the past, Macy's had treated factors—who bought retailer payables at a discount—with contempt, rarely responding to phone calls, and never providing the critical, up-to-the-minute financial data that the factors needed in order to determine the company's stability.

Only a week after Baker joined the company, Macy's went on the offensive. Intent on mending fences, it invited executives from eight of the most powerful factoring firms to meet with Finkelstein, Ullman, and Baker. It was a good decision, especially since most executives in the small, close-knit factoring community had worked together at one point in their careers and frequently shared information. By week's end, having been properly stroked and catered to, the factors announced that they had been favorably impressed, particularly with Baker, who spoke their language and promised fast, accurate assessments of Macy's finances. When she kept her word, the factors backed off and goods began to flow again. She then met with hundreds of vendors during the following six months.

Finkelstein also needed to restore Macy's luster on Wall Street. Invited to address a retailing conference organized by the investment banking firm First Boston in June, Finkelstein confidently dismissed Christmas 1989 as an "aberration" and asserted that Macy's was in "good shape."

He then detailed a Job-like series of calamities that had afflicted the company. Federated and Allied had put everything on sale, which forced him to follow. An earthquake in northern California disrupted sales. And high unemployment in the Northeast, where Macy's had a major presence, had crimped holiday spending in that crucial market.

Reluctantly addressing what he described as "the D word," Finkelstein acknowledged that the company was heavily leveraged. However, he emphasized that "Mismanagement, not debt, is almost always the primary culprit in the failure of a business," and attributed the recent bankruptcy filings of Federated and Allied to the fact that both were in the hands of a real estate man, not experienced merchants.

He also reminded listeners that Macy's managers owned equity in the business. Unlike the bunch at Federated and Allied, he said, his executives had plenty of personal motivation to succeed.

Playing to his audience, Finkelstein singled out Mike Ullman for praise, explaining that Ullman brought a new level of "sophistication" to Macy's non-merchandising efforts. Moments later, he pointed at favorable results in the third quarter, and promised that Macy's would perform even more strongly in the quarter ending July 28.

It was the Ed Finkelstein that Wall Street knew and admired: assertive, defiant, and inspired, a dedicated merchant who knew how to solve problems and deliver results. Fittingly, he finished on a high note. "Just how well we'll do at Macy's as a result of our LBO is not yet determined," he said. "But there comes a time when one senses instinctively that the most difficult part is over and the best is yet to come. I sense that now."

And at first, Ed Finkelstein's senses appeared to be serving him well. Early on August 2, Macy's disclosed that it had sold a 1 percent equity stake in the company to Corporate Property Investors, a real estate developer, for $15 million. The price effectively valued all of Macy's at $1.5 billion, which was the same figure that Finkelstein used during his negotiations with The Limited's Leslie Wexner. Considering that Macy's now had more than $5 billion in debt and had just experienced its worst Christmas in recent memory, Corporate Property Investors had paid a seemingly generous price. (Rival real estate executives understood: Macy's operated stores in twelve of Corporate Property Investors's twenty-eight malls nationwide. The investment, says one real estate executive, was a cost of doing business.)

Still, the emergence of Corporate Property Investors was a glimmer of bright news. So, too, was the decision of Macy's key banks to reduce the cash flow ratio coverage covenant relative to debt from 1.5 times to 1.2 times. (The covenants, a financial promise, were put in place by lenders to protect their loans.) This was the third time in as many quarters that the banks had done so, proving the old adage: lend me $100, and you own me; lend me $1 million, and I own you. Although the covenants had been written into the loans to protect the banks, the only alternative to amending them was to declare Macy's in violation and force it into bankruptcy.

This was not a solution.

Eventually Macy's violated its bank covenants more than twenty times. Each and every time, the banks dutifully announced amendments.

But Macy's satisfaction in the twin developments—the $15 million investment, and the solicitude of its banks—would be short-lived. Less than twenty-four hours later, Iraq invaded its neighbor Kuwait, sending oil prices rocketing, and fraying the nerves of millions of Americans. President George Bush quickly barred all oil from Iraq and Kuwait, and then committed American troops to the Persian Gulf.

Within two weeks, a survey of economists found that "the U.S. appears headed for significantly higher unemployment and little or no economic growth in the next year." By the end of that month, retailers nationwide were expressing fear that the upcoming Christmas season might be even worse than the one that preceded it. Fueling their concern was a report by the Conference Board, a nonprofit research organization, that found consumer confidence had fallen to its lowest level in seven years.

The gloomy economic news continued as Christmas neared. Housing starts were falling, manufacturing was slowing, and capital spending was down. Although the Bush Administration denied it, a consensus was building that a significant recession was under way.

By all rights, Ed Finkelstein should have been deeply depressed. Instead, Macy's was rallying. Together with Baker and Ullman, he had sketched out a three-pronged plan to restore the company's credibility, one that called for Macy's to raise more cash, retire debt, and demonstrate to skeptics that Macy's still had a tremendous future.

He started by using the $15 million from Corporate Property Investors to buy back Macy's own 16.5 percent zero coupon bonds with a face value of $45 million—at the greatly reduced price of only twenty cents on the dollar. He also bought $5 million worth of Macy's 14.5 percent junior subordinated debentures at forty-five cents on the dollar. "We never dreamed we'd have the opportunity to buy bonds at such a discount," chortled Mike Ullman.

Presumably the Macy's investors who originally paid face value for their bonds felt the same way.

Although the buyback was insignificant in comparison to the amount of debt outstanding, the move restored some confidence among Macy's vendors and bank lenders. And then, in early October, Macy's announced it was selling its credit card business to General Electric Co. for an estimated $100 million. General Electric, Macy's largest equity investor, already managed thirty-seven million customer credit cards for more than two hundred retailers, making it one of the largest in the world in that lucrative business.

Finkelstein had long fought against selling Macy's credit card business, arguing that it was a mistake to put it in the hands of a third party.

He wanted Macy's own employees answering questions from the customers—and resolving their problems—rather than an outsider. At least eight million shoppers carried Macy's charge cards, making it one of the biggest such businesses in the country. If they were treated shabbily, Macy's would suffer as a result.

Still, the retailer needed cash, and Finkelstein finally gave in. The sale, he announced, would be concluded in January 1991. When it did, it would remove $1.5 billion worth of debt from Macy's books related to Macy Credit Corp. and Macy Receivables Funding Corp.

Although Macy's had surrendered a key asset, bondholders greeted the development with relief. Macy's bonds had fallen drastically during the previous four months, in part from concern that the coming Christmas would be terrible. Since Macy's was expected to use the new $100 million to buy back yet more junk bonds, prices on all three Macy's issues rose.

Finkelstein's forceful campaign to restore Macy's credibility was so successful that even after he disclosed in mid-October that Macy's losses for the fiscal year ended July 28, 1990, had more than tripled to $215 million on $7.27 billion in revenues, many vendors continued to voice support. Still, some apparel suppliers began asking for special payment terms, and a handful of Japanese consumer electronics makers flatly refused to ship goods until special arrangements could be worked out. Macy's also stopped doing business with several firms, including Spode, the china company whose Christmas collection had been an important holiday seller for many years.

It had been a challenging year, forcing Finkelstein to make difficult, painful decisions. And yet Macy's had somehow moved forward, paying $717 million in interest payments, or $21 million more than in 1989, and $125 million more than in 1988. These were big numbers, and they illuminated the mistakes Macy's had made since going private, as well as the challenges Finkelstein faced in the near future. The increase in the size of the interest payments between 1988 and 1989 reflected the purchases of the two Federated divisions, while the rise between 1989 and 1990 mostly reflected an increase in working capital borrowings.

In other words, because of Finkelstein's huge bet on Christmas 1989, Macy's had suffered twice. Not only had it lost money during its Christmas quarter, but it had paid dearly to stock that inventory, borrowing money at an interest rate that reflected its highly leveraged situation. Overstocking the stores had been a dangerous gamble—and one that Finkelstein lost.

The size of Macy's losses, coupled with the prospects of yet another difficult Christmas season ahead, finally galvanized the board. Realizing that they would have to act, or watch their investment disappear, four of the company's largest preferred shareholders—General Electric Capital Corp., Loews Corp., the Mutual Series mutual fund group, and Taubman Investment—agreed in early November to provide as much as $150 million in new equity. The money, they said, would be used to buy Macy's junk bonds, which in turn would reduce its crippling interest charges.

It was a bittersweet moment for Ed Finkelstein, and for all of Macy's management investors, since the new capital would dilute their stake by one-third.

Tellingly, when Leslie Wexner wanted to merge with Macy's in early 1989, Finkelstein valued Macy's equity at $1.5 billion, or five times the $300 million that its shareholders invested in July 1986. As recently as August 1990, he had charged Corporate Property Investors $15 million for its 1 percent stake, placing that same $1.5 billion value on Macy's equity.

But now, only two months later, Macy's original partners were buying new shares at the exact same price they had paid in July 1986. To these hard-nosed investors, Macy's stock hadn't gained a cent in value during the company's first four years as a privately held business.

Rather, their move suggested that Macy's equity was only worth $450 million—the $300 million that had been invested originally, and the new $150 million that they were going invest. For Corporate Property Investors, this meant that its recent $15 million investment had already lost four-fifths of its value.

But on a larger scale, it was public recognition that Ed Finkelstein had frittered away more than $1 billion in perceived value. His move to buy Federated Department Stores, prompted largely by visions of grandeur, had saddled Macy's with more than $100 million in related expenses at a time when it should have been conserving every dime. More tellingly, he had spent a tad over $1 billion to buy the Bullock's/Bullocks Wilshire and I. Magnin stores. Presumably, without those stores Macy's would have been worth at least $1.5 billion, perhaps more when the related expenses and interest costs were excluded.

The good news, then, was that Macy's deep-pocketed investors were going to write yet more checks, saving the company from collapse.

The bad news was that Macy's business was still weak. As the recession deepened in the Northeast, the retailer disclosed that it had lost $66 million for the quarter ended October 31, or twice its losses in the same quarter a year earlier. Meanwhile, same store sales fell nearly 10 percent.

The very next day, all $2.5 billion worth of Macy's junk bond debt was downgraded by Standard & Poor's, the credit ratings agency. In a particularly blunt assessment of the retailer's immediate future, Joanne Legomsky, an S&P analyst, predicted that Macy's would "find it impossible" to meet its debt obligations without a sharp upturn in business or a major restructuring.

"In the last several quarters, Macy's has performed substantially below our expectations," she said. "Neither do we have high hopes that this will be a good Christmas."

It was, for Ed Finkelstein, the last straw.

In early December, Macy's bought a full-page advertisement in *Women's Wear Daily,* the influential trade publication. In an angry tone, Finkelstein addressed the widening speculation that Macy's would either file for bankruptcy protection or be forced to sell off some of its businesses, including its stores in the Atlanta region.

"No 'miracles on 34th Street' are required this Christmas," Finkelstein wrote, referring to the holiday movie that starred Macy's Herald Square. "The season will not make or break Macy's. We expect it to be slow, and we are prepared for it."

The ad was intended as much to raise company morale as well as to quiet the concerns of suppliers. Yet its odd mixture of anger, wounded pride, and boastfulness—Federated and Allied weren't "run by merchants who have seen hard times before and know how to plan for them"—indicated that Finkelstein was feeling the strain of managing a $7 billion (revenues) company where the first ten cents of every sales dollar went to cover interest expense.

And then, as if in a scene from *Miracle on 34th Street,* the movie that Finkelstein had only a few weeks earlier mocked, Macy's and its investors were blessed with their own Christmas miracle.

Sir Run Run Shaw, the eighty-three-year-old entertainment mogul whose Shaw Brothers studio was credited with making more than one thousand movies, many of them action-packed kung fu thrillers, had decided to invest $25 million in Macy's at $31.81 per share, with an option to buy another $25 million worth of preferred shares the following March.

The film executive, whose vast philanthropical efforts led to his being knighted in England, originally met Ed Finkelstein at Mitchell Finkelstein's wedding to actress Hui Ling, who had appeared in some of Shaw's films. Executives familiar with Finkelstein say he and Shaw struck up a casual friendship, with Shaw favorably impressed by Finkelstein's verve.

For the Hong Kong financier, the Macy's shares represented an opportunity to develop a significant asset in the United States at a time when his own island's future was growing increasingly cloudy. And though the investment ultimately made him Macy's fourth-largest shareholder, it represented only a small fraction of his vast fortune.

The emergence of Sir Run Run Shaw as a major shareholder was disclosed a week before Christmas Day. Clearly exuberant, Finkelstein said Macy's had raised $187.5 million in new capital, presuming Shaw exercised his option. (He did.)

And in addition to Shaw's investment, Tisch, Taubman, Price, and General Electric agreed to provide $119 million in new funds, also at $31.81 per share. Other investors included a group of mall developers, Corporate Property Investors among them, who agreed to buy $18.6 million worth of preferred shares.

In what amounted to a corporate game of "chicken," Macy's had come perilously close to collapse before being rescued by its board. It was a lesson Ed Finkelstein wouldn't forget.

Christmas that year went almost exactly as Macy's predicted. The customers were skittish, and waited for bargain prices. But Federated and Allied were no longer offering 50 percent sales every week, and neither did Macy's.

As a result, Macy's made money in its second quarter ended February 2, 1991, earning $78 million compared with a $39 million loss in the same period the previous year. Revenues fell 10 percent to $2.2

billion, and same store sales dropped 13 percent, but since Finkelstein had purposely reduced Macy's inventory, the decline was expected.

Still, Macy's Christmas profit resulted entirely from the repurchase of $85 million worth of its own bonds at a discount. Excluding those gains, Macy's lost $7 million. At Christmas. Again.

Chapter 12

"Department stores in general didn't want to change, because change involves pain."

What a difference only a few months made.

As Ed Finkelstein's tuxedo-clad guests looked on in amazement, a remote-controlled silver flying saucer hugged the ceiling on the main floor at Macy's Herald Square. The sight delighted hundreds of cosmetics executives and clothing suppliers who were sipping champagne and enjoying cheese canapés, caviar, and lox on brown bread. Also on hand were members of Macy's all-star board, including Jimmy Weinberg of Goldman, Sachs & Co.

They gathered in the middle of May 1991 to celebrate Macy's remarkable recovery. By now the retailer had purchased $371 million worth of its junk bonds for less than half of face value, slashing its interest obligations. By comparison, one of Macy's most vibrant competitors in southern California, Carter Hawley Hale Stores had filed for Chapter 11 bankruptcy protection in February, unable to cope with the huge debt it had assumed while battling Leslie Wexner.

As Carter Hawley Hale began a bitter reorganization, the Macy's crowd was partying. After finishing their drinks, Finkelstein's guests took the elevators to the ninth floor, where a small stage, podium, and viewing screen were set up. "Tonight, we want to convey to you our excitement and enthusiasm about Macy's future," he began. "We want you to understand that Macy's is back. And Macy's is ready."

Moments later, several dozen senior Macy's executives and others rose from their chairs in the back row and, to the astonishment of onlookers, burst into song. Although the words have been lost in time, one of those who sheepishly sang that night recalls that the verses were penned by a fellow Macy's staffer, and that they praised the vendors who had supported Macy's during its recent, turbulent period.

After they finished this goofy performance, the Macy's team sat down, and Finkelstein resumed his speech. "A year ago, when the press was at its most critical and when the rumors were flying, I received a letter from one man I'd never met, saying, 'Every so often I glance at the enclosed philosophy and it always gives me a lift. I hope it will do the same for you.' "

Finkelstein then read the following: "Far better it is to dare mighty things, to win glorious triumphs, even though checkered by failure, than to take rank with those poor spirits who neither enjoy much nor suffer much, because they live in the gray twilight that knows not victory nor defeat." The quote was from a speech Theodore Roosevelt gave in Chicago in 1899.

Nodding his head with appreciation, the Macy's chief continued. "I couldn't agree more with those words. You can either fumble along the fringes, or you can aspire to greatness. And we've always believed that Macy's is, and will be, a great store, doing great and daring things."

He then made a series of extraordinarily upbeat predictions. Macy's, said Finkelstein, was about to launch an aggressive, five-year expansion program that would add $3.6 billion of revenue by 1996, bringing Macy's total annual revenues to more than $10 billion. The department store company was also investing $65 million in new technology designed to speed reorders with suppliers.

"You're probably thinking 'promises, promises, promises,' " he continued. "But just as you've delivered to us, we deliver on our promises too. We said we'd pay our bills promptly and we did. We promised we'd reduce our debt and we did—by over $2 billion. We promised we'd raise new equity and we did that too, over $200 million worth. So when Macy's promises, you know you can rely on it."

He then explained that about $700 million would come from eleven new Macy's and Bullock's stores set to open during the next four years in such markets as Florida, California, and Texas. In recent years, he said, Macy's had invested $300 million in modernizing its older stores. An additional four stores were on the drawing board, he said, but since the developers weren't yet sure of their financing, he didn't want to say too much about them.

And he wasn't finished. That night, he said, he was announcing Macy's first credit promotion with Citibank's Visa card, a campaign that would involve a mailing to three million cardholders who currently didn't have a Macy's charge account.

Finkelstein then recalled recent trips to various malls around the country that he had made with Mike Ullman and Mark Handler. The real competition out there, he said, was the Limited and Gap chains. He knew, however, that a department store company could successfully compete because of the value, convenience, and fashion that it offered. The problem was getting that message to the customers. "We know our customers don't read newspapers the way they used to," he said. "But they do watch television. That's something that McDonald's and Coca-Cola learned years ago. Since Macy's is a brand just like they are, we decided Macy's should be marketed in the same way."

Moments later, he turned and gazed at the screen behind him as Macy's new television commercials began to play. Only a few months earlier, Finkelstein had gambled on a TV campaign with the theme "The Magic of Macy's—We're a Part of Your Life." The $150 million effort, which featured singer Melissa Manchester, represented a fivefold increase in what Macy's had been spending on television. The commercials had been prepared by one of Madison Avenue's leading agencies, Lintas: New York. It was the first time in recent memory that Macy's had turned to an outside firm to create its advertising.

"Our campaign, which kicked off last month, will be massive," Finkelstein added. "There won't be a Macy's market that is untouched by it. We want the customers and you to know that Macy's is back, Macy's is ready, and we intend to succeed."

The crowd, impressed and reassured, broke out into spontaneous applause. Then they went downstairs to The Cellar, where Glorious Food was catering a lavish dinner, Ms. Manchester entertained, and the Peter Duchin Orchestra played romantic ballads. Macy's did business with so many suppliers that it had to play host for two nights that week to avoid bruising anybody's feelings by leaving them out.

The events created massive goodwill and were the talk of New York's garment center. The euphoria, however, lasted barely as long as it took that flying saucer to make its way across Macy's main floor. The very next week, Macy's revealed that it had lost $101 million on a 7 percent decline in sales for the third quarter ended May 4, 1991, compared with a $63 million loss a year earlier. It was the largest single quarterly loss in the retailer's history, a breathtaking reversal as unexpected as it was disturbing.

Macy's attributed about $25 million of the loss to the sale—finally completed after numerous complications and delays—of its credit card operation to GE Capital for just over $100 million. At the same time, Macy's also benefited from a one-time gain of $15 million related to the repurchase of more debt at a significant discount. What this meant was that Macy's direct losses from operations totaled $91 million.

Even as he described the performance as "unsatisfactory," Finkelstein gamely found a few bright spots. Macy's had reduced its total debt by $2 billion in the past year, he said, while lowering its cash interest payments by $213 million. (The $2 billion figure included the sale of the credit facility, which removed about $1.4 billion in debt from Macy's balance sheet.)

And Macy's was soon going to go on the offensive. In hopes of luring back three million customers who hadn't used their charge cards in ages, Macy's would be offering them a sizable discount on their first purchase. There would be a commission plan for employees who coaxed other shoppers into signing up for the cards. The retailer's big advertising campaign was also going to kick in, Finkelstein said, bolstering the retailer's revenues within months.

But on Wall Street, the mood was gloomy. "These results are worse than I expected," said Thomas Razukas, an analyst with Fitch Investors Service Inc. "People got euphoric about the Macy's buyback of debt but forgot to watch the fundamentals."

Macy's woes were partly related to geography. The Northeast, where the retailer produced about half its revenues, was gripped by recession. Housing prices were falling, unemployment was up, and many local economies were in a shambles. Those who hadn't lost their jobs knew someone who had, lowering consumer confidence and resulting in weaker sales. The economy was also deteriorating in southern California, where the retailer now had a major presence. For years, Los Angeles's exploding real estate market had helped nourish the conviction that opportunities remained limitless. But now, with housing prices falling at a mind-numbing, double-digit rate, many of those same properties were unsellable, causing some owners to walk away.

The downturn also affected home owners who didn't want to sell, but who now felt poorer because their biggest asset was depreciating so rapidly.

Macy's had weathered many recessions during its history, mostly by cutting back on inventory. But in 1991, the company was saddled with more than $3 billion of debt. It wouldn't be able to survive by hunkering down and waiting for the economy to improve as it had in the past. Macy's needed the very sales gains that Finkelstein had promised to his suppliers in order to generate the cash flow necessary to meet debt obligations.

Whether spending $150 million on a feel-good, image-oriented advertising campaign at such a time was a wise move would be debated hard in the months ahead.

As Finkelstein wrestled with these latest setbacks, Federated and Allied Stores, free of Robert Campeau and the billions of debt that he had created, were emerging as strong, creative department stores.

Much of the credit for that revival belonged to James Zimmerman, Federated's president, who in late fall of 1989 made the difficult but right choice of preparing for a Chapter 11 bankruptcy filing. He later received little public credit for this, but his willingness to confront the problem enabled Federated/Allied to build a firm foundation for the future.

His first decision had been to call in David Heiman, who headed the fifty-five-lawyer bankruptcy practice at Jones, Day, Reavis & Pogue in Cleveland, and ask him to begin contingency planning. Although Federated/Allied soon after received an emergency $250 million cash infusion from Olympia & York, Zimmerman worried that it wouldn't be enough to avoid a filing. And if that happened, he wanted to be prepared.

Heiman, a decent, soft-spoken man in a field mostly dominated by bullies, began spending an increasing amount of time in Cincinnati, establishing more than a dozen individual teams that specialized in business, law, investment banking, accounting, and personnel. If Federated/Allied had to file, he felt, it would be critical to immediately establish a "business as usual" atmosphere in the stores so that the customers wouldn't lose confidence. There were dozens of issues that would have to be addressed in bankruptcy court the first day, including return policies, layaway agreements, and leased departments. At the same time, Heiman and Zimmerman began to focus on how store personnel would react; at that point Federated/Allied had more than 100,000 employees, all of whom would have to be reached as soon as possible. They launched a massive effort involving Federal Express, preparing videotaped explanations and packets of information for store supervisors, divisional managers, and senior management, so that all would be able to explain what was happening, why, and what the filing would mean in terms of going forward. Carol Sanger, Federated's public relations head, even prepared a glossary of bankruptcy terms which were distributed internally and to the press on the day of the filing. In addition, teams of lawyers were stationed in all of Federated/Allied's major regions to work specifically with divisional heads, including Bloomingdale's in New York and Rich's in Atlanta.

Simultaneously, Zimmerman and Heiman quietly began negotiating with the banks so that adequate financing would be immediately available. All relevant taxing authorities would have to be contacted as well. Eventually there would be a tax group, a litigation group, a financing group, a core bankruptcy group, and even a corporate chart complete with the names of individual team leaders. By late November, the law firm had taken over an entire floor at the Federated headquarters building in Cincinnati complete with computers linked to other Jones, Day offices. "What made this work was that Federated wasn't afraid to go with the experts," says Heiman. "They didn't accept everything that was said. But they wanted to hear everything. That's a sign of strong management."

When they finally filed—because of too much debt—Federated/Allied had more than $200 million in cash on hand, plus commitments for another $1 billion. The only big mistake: shortly before the filing, Federated/Allied sent checks to vendors, and seven in ten checks bounced. As a result, many loyal accounts now found themselves on Federated/Allied's long list of unhappy creditors. For the banking community, however, the substantial cash on hand signaled that the battered department store retailer had a sturdy financial base on which to build.

One of the few advantages of Chapter 11 bankruptcy protection was that it provided an opportunity to close unprofitable stores without having to pay off the remainder of the lease. Under the code, bankruptcy judges were empowered to declare such leases null and void. While this hurt developers, especially during a recession when most retailers were cutting back on expansion, the bankruptcy process was created to enable companies to emerge in the strongest possible financial position while rewarding patient creditors. Federated/Allied chairman, Allen Questrom, focused on the problems ahead, had already closed fourteen stores, and more would follow.

Meanwhile, same store sales at Federated/Allied were showing steady growth. Indeed, the combined companies were doing so well that in late April 1991 Questrom confidently predicted that the department store companies would emerge from Chapter 11 in early 1992 by going public again. "This isn't pie-in-the-sky thinking," insisted Questrom. "The worst is behind us. Operationally, we're performing as well or better as all our major competitors." At the time he made these remarks, Federated/Allied had $7.2 billion in claims against them.

Questrom, whose hefty $12 million contract had been widely criticized by creditors, was now proving that he was worth every cent. For decades, each of the nine department store divisions he now oversaw had operated independently of each other, complete with their own buyers, advertising programs, and distribution network. Not any longer.

If the combined company was going to survive, Questrom said, it would have to do business more efficiently. Divisions would be merged—including all three Florida chains, eliminating 145 jobs—and payrolls pared. Federated would also have to rely on more centralized buying, which meant less autonomy for each of Federated/Allied's department store divisions.

"Department stores in general didn't want to change, because change involves pain," says Questrom. "Even as other formats with smaller cost structures began to compete, they continued to operate with higher expense margins. First the small regional department stores went out of business because they didn't want to deal with what it takes to stay around—and what it takes oftentimes isn't pleasant. It causes trouble, all kinds of trouble.

"If you start off with a great selection, but your costs are too high in other areas, you're going to end up losing. Although all of Federated's divisions were profitable, I don't believe that it would have succeeded unless it filed for bankruptcy protection. You had to get away from autonomous operations, and you had to get costs down. The bankruptcy caused us to deal with that. Either we would get things fixed, or we wouldn't be around. The bankruptcy forced us to make changes that back in Howard Goldfeder's day we weren't prepared to do. We weren't prepared to come to the fact that we were sitting in corporate offices looking at corporate strategies that weren't working. We weren't asking the questions. Eventually we would have gone out of business."

His point man was Roger Farah, whom he named chairman of Federated/Allied Merchandising Services that summer. Farah, a six foot five inch former basketball player at the Wharton School of the University of Pennsylvania, had built a sterling reputation, beginning at Saks Fifth Avenue, where he helped build a solid men's designer business with such names as Hugo Boss and Giorgio Armani. Smart, unaffected, and hardworking, Farah was one of Saks's top young merchants. He was also ambitious, and after concluding that his path to the top job was blocked, he began looking elsewhere. Federated hired him in September 1987 as president of Atlanta-based Rich's, and promoted him to chairman and chief executive in 1988.

Three years later, he was hungry again for a new job, and met with Questrom to discuss his future. Although Farah says he was offered the chairmanship of Bloomingdale's, he instead accepted the chairmanship of the Federated Merchandising Services unit based in New York. Questrom, determined to modernize the business, had already implemented a team-buying approach that covered nearly twenty major merchandise categories, and intended to increase the amount of goods bought that way from 50 percent of all merchandise to 70 percent.

"Based on what I knew, I said I wanted the Bloomingdale's post," says Farah. "But Allen said the Federated job would be better, because I would be involved with all divisions."

As Federated/Allied's fortunes were improving, Macy's were in freefall. With losses mounting and sales declining, Finkelstein decided in August to merge his department stores into two major groups in a desperate effort to reduce expenses.

In a move that had far-reaching consequences, he created two new divisions: Macy's East, which included the former Macy's South and

Macy's Northeast stores, and Macy's West, which consisted of the Macy's California stores, the Texas stores, and the Los Angeles–based Bullock's department store group. Daniel Finkelstein, chairman of Macy's California, was named chairman of Macy's West, whose fifty-two stores generated $2.6 billion in revenues. It was a massive challenge. The young Finkelstein and his team of buyers would now be responsible for overseeing all merchandising decisions affecting those stores. It would take time to familiarize themselves with the new markets, as well as the customers who shopped there, increasing the pressure on quiet Dan Finkelstein.

The struggling I. Magnin speciality store chain continued to operate independently, although it now received some new blood, with Don Eugene, a Macy's senior vice president in New York, named as president. By now Magnin's twenty-three stores—all but four of them in California—were racking up big losses. True, Rose Marie Bravo, who had replaced Barbara Bass, had brightened the stores and improved relationships with vendors. But it wasn't enough. The older, wealthy customers who valued I. Magnin's emphasis on service were fading away, and the store wasn't attracting young shoppers in their twenties, who preferred to shop instead at Saks Fifth Avenue or Neiman Marcus.

The second new division, Macy's East, included the stores that comprised Macy's South and Macy's Northeast. Art Reiner, who had been chairman of Macy's Northeast, was named to head the new unit, which had sixty-eight stores and $3.7 billion in revenues. Harold Kahn, the chairman of Macy's South, would report to Reiner as chairman of merchandising for Macy's East.

For Kahn, who had believed that he would one day succeed Finkelstein as chairman, the move constituted a major demotion. What particularly infuriated him, say former colleagues, is that Ed Finkelstein hadn't offered him a chance to go home to San Francisco. He had much greater experience than Dan Finkelstein, and his family still lived in Hillsborough, an affluent suburb. He was also the only Macy's executive who was familiar with the Macy's California stores, the Bullock's group, and the Texas stores.

But Finkelstein wouldn't be swayed. His son was doing such a fine job that there wasn't any reason to make a change, he insisted. Danny was growing, he had command of the business, and he would be able to handle the new responsibilities. If Hal Kahn wanted to stay with the company, he would have to return to New York as Reiner's lieutenant.

As Kahn was losing influence—he would resign before year-end—Mike Ullman was gaining new prominence. Having won Finkelstein's loyalty and trust with his intensity and grueling hours, Ullman was rewarded by being named a corporate vice chairman. Although Mark Handler still ranked ahead of him on the organizational ladder, Ullman was in effect now Macy's second-in-command—and only three years after joining the company. "You've got to understand that when Ullman came in, he was an operations guy who didn't know merchandising," says one former Macy's executive who asked not to be identified. "Finkelstein was a merchant who didn't know operations. So when Ullman added new computer systems, and supported everything he did with beautiful charts, graphs, and slides, Ed was impressed. Don Smiley, the former chairman, just talked and had a piece of paper. With Ullman, it was reports, pamphlets, and these impressive presentations. And once Ed backed him, whatever Ullman said went. If he said cut the budget, we cut the budget. There was never any disagreement." Finkelstein's endorsement of Ullman was so strong that at one point he turned to a fellow Macy's colleague and said, "Mike Ullman is the straightest shooter since Roy Rogers."

On Wall Street, the decision to meld Macy's into two major operating groups was applauded, mostly because analysts expected significant savings to result from the inevitable layoffs. Inside the company, however, it created doubt and confusion. For decades, Macy's had been a stable business with clearly marked lines of responsibility and opportunity. Now, for the second time in two years, all of Macy's department stores were being reorganized into new structures. Whatever continuity had been established during that period was now being squandered.

Less than a week later, Macy's issued its rosiest projections in a long while. For the six months ending February 1, 1992, the retailer predicted, revenues would climb 8.3 percent to $4 billion, while operating profits would increase to $260 million against $156 million in the same period a year earlier. That forecast, coupled with a pointed reminder that Macy's had never once missed a payment to its vendors, helped create the impression that Macy's was finally back on track.

Although it wasn't widely understood at the time, the forecast was a public disclosure of what was in effect Macy's biggest bet since Finkelstein had bought Bullock's/Bullocks Wilshire and the I. Magnin business. In a desperate roll of the dice, Macy's was betting on a minimum of an 8 percent sales gain for the upcoming Christmas holiday season, which meant its merchants were buying enough goods to generate a 10 percent gain.

If it was a healthy Christmas, Macy's would generate substantial cash flow. It would also be in a much stronger position to renegotiate terms with its banks and other lenders. The struggling retailer would have to pay more than $500 million in debt service in 1992, well beyond its present abilities. But a strong holiday season would be convincing proof that Finkelstein had finally regained his magic touch, restoring confidence in the company's future among bondholders and suppliers alike.

Once again, Finkelstein was betting heavily against the odds. There would be six fewer Christmas shopping days this year. And consumers, frightened by the lingering recession and high unemployment, were cutting back on spending. A national survey conducted in late October by Fairfield Research, based in Lincoln, Nebraska, found that consumers planned to trim their Christmas spending by about 4 percent compared to the prior year.

While it was a small number—and shoppers were notorious for spending much more in December than they expected—it accurately reflected the country's mood, which was pessimistic and grumpy.

Two months later, on November 4, Macy's shareholders realized how important the holiday season would be. Despite Finkelstein's boasts in May that Macy's was finally on track, the retailer reported a 7 percent revenue decline to $6.76 billion for the fiscal year ended August 3, with same store sales falling 8 percent. Worse still, Macy's suffered a loss of $150 million. Although this was less than the $215 million that it lost a year earlier, many of Macy's vendors, as well as the factoring companies that approved orders of new goods, were staggered. Macy's cash flow, the financial measure that reflected the retailer's ability to pay its debts, fell to $555 million, compared with $722 million a year earlier. Although an estimated $100 million of that decrease was attributed to the sale of its charge card business, the performance was abysmal.

Yet in August, same store sales climbed nearly 2 percent. In September, same store sales jumped 4 percent. And though it didn't disclose the actual number, Macy's said that same store sales had increased again in October.

Two more months like this, and maybe Macy's would be over the last hurdle.

Even as Finkelstein and Ullman were putting in longer and longer hours, much of it in the stores to raise the spirits of their employees, one of the country's largest factoring companies, Heller Financial Inc., a unit of Fuji Bank of Tokyo, disclosed only two weeks before the beginning of the Christmas holiday season that it would no longer approve shipments of new goods to Macy's.

Heller's decision couldn't have come at a worse time. The daily newspapers were filled with stories predicting that consumers would spend less than ever during the Christmas season. The prices of Macy's junk bonds were falling almost every week, and some manufacturers were complaining that Macy's was not paying its bills on time. And now Heller was flatly advising its suppliers that if they shipped merchandise to Macy's, it would be at their own risk.

Determined to convince other factoring companies not to follow Heller's lead, Ullman said, "We're paying our bills promptly and we have excellent relationships with our vendors and the factors. We didn't fail last year, and we won't fail this year."

Soon afterward, Ullman received an unexpected phone call from an executive at the Prudential Insurance Company of America. Prudential was Macy's single largest lender, with about $800 million in mortgage loans that were backed directly by Macy's stores.

As part of its loan agreement, Prudential had received what was described as a "kicker," a provision that entitled it to share in revenues over a set limit at certain stores. The formula was complicated, but it basically obligated Macy's to share revenues it otherwise could have kept for itself.

Now the Prudential men were interested in a deal. What they wanted, they said, was for Macy's to buy back the kicker for $50 million, which Prudential would then be able to enter on its balance sheet before year-end. In turn, Prudential would restructure the original terms of the loan agreement at more favorable terms for Macy's. Prudential was also willing to allow Macy's to delay a $40 million payment due in November until the talks were over.

But an agreement was never realized. When Prudential decided it had found a different solution to its problems, the talks came to an abrupt end. "When they came to us, they wanted earnings for their year. A few weeks later, they didn't care anymore." Ullman, furious when the talks abruptly broke off, says he felt betrayed by Prudential. "We had a deal, and then they said 'never mind,' " he recalls.

Macy's had now lost an opening to renegotiate some of its debt. More important, it had missed a critical opportunity to strengthen ties with its biggest lender. That would come back to haunt Macy's—and particularly Ed Finkelstein—only a few months later, when Prudential held Macy's fate in its hands.

Despite all that had happened, Ed Finkelstein remained certain that Macy's was on the cusp of turning the corner. Although some of his lawyers had recommended that the company begin to plan for a Chapter 11 bankruptcy filing, Finkelstein refused to even consider that option. He had unshakable faith, not only in himself but in Macy's and all that it had meant, its decades of having met payroll after payroll, and the fact that it had paid each and every bill to the penny. Macy's had never welshed on an obligation; it wouldn't do so now.

So in late November, when he learned that a businessman named Fouad Jaffer was interested in selling about $6 million worth of Macy's preferred shares on the open market, Finkelstein knew what to do. Most of Macy's holders of preferred shares paid $39.62 per share when the retailer went private in July 1986, with Macy's retaining rights of first refusal on any subsequent sale. Jaffer, honoring those conditions, said he would be willing to accept $25 per share, or 39 percent less than what the stock commanded at the time of the buyout. Jaffer worked for the London-based Kuwait Investment Office, which oversaw various investments made around the world by the oil-rich country.

Ed Finkelstein thought the $25 price was a bargain. One by one, he called about one dozen of his most trusted lieutenants into his office and told them that an investment opportunity had come along that they couldn't afford to pass up. Among them: Mark Handler, Mike Ullman, Diane Baker, and Art Reiner. Finkelstein also urged his sons to invest in the opportunity.

"What he said was that it wouldn't be good for us if the stock fell into the wrong hands," says one executive Finkelstein approached. "He said he was going to make a major purchase, and he wanted our help."

The response was not what he expected.

Mark Handler begged off, explaining that he had already invested $2.1 million and felt it was enough. Mike Ullman also passed, explaining he had to pay college tuition bills for his kids. Besides, he had already invested $150,000 in Macy's stock. Art Reiner offered to buy one thousand shares, only to have Finkelstein scream at him that one thousand shares wouldn't help. (Reiner, who says he can't recall his immediate reaction to the offer, returned and agreed to buy more shares.)

On December 3, each of the Macy's executives received a letter from in-house counsel Herb Hellman confirming their individual purchases of the preferred shares and advising them that the sale was expected to close on or before January 6, 1992. Payment was to be by bank or certified check. The Macy's members were asked to sign the letter and promptly return it. Which they did.

They were all now on the line for tens of thousands of dollars' worth of Macy's stock.

(Later, after Macy's collapsed into bankruptcy, the executives who had agreed to buy those shares were furious at Finkelstein, believing that he had pressured them into buying the stock. And their rage grew substantially when they were contacted by representatives of the Kuwait Investment Office and told to pay up. Finally the small group, while staying at the Four Seasons Hotel in Newport Beach, California, on Macy's business, gathered at 8 A.M. to discuss their options at poolside. Some suggested negotiating a settlement, writing a check, and putting it behind them, especially since their own lawyers said they were obligated to buy the stock. Most of the conversation that morning was in careful, measured tones. Yet before the meeting ended, two senior executives suggested suing Finkelstein personally because they felt he'd had better financial information about Macy's than they did.

The negotiations would continue for months, with the Kuwait Investment Office initially agreeing to accept $20 per share instead of $25. By August 1993, the demands were reduced to only $12.50 per share. And then . . . nothing. Nobody was sure whether the money was too insignificant to interest the Kuwaitis, or if they had simply forgotten while their attention was focused on a disastrous investment in Spain. In any case, the Kuwait Investment Office stopped pressing for payment, and the matter faded away.)

·   ·   ·

Slowly but surely, it was all beginning to spin out of control. Macy's same store sales rose in October, and then again in November. But revenues weren't as strong as expected, and the price of Macy's bonds continued to fall. A one-day sale expected to generate $70 million instead produced only $60 million, putting the retailer in a bind from which it wouldn't recover. "It didn't take a brain surgeon to see that we weren't going to have a great month," says Ullman. "And how many sales days can you add on?"

Macy's thirty-nine-member bank syndicate, led by Manufacturers Hanover Trust Co. and Bankers Trust Co., recognized they had a serious problem. Under terms of Macy's revolving credit agreement, the retailer was required to repay all of its $587.7 million of its working capital facility by the end of December, and not to borrow any additional funds for any thirty-day period from December 16 through February 15.

That was going to be impossible.

Instead, Ullman and Baker asked their banks to amend their loan agreement for the twenty-second time since the original buyout. And on December 10 the banks agreed. Instead of being held to the original terms, Macy's would be required to reduce its revolving-credit borrowing to $75 million for one week, and to $150 million for thirty days at any point between December 16 and February 15.

When Ullman was later asked why he didn't ask the banks to allow Macy's to owe $250 million for that thirty-day period, he replied, "We thought the numbers were doable based on our revenue trends and our expenses. We had a cash model that Diane Baker had developed, and it was very efficient. We thought we had a safety net, based on estimates from our merchants."

But that net would have more holes than anyone expected. In the middle of the month, Macy's reported that its losses for the quarter ended November 2 had more than doubled to $155.4 million. At the same time, revenues rose only 3.6 percent to $1.6 billion. It was yet another disappointing performance, particularly since Finkelstein had predicted in late August that Macy's sales would jump 8 percent for the period. Macy's buyers had increased their inventories accordingly in order to achieve the gains. Now they were once again stuck with enormous quantities of goods at a moment when shoppers were cutting back on their spending.

Meanwhile, inside the stores there was a growing sense of panic and chaos. One senior executive who worked at Macy's Herald Square says she knew by Thanksgiving Day that Macy's had fallen millions of dollars behind plan. "The customers wouldn't buy anything unless it was marked fifty percent off," she says. "Despite that, we had piles of private label goods from Hong Kong that couldn't be sold. We'd cut our security team by forty percent, and the theft that resulted was just astronomical."

This executive says a sense of confusion and uncertainty affected every aspect of daily business. Often new goods were shipped without an invoice, which meant that buyers no longer knew what sizes or styles they were receiving. That widening sense of disorder carried over onto the sales floor, too, where a new system had been created that promised to reduce costs while giving more responsibilities to the cashiers. This, too, was a debacle. Sales people were given the power to cut through red tape and provide cash refunds for up to $50 without requiring a senior manager's signature. This sounded smart, but a new gift certificate program had recently been put in place, one that enabled cashiers to sell certificates. Those certificates, which were in effect cash, were sometimes left by the sides of individual registers, with many subsequently stolen. Thieves filled them in, went to a Macy's café, spent a couple of dollars, paid with the certificates, and received cash in return. Although the certificates weren't entered into Macy's tracking program, the cashiers invariably cashed them in order to avoid insulting a customer. "In the old days, Macy's would have gift certificates delivered by armored carrier, and then have them signed for in a vault, and they would be sold at a service desk. Now they were actually using Federal Express to ship certificates. Supposedly, they weren't live until they were issued by the store. But in our system, they were live because we weren't prepared. And executives in the high positions didn't care. It was immoral. We saw this coming and we called it out to the controller, to the people in charge of inventory, to security, and the systems committee. But nobody was concerned because nobody was responsible."

Every day brought new problems, she adds. One of the biggest issues was the lack of help. In order to pare back expenses, Macy's reduced its holiday hirings. As a result, there weren't enough clerks on the selling floor. Goods quickly piled high on tables, spilled out over onto the floor, and were then tossed back. "I got attacked every time I walked on the floor," she says. "Customers came and screamed and asked me to take their money." Although she was working eighty-hour weeks, it still wasn't enough to preserve a sense of order in her department. "And nobody seemed to care about the problems," she says. "It was very sad. And the name is still a gold mine. People love Macy's. There is something entrenched in their subconscious from the time they saw *Miracle on 34th Street.* You can't take it out of them, and Lord knows we've tried."

A second, higher ranking Macy's executive acknowledges that the observations are accurate. That Christmas, he says, major changes were implemented involving the selling floor system. In the past, when customers wanted a refund, they needed a signature of a manager; otherwise a cashier could write out refunds to friends. The purpose of the old system was to include an independent third party. But under the guise of customer service, Macy's now allowed the clerks to issue refunds on the spot rather than having to go to a service desk—the same location that had once supervised the sale of gift certificates. "I remember speaking to the head of security before the changes took place, and he was scared," says this executive.

Then, as the Christmas season reached its frenzy, Macy's lost whatever chance it might have had of salvaging the holiday period. In an unexpected move, General Motors Corp. announced on December 18 that it was closing twenty-one factories, firing 74,000 people, and reducing its capital spending. The big automotive maker also said it was putting a freeze on hiring in 1992.

The belt-tightening, following on the heels of similar restructuring moves by International Business Machines Corp. and TRW Inc., threw a scare into Christmas shoppers from coast to coast.

Ed Finkelstein had been at Macy's for decades, to the point where he could predict the retailer's business to within a half a percentage point after the first ten days of December. Although he realized that Christmas wasn't going to be as strong as hoped, the General Motors announcement, coming with the seven best shopping days of the month still remaining, was a knockout blow. The slight sales momentum that Macy's had enjoyed since late summer now came to an abrupt halt. Macy's would finish the month more than $150 million in sales behind plan.

Chapter 13

"We've seen this movie before; we know how it ends."

In the early days of January 1992, Ed Finkelstein, exhausted by the disappointing Christmas selling season, flew to Barbados for a vacation. He knew he'd be speaking to Mike Ullman every day by telephone, and if an emergency developed, he was only a short flight away. Diane Baker, Macy's chief financial officer, also went on holiday, to St. Bart's.

Elsewhere in the city, however, an elite group of highly paid lawyers and bankers were focusing on Macy's deteriorating finances. As Finkelstein departed for the Caribbean, Joel Zweibel, a senior partner and cohead of the creditors' rights department at the law firm O'Melveny & Myers, received calls from Manufacturers Hanover Trust Co. and Bankers Trust Co., the two lead agents for Macy's thirty-nine-member bank syndicate.

They didn't have to tell an experienced bankruptcy lawyer what was on their minds.

In recent years, Zweibel had worked on behalf of principal creditor groups in such high profile reorganizations as Texaco Inc., Eastern Airlines, and Public Service Co. of New Hampshire, the utility that owned the Seabrook nuclear plant. He also represented major bank groups in other complex bankruptcies, including the long-running Chapter 11 filing of Dallas-based LTV Corp., the steel, aerospace, and defense giant.

As he quickly learned, Macy's was in a so-called clean-down period

of its revolving credit agreement, the time frame in which it was obligated to repay its loan. After agreeing in December to reduce the
terms of that facility, the banks had grown increasingly anxious when
the retailer's Christmas business deteriorated. What concerned them
now, they said, was the likelihood that Macy's would meet its clean-
down obligations, and on January 25, demand a new $250 million fa-
cility.

Normally this wouldn't have been a problem. But the bankers suspected Macy's would be filing for Chapter 11 bankruptcy protection
within months, if not weeks. What they needed to know from Zweibel
was whether they were obligated to provide more funds if Macy's
somehow met its clean-down requirements.

Within days, Zweibel's New York office was filled with stacks of
complex bank loan papers. Together with a small team of financial
and real estate experts, he worked his way through the original bank
agreements, plus the accompanying modifications.

When they were finished, Zweibel called his clients and said he
thought he'd found a solution.

Although the banks were technically obligated to provide funding
after the clean-down period, it appeared that Macy's was no longer
in compliance with key financial covenants related to its performance
for the quarter ending January 26. Although the quarterly results
wouldn't be available until March, Zweibel was confident that Macy's
poor December performance, coupled with press reports that some
vendors were no longer shipping new goods, were enough to suggest
that the retailer was in technical violation of its loan. When this had
happened in prior years, the banks had simply amended Macy's loan
covenants.

But this time, Zweibel counseled, Macy's lenders would require
Mike Ullman and Diane Baker to submit officers' certificates with
their new borrowing request. The certificates would state that Macy's
wasn't in default of any covenants, and that there hadn't been mate-
rial adverse changes in its business. On the side, Macy's bankers would
also quietly let it be known that if Macy's was later discovered to be
in violation, they would deal with Macy's two top financial executives
accordingly.

It was an unusual but effective strategy. Ullman and Baker were
each well-known in New York's clubby financial community, and nei-

ther wanted to risk tarnishing their personal reputations. The certificates went unsigned.

With Diane Baker back from holiday, Macy's now began a series of intense negotiations with its bank lenders. Others had told Joel Zweibel that Baker was an authoritarian personality, very bright, brusque, and difficult. But in those early meetings, Zweibel found himself impressed with her firm command of Macy's finances. With her nerves obviously frazzled, sometimes she would speak for long periods without stop, but Zweibel, bemused, simply sat back and listened, eager to learn anything that could be helpful. He also felt that Baker and Ullman, despite the intense pressure, were trying hard to avoid a confrontation.

For Joel Zweibel, the stakes could not have been higher. Not only had the banks asked for a quick decision involving hundreds of millions of dollars, but there was also the very real possibility that if his advice was wrong, and it was later determined that the banks had inappropriately declined to honor a borrowing request that contributed to a filing, his firm could face a potential liability of major consequences.

After several weeks of daily talks, Baker said that Macy's wouldn't be asking for any more money from the banks—regardless of whether the retailer was in compliance with its bank loans or not. Although nobody acknowledged it, the decision was tantamount to declaring that Macy's would soon be filing for bankruptcy, since it couldn't operate without a new credit line.

"Given where we were at that point, I'd have needed $225 million just to pay our bills," says Baker. "And we wouldn't have had anything left over to buy spring merchandise. Either I paid our winter bills, or I bought spring, but I couldn't do both. And we didn't have any cash, and I couldn't borrow."

Although Macy's could have withheld payments to its suppliers, Finkelstein and Baker didn't want to hurt those who had continued to ship them new merchandise. So Macy's paid its bills, further emptying its coffers.

Later, Zweibel would say that what surprised him most about that period was the fact that Macy's was still not preparing for a filing. Normally that process would take weeks, if not months. Not only did it require massive amounts of documentation, but companies also normally negotiated in advance a debtor-in-possession financing facility, a line of credit that would cover all operating needs in Chapter 11.

But Macy's wasn't taking any steps. When the subject was broached, say former executives, Finkelstein insisted Macy's would never file and refused to approve any work, partly because he feared word would leak out.

"Nobody was sleeping, and Ed was in a state of denial," says Baker. "The merchants realized, finally, they had no money. I had anguished phone calls from Ed, saying can't you do anything. I had no patience, but I could hear the anguish. That was the human tragedy part. Whatever his hubris, the tragedy of Ed was beyond belief. It was awful. He couldn't understand why we couldn't pull it out one more time. He was simply devastated during this period. Mike was distancing himself from Ed, and Ed was reaching out for consolation, be it me or Ira. But he wasn't getting it."

It wasn't as though Finkelstein was being kept in the dark, either. Finkelstein spent every day in December with Mike Ullman, discussing the business, weighing various debt restructuring plans, reviewing their options. They spoke in the morning, they ate lunch together, they spoke at night. Macy's had framed each corner of Finkelstein's life. Two of his children worked there, his social circle revolved around friends he made during his years on the job, and he tied up much of his own personal fortune in the company's stock and junk bonds. Even when Finkelstein was in Barbados, he spoke with Ullman four times a day.

Yet Macy's chairman refused to discuss the possibility that Macy's might have to file. Although Federated had planned its bankruptcy four months in advance, Finkelstein turned on Ullman every time he brought it up. And Ira Millstein, Finkelstein's lawyer and closest outside adviser, was treated the same. The matter was closed. Finkelstein was so insistent that Macy's wouldn't file that Ullman didn't meet Harvey Miller, Weil, Gotshal & Manges's lead bankruptcy attorney, until January 24, only three days before the company filed. "At some point, Ed stopped listening," says Ullman. "He stopped listening to his customers, to his associates, and to logic for the most basic things, be it private label, Macy's relationships with its vendors, or expenses. He was looking at the finish line and didn't want to hear about anything else."

•   •   •

New York's bustling garment industry had its own rules, including a payment method that encouraged retailers to pay their bills on time. The terms were 8–10–E.O.M., which meant that buyers received an 8 percent discount on all bills paid by the tenth of the following month.

In Macy's case, this meant that most of its apparel suppliers expected to be paid for December shipments totaling about $200 million on January 10, 1992. But that morning, Macy's didn't issue any checks. Instead, wild rumors swept the marketplace to the effect that the department store retailer was halting all payments until a new working capital facility was approved. By late afternoon, frantic vendors were sharing a telephone number for Macy's San Francisco accounts payable department. Those who dialed heard this prerecorded message:

"For your information we are meeting the technical clean-down provisions of our bank agreement and sending out vendor checks on January twenty-fifth. The company's clean-down requirement ends at that time and the full working capital facility is once again available for the company's use."

In common English, this meant that Macy's was stiffing its vendors for at least two weeks.

That weekend, Kurt Barnard, a retail consultant, drew comparisons to Federated Department Stores, which had filed for Chapter 11 bankruptcy two years earlier. "First you had all the rumors," he said. "Then there was the failure to receive payment for goods already shipped, followed by a sense of concern pervading the garment center. In the case of the Campeau stores, there was absolutely no alternative. In the case of Macy's, we have a super powerful board of directors that includes Larry Tisch, Alfred Taubman, and Henry Kissinger. These are people who theoretically have access to enormous pools of money, and it is within the realm of possibility that they will pull a rabbit out of the hat to prevent a filing." Richard Hastings, a young analyst at a factoring company, simply said, "This means they stink."

Although some of the retailer's largest suppliers, including Leslie Fay Cos., were informed late Thursday about Macy's plans, most were caught by surprise. Steve Stoller, president of Karin Stevens Apparel Group, a dress house, worried that his company was at risk for half of the goods it had shipped. At Chetta B Inc., a maker of expensive women's clothes, Howard Bloom complained, "I suppose I'll ship them new goods—but after I receive my January payment." Laney Thornton, chairman of Eileen West Inc., a San Francisco maker of women's lingerie and dresses, said he was owed in excess of $100,000. "We've been through this before with Federated," he said. "The real problem is that Macy's isn't making any money."

He was right. Macy's holiday performance had been much worse than expected. In early December, when Mike Ullman went to the banks and asked to renegotiate the terms of Macy's working capital facility, he asked to reduce Macy's borrowing to $75 million for one week, and then to $150 million for thirty days from any point between December 16 and February 15. Although the retailer was obligated to reduce that facility to zero by December 31, the banks agreed.

By the end of the first week in January, however, Ullman realized Macy's wouldn't be able to comply with even those terms. December had been such a brutal month that the retailer wouldn't have enough cash on hand to pay its vendors and its bankers.

By now he was in delicate negotiations with the banks. Rather than risk further alienating them, Ullman chose to force Macy's suppliers to wait an additional fourteen days for payment. He knew they would be upset. Still, they had little choice but to go along. Macy's was still a retailing giant with 251 stores nationwide.

Its suppliers needed Macy's as much as Macy's needed them.

His decision made, Ullman called Ed Finkelstein in Barbados on January 9 and asked his permission to freeze payments. Finkelstein agreed, and flew back to New York two days later, on a Saturday. In an interview with two *Wall Street Journal* reporters that day, Finkelstein waxed philosophical. Looking tanned, rested, and fit, he confidently predicted that Macy's would weather this latest crisis.

In a relaxed voice, he said that while Macy's suppliers were anxious, they were also supportive. The same was true of the banks, and the factoring companies that Macy's had curried favor with over the past eighteen months. And though it had been a tough Christmas season, he was convinced that "reason will prevail," and that Macy's would be allowed to work out its problems.

Asked whether he believed Macy's would have to file for Chapter 11, Finkelstein insisted such a move wasn't in the best interests of the company. "It runs against our grain," he said. "We think we know what we have to do to meet our financial obligations, and we're prepared to do them."

Instead, he said, Macy's would look to raise additional equity capital, and use that money to retire more of its debt. The options included the possible sale of certain stores, or new equity investments from the retailer's holders of preferred shares. "I know what dealing with change is about," he said. "I'm not an outside predator coming to the retail business. I've spent my entire life running retail businesses, fixing divisions up. I've been through some pretty discouraging times before that we worked our way out of. We're really trying to do things to get ourselves ready to be a preeminent department store. . . . We have a far stronger team than five and a half years ago. And fortunately we have some investors who feel the same way about the franchise. So far they've been very encouraging that we're doing the right thing. We know how to play the game pretty lean."

It was a brave performance, one in which Finkelstein returned to familiar themes: Macy's had been hurt by the awful economy and other events outside its control, but its management had the answers.

Still, Macy's faced daunting challenges. The retailer owed more than $3.4 billion. In April, it would have to pay $27.5 million to holders of its senior subordinated bonds. And in May, it would owe $48 million to Prudential Insurance Co., as well as a $27.8 million payment due holders of the retailer's junior subordinated debt. Altogether, Macy's would have to pay out $500 million in interest expense alone in 1992.

Meanwhile, as Macy's slid closer to Chapter 11 protection, a bankruptcy judge in Cincinnati was blessing a plan that called for Federated to emerge as a publicly traded company in early February.

The plan eliminated about $4.7 billion in debt from the retailer's books, reduced annual interest payments from $800 million annually to about $400 million, and ended the retailer's ties to the Campeau Corp. The revitalized company would emerge with about $3 billion in debt, $2.1 billion in equity, and eight divisions that included Bloomingdale's; Jordan Marsh; Burdines; Lazarus; Bon Marché; Stern's; Abraham & Straus; and Rich's/Goldsmith's. Federated would also issue nearly eighty million shares of common stock to creditors. All non–department store holdings were gone, including Ralphs Grocery Co., the Los Angeles–based supermarket chain that was now majority-owned by developer Edward J. DeBartolo.

Federated had also shut forty-three unprofitable department stores, merged some divisions, and instituted a team buying approach that accounted for 60 percent of all purchases. Macy's most important competitor would soon be free of the costly and cumbersome court restraints created by the bankruptcy process, where every major decision required judicial approval.

Going forward, Federated's efforts would focus solely on business rather than its creditors and the court.

During January 13, 14, and 15, Macy's board of directors talked informally about what they were going to do. To Laurence Tisch and Gary Wendt, a senior executive at GE Capital, it was apparent that Macy's wouldn't be able to survive with its existing capital structure. Unless something was done immediately, Macy's would be forced into Chapter 11 bankruptcy protection, wiping out their entire investment in the company.

On January 16, a Thursday, the full board met for the first time that year. On the agenda was raising enough cash to survive the next few months, and then buying back a large portion of Macy's high-interest debt.

The following day, Gary Wendt said that GE Capital would be willing to lend Macy's $250 million. The funds would be treated as the equivalent of senior bank loans, he said, with $40 million going to buy back half of GE's equity position in the company. In effect, GE Capital would only be investing $210 million but would be credited with a senior bank claim of $250 million. At the same time, GE Capital would be reducing its own equity exposure by half.

It was, at best, a short-term solution. Still, it would send a powerful message to the outside financial community that Macy's deep-seated investors remained committed to the company, providing a badly needed psychological lift. In hopes of buying time and raising Macy's credibility, the board voted their approval.

The next day, however, Wendt returned and revised his offer. Instead of buying back $40 million worth of equity, Wendt said, GE Cap-

ital now wanted $80 million of its $250 million loan to be used to retire GE Capital's equity.

The revised proposal was immediately rejected. Not only would it
clearly have benefited only GE Capital, but Macy's board was furious
that Wendt was trying to renege on his earlier offer.

A few hours later, Louis Page, who represented Sir Run Run Shaw,
the Hong Kong–based entertainment mogul, made several new pro-
posals, including the possibility of advancing $250 million as a two-
year working capital facility in exchange for an option to increase his
ownership in Macy's to 50 percent of the common. In exchange, Sir
Run Run Shaw would receive an option to buy GE Capital's preferred
shares for $80 million.

It was a generous offer, since the full $250 million would be used
for working capital. But after consideration, it, too, was rejected, because some directors felt it would give Sir Run Run Shaw an opportunity to take control of Macy's on the cheap. Adding to their doubts
was the fact that few directors knew Sir Run Run Shaw personally, or
had many outside dealings with Page.

It was at that critical moment that Laurence Tisch began to think
seriously about buying the company himself.

The Brooklyn-born son of a children's clothing maker, Tisch was
a gifted student who graduated from New York University when he
was only eighteen years old. After a short stay at Harvard Law School,
he urged his family to buy Laurel-in-the-Pines, a hotel in Lakewood,
New Jersey. One resort begat another, which begat hotels in New York
and Atlantic City, followed by control of the Loews theater chain. The
Tisch clan renamed their new prize Loews Corp., and then scooped
up a garden variety of companies including Lorillard, the maker of
Kent and Newport cigarettes, and CNA Financial, an insurance business.

Intrigued by the sight of early bird shoppers lining up before the
doors opened, Tisch offered $900 million for the Saks Fifth Avenue
and Gimbel Brothers chains in 1973, only to see both snatched away
by a British tobacco conglomerate. Disappointed, he focused on more
mundane businesses, purchasing the Bulova Watch Co. and a small
fleet of oil tankers.

Mostly, though, only his shareholders paid attention, which was how
he liked it. Then Loews began accumulating shares in CBS Inc., the

troubled television broadcaster. By the summer of 1986, Larry Tisch's gnomelike presence created a stir wherever he went, public acknowledgment that he would soon be shaping the news, sports, and comedies beamed into millions of homes daily.

Now he was weighing a decision that would change Macy's character as well.

A̲t about 3:30 P.M. on Tuesday, January 21, Greg Milmoe, a white-haired, experienced deal attorney with Skadden, Arps, received a phone call from Laurence and Jim Tisch, a key adviser to his father who worked at Loews Corp. Milmoe had known Jim Tisch very casually through their children, both of whom played on the Rye Rangers hockey team.

When Milmoe picked up the phone, he heard Jim Tisch introduce himself, and say he was there with his father. A moment later, Milmoe heard, "Hello, hello, it's Larry Tisch. Call me Larry. You busy?"

"You know, the usual."

"Well, we'd like you to help us."

"Oh yeah, I'd love to. With what?"

"We want to buy Macy's. Got any conflicts?"

"I don't think so, but let me check."

There were no serious problems. Twenty minutes later, Milmoe called back and said, "Okay, what do you want to do?"

Jim Tisch said, "We have a meeting at Macy's at five P.M. Why don't we pick you up and fill you in on the ride down?"

On the ride to Macy's Herald Square, Larry Tisch explained that he had been a Macy's director for a long time, that the board was largely composed of representatives of the leading investors and management, and that Macy's hadn't paid its trade creditors but would pay them.

The Tisches also mentioned that there had been a brief negotiation with GE Capital, but those talks were over. Larry said he felt it would be terrible for Macy's to file for bankruptcy, and that he intended to prevent it if possible by buying the business. They had been working on a proposal that included a substantial cash offer, a plan that would pay off all creditors in cash with the exception of senior banks and the senior secured debt holders. The Tisches intended to deal with those groups directly.

All of this was jotted down on about a page and a half of notes.

There were two major chunks of senior bank debt. One involved the Swiss Bank piece of about $300 million. The Prudential stake, valued at $800 million, was the second. In light of Macy's desperate financial condition, the Tisches believed that the 12 percent annual interest rate on the Prudential debt was too high; 9 percent would be a more accurate reflection of Macy's condition.

Also at issue were the revenue kickers that Prudential had earlier tried to sell back to Macy's. Those, too, would have to be sharply reduced.

It was a fine plan, the Tisches continued. But negotiations with Prudential often involved months of work. It was time they didn't have. Prudential would either accept a lower interest rate, and eliminate the kickers, or the Tisches would walk away, and take their $1 billion with them.

"The company is absolutely on the line here," said Larry Tisch. "If we can save it, I've got to do it quickly and cleanly. And I will pay a lot for that, but I won't, under any circumstances, get drawn into a long drawn out negotiating fiasco. I'm telling you right now: I want to do this, do it creatively, effectively, and get it done. But if I can't do it, I'm out. By the way, I'm going to make one offer to the bondholders. It will be a take it or leave it thing; I have no interest in negotiating with committees and so forth."

Before he left his office, Milmoe had discussed the Tisches' interest with some of his colleagues, who in turn began to gear up for what they expected would be a terrifically intense week.

After they arrived at Macy's Herald Square, Larry Tisch began by saying, "This is a terrible situation, but I think I can be helpful. Here's Greg from Skadden, Arps, who has done this kind of thing before. What I want to know is whether you think I should go forward. I'm not going to do anything without the support from the board and stockholders, because I don't intend to be hanging in the wind. Do you want me to do this?"

The board members said yes, go forward, we're interested, let's get this moving.

At about 8 P.M. that night, Milmoe returned to his office and began drafting a proposal. By then his colleagues were identifying key issues. The gist of the plan, however, was simple. Larry Tisch had a lot of cash, or had access to a lot of cash, and he was prepared to make an offer conditional upon the cooperation of the interested parties.

A hallmark of the plan was that he would pay one hundred cents on the dollar to the trade upon confirmation. He would also pay the public debt in cash at prices significantly above market, which he also felt was fair. The more ticklish issue was whether the Tisches would pay anything to Macy's shareholders, including the company's employee investors. There was a sense there would be something for them as well. But everyone would suffer some pain.

As part of the Tisch plan, Macy's would file a prepackaged bankruptcy, emerging from Chapter 11 a month later. If the investors took it, great. Otherwise, adios.

The following morning, Milmoe and Larry Tisch went back to Macy's, and met with Prudential and the bank group. The meetings basically let everyone know that the Tisches had a plan, and they would keep everyone informed.

By Wednesday night there were a horrendous number of things to do. At least fifteen people inside Skadden, Arps, were now working on the project, including the preparation of a formal proposal letter that ran six or seven pages. It primarily addressed the Prudential, since the Tisches were asking the insurance company to accept market rate interest on their loan, and to forgive an equity kicker valued at $30 million to $50 million.

At one point earlier in the day, Milmoe had turned to a senior Macy's staff lawyer and said, "Can we have a copy of the Prudential agreement?" And he said sure, waving him toward a full bookcase containing the Prudential documents.

"I remember having a preliminary conversation with a lawyer who represented the Prudential," says Milmoe. "When we outlined the deal, he asked if we were asking anybody else to cut their returns. We said no. Then he asked about the banks, including Swiss Bank, saying why should Prudential have to suffer if the banks weren't going to suffer as much pain."

Milmoe replied, "To get the deal done."

The lawyer, skeptical, said, "Thank you very much."

On Thursday at 1 P.M., the Macy's board met formally to listen to the Tisches' presentation. Only Prudential sounded less than enthusiastic.

They had good reason. At the time of the Macy's buyout, they had cherrypicked Macy's best stores. Now they were confident that even if Macy's went bankrupt, they would be adequately protected. Prudential had already weathered several other retail bankruptcy filings, and understood how the process worked. Tisch's demand to retire the Prudential mortgage facility at par, for example, represented a major sacrifice, since Prudential valued it at $200 million above par.

Instead of rejecting Tisch's offer outright, however, Prudential executives said they would give the Tisches half of what they had asked for.

Prudential's point man was Frank MacDougal, a veteran real estate man who had successfully steered Prudential through the Allied bankruptcy. He was soft-spoken but firm, and he didn't like being pushed. So when Jim Tisch called him late Thursday evening and said, "This is it. Either you consent to a reduction in interest and the elimination of the equity kickers, or we're out," MacDougal didn't panic.

Instead, he said something Tisch would never forget. "We've seen this movie before," MacDougal replied. "We know how it ends."

At 10 A.M. the following morning, Friday, January 24, Jim Tisch called the Prudential for the last time and said, "Hey, we haven't heard from you. We need to know where you stand by eleven-thirty A.M. because there is a one P.M. board meeting scheduled. If you aren't with us, we aren't going forward."

MacDougal called back within an hour, and said, "We're sorry, but we can't do business with you. It's not fair to us. Our assessment is that we'll do better in bankruptcy."

Still, there would be one last frantic effort to reach an accord. Just before the board meeting began, Ed Finkelstein called MacDougal. Although they knew each other, Finkelstein said, he had purposely stayed out of the financial negotiations. But now he wanted to know if they couldn't work something out.

"All it's going to take is for the other side to give up some of the upside," MacDougal said.

Excited at the possibility of a last-minute breakthrough, Finkelstein patched Larry Tisch into their conversation.

But for Tisch, the subject was closed. "We've gone as far as we can," the financier said. "There's not enough juice left in this."

With that, the conversation ended. In the weeks ahead Prudential would be attacked for having pushed Macy's into bankruptcy by failing to agree to Tisch's offer. Frank MacDougal, however, felt otherwise. "Even if we'd agreed, there were another dozen or so classes that had to be won over," he said. "But we weren't inflexible. In most negotiations, the more you talk, the more both sides soften their positions. The forty-eight hours we had was too short."

By the time the 1 P.M. board meeting started, Larry Tisch wasn't yet back from a trip to Washington, D.C. Instead, he participated by phone, as did several other directors, including Henry Kissinger. Harvey Miller, the Weil, Gotshal & Manges lawyer, now took them through an extended course in bankruptcy, explaining their fiduciary responsibilities as directors, the implications of a filing for creditors, and how long it would take for the firm to prepare the necessary papers.

For Greg Milmoe, who had worked around the clock on one night, and nineteen hours on another, the disappointment was considerable. "In other circumstances, with another couple of weeks, I'm sure we could have gotten a deal," he said, a few years later. "By the time the talks were finished, I'm not even sure that we'd read all the necessary real estate documents. But I'm reticent to paint Pru with too black a brush."

Although the Tisches were frustrated, they were also impressed by how well-versed Mike Ullman was at every meeting. Until that point the Tisches had dealt mainly with Ed Finkelstein. But during the negotiations, Finkelstein had been primarily a stage setter, with Ullman providing the hard financial data. "You'd have to say that Ullman came off as looking very good," says Milmoe. "He was calm, unflappable, a producer. Everyone was impressed."

Months later, when the Tisches would have to decide whom to support, Finkelstein or Ullman, they would remember how well Ullman had done that week.

At 4:30 P.M. that Friday afternoon, the phone rang in the office of Darla Moore, a thirty-seven-year-old managing director at Chemical Bank, and the unofficial queen of debtor-in-possession financing. Under the bankruptcy code, companies in Chapter 11 were allowed to borrow new working capital, loans which were then considered more secure than any secured claim.

It was as close as possible to a risk-free business, and in the years that Moore, a stylish blonde from South Carolina, had been involved with bankruptcies, she had never lost a penny.

Moore had already met briefly with Diane Baker to discuss generally what would be involved in financing a bankruptcy. Afterward, Chemical Bank had done some follow-up work—just in case.

Now Baker was calling to tell her that the Tisch offer had fallen through, and that Macy's would likely need as much as $600 million in financing.

A few hours later, Moore set out for the offices of Weil, Gotshal & Manges, which had now become the hub for Macy's bankruptcy activities. She would spend almost all night there, and virtually the entire weekend trying to pull together the financing.

By now, nearly an entire floor at the law firm was dedicated solely to Macy's. Wood-paneled conference rooms were filled with associates and junior lawyers, working on the documents necessary to file petitions for Macy's and its nine affiliates. "They had real war rooms set up," says Moore. "The biggest conference room was designated for documents, and it had a table the size of a football field."

It was a wild scene, with popcorn bowls, coffee cups, and paper plates scattered everywhere. Before they were done, Harvey Miller, the bankruptcy attorney, described it as "a seven-pizza deal." There was so much tension that the weekend developed into an "eat-a-thon" with people gobbling down food simply to reduce the pressure. In one room, lawyers reviewed the Macy's credit card facility purchased by General Electric. Chemical Bank also had a room, as did the real estate team. At any one point, six to eight conference rooms were filled with people, with Harvey Miller overseeing the Weil, Gotshal lawyers, and Diane Baker handling the financial side for Macy's.

Within hours, Chemical Bank would need people in the field to evaluate Macy's assets in California, Texas, and much of the South. The giant retailer wanted $600 million in debtor-in-possession financing, and it needed to have those funds secured within seventy-two hours, when it filed for Chapter 11 bankruptcy protection on Monday afternoon.

That night, Moore helped write credit agreements and terms sheets. She was also frantically trying to reach Bankers Trust, which she hoped would join Chemical as a partner. All the while, fees, fee letters, commitment letters, and dozens of other issues remained to be negotiated. And it was slow going. Whenever a key player was pulled out of a meeting to go into another conference room, work in the first room would often slow to a halt until the person returned. And it could be any person, at any given time, a lawyer, Diane Baker, a number cruncher. "Whoever left that room, I guarantee you that you needed to keep moving," says Moore. The only bright spot was that Moore finally reached Bankers Trust on Saturday morning. Although the bank was interested, it would have to send over its own lawyers and bankers. All would be starting from scratch.

Darla Moore was accustomed to working helter-skelter. But for her new husband of less than ten weeks, Richard Rainwater, the Texas financier who had been a close adviser to the Bass family, it was bewildering. On Saturday night he brought in an armload of sandwiches from a nearby deli, hoping to lure his bride outside for a half-hour stroll. "He's a deal guy," says Moore. "This round-the-clock stuff of forty-eight hours or seventy-two hours and only sleeping two hours a day flabbergasted him."

On Sunday morning, everyone assembled back at Weil, Gotshal and cranked it up again. They would go all day, into the night. By the time Moore, and several other Chemical Bank executives left, it was 4 A.M. Instead of heading home, however, they trundled back to Bankers Trust, where they had to resolve one more term sheet. Macy's intended to file the following afternoon, but nothing would move if the documents weren't completed.

Finally, at 6 A.M., Chemical Bank and Bankers Trust reached an agreement on providing Macy's with the $600 million it wanted.

A few hours later, the Chemical Bank team met at yet another law firm for a final reading with Bankers Trust. To Moore's disappointment, Bankers Trust now insisted that it needed one more executive signature.

"We were all crazy with tension and nerves, because the deadline was twelve noon," Moore recalls. "Twelve-thirty comes. Nothing. One P.M. comes. Nothing. By now Harvey Miller, Diane Baker, everyone is at the board meeting, waiting for us to sign off. And they are calling every few minutes."

Moore, in turn, was calling Bankers Trust, but each time she reached voice mail. At 1 P.M., Harvey Miller called again for Moore, who by then was sweating. Tisch, Taubman, everyone, was waiting for them.

As soon as Moore picked up the phone, Miller said, "Where are you?"

"We're committed, we're waiting for Bankers Trust, and there's nothing else I can tell you," replied Moore.

"Well, I've got words for you, and they aren't 'Happy Birthday.' "

About five minutes later, executives from Bankers Trust called and said they were on board. By now, however, Darla Moore wasn't going to take their word. Instead, she wanted signatures on a signature page. So she faxed it over. It came back at 1:10 P.M.

Moore then called Miller. "It's done," she said.

"Okay," grunted Miller, and slammed down the phone.

Exactly twenty-seven minutes later, Macy's filed for Chapter 11 bankruptcy protection, listing nearly $4.95 billion in assets and $5.32 billion in liabilities. In its legal papers, Macy's referred to "the Christmas that never came" as a key factor. Indeed, during Macy's Christmas quarter, which ended that previous Saturday, the retailer had generated less than $135 million in cash flow, only half of what Macy's had produced during the same period a year earlier.

In its filing, Macy's indicated that it had an estimated $275 million in unpaid trade bills—vendors who had shipped goods but hadn't been paid. Among them were Sony Corp., the consumer electronics company; Estée Lauder Cos., the cosmetics house; and Liz Claiborne Inc., the sportswear maker.

In a statement, Ed Finkelstein said, "Our business is basically sound. It's our capital structure that needs rehabilitation."

Macy's senior executives later estimated the company's net worth at the time of the filing at $1.8 billion to $2 billion, or slightly more than half of the $3.5 billion that Finkelstein paid to buy the company in July 1986. Since then, of course, he had paid an additional $1.1 billion for Bullock's/Bullocks Wilshire and I. Magnin, and preferred shareholders had invested slightly more than $200 million in new equity.

It was a fiasco. Every cent invested by Macy's more than four hundred managers was wiped out. Many still owed sizable amounts related to their stock purchases, including Mike Ullman, who had borrowed $150,000 to buy his shares. The preferred shareholders, too, were wiped out. On Wall Street, Macy's $1.3 billion in junk bonds fell to new lows.

For Darla Moore, however, the filing had been a triumph.

The fact that Chemical and Bankers Trust had agreed to provide $600 million in financing didn't mean that the two banks would write checks for that amount. Instead, most of the financing would be syndicated. So on February 14, Valentine's Day, Moore invited possible lenders to a meeting at Chemical's auditorium at 55 Water Street. Every seat was taken, some by bankers caught up by the Chapter 11 filing, and many others who didn't have any exposure.

The meeting began promptly at 8:30 A.M. After Moore gave a brief introduction, a group of Macy's executives, including Ed Finkelstein, Mike Ullman, and Diane Baker, spoke about different aspects of the company.

Finally, Darla Moore returned to the stage. Until that moment, she had painted the bleakest possible picture of Macy's future, in large part to justify Chemical's fees. Now, in a complete reversal, Moore said there were some things in America that were sacrosanct: General Motors, the Statue of Liberty, and Macy's. It was a rousing performance, capped by Moore's boast that the Macy's debtor-in-possession financing was the best piece of paper Chemical had offered to date.

Minutes after the meeting ended, Harvey Miller, the bankruptcy attorney who had approved Chemical Bank's fee structure, approached Moore and dryly said, "Okay, I want my money back."

In the weeks that immediately followed the filing, widespread bitterness swept Macy's executive suite, with much of it directed toward Mike Ullman. The reason: as he was negotiating with the banks to save the company, Ullman was also quietly discussing the possibility of landing a new job.

Although Ullman had maintained an upbeat public tone, his private doubts about Macy's future stretched back to the summer of 1991. Sensing his concern, Finkelstein invited him to dinner in mid-July, the first such meal they'd shared together since Ullman had joined the company.

After they ordered, Finkelstein said he wanted to know what was on Ullman's mind. And Ullman told him.

"Ed, there are only a couple of things," Ullman began. "First, I don't have a contract, and you and Mark do. Second, I don't have the title of chief operating officer, even though I am doing the work. Finally, you keep talking about naming a successor, but nothing's been done."

Ullman then said he had five children to take care of, and that he was concerned about Macy's future. If something happened to Finkelstein, Ullman continued, it looked like Handler would be named to succeed him. And Ullman wasn't sure he could accept a job where he had to report to him.

After Ullman finished, Finkelstein said that he understood, and assured him that they would address every issue in the weeks ahead.

But nothing was ever offered to him. Then, in early fall, Ullman was approached by a search firm representing a major retailer. Although the company wasn't identified, the opening involved the post of vice chairman and chief operating officer. After listening, Ullman declined, explaining he was committed to Macy's. But by late December, he was feeling more tentative. He still didn't have an employment contract and Macy's future was now in serious question. And when he was approached by the same headhunter again, Ullman agreed to meet with the company—Dayton Hudson Corp., based in Minneapolis—to hear what they had to say.

As it turned out, both sides liked each other, and Dayton Hudson offered Ullman the job. Once again, however, he hesitated, explaining that he wanted to stay with Macy's until the immediate crisis was resolved one way or another. So while the desperate January events were unfolding, Ullman was also weighing whether to leave Macy's at the end of the month.

Ullman finally confided in Ira Millstein, who promptly advised him to tell Finkelstein. During the meeting that followed, Finkelstein listened as Ullman explained his situation. When he was done, Finkelstein snapped, "I think you ought to go."

Ullman said he agreed. But when he relayed the events to Millstein, the lawyer said, "No, Ed can't tell you that. It's a board decision." Millstein then pressed Ullman about what it would take for him to remain in place.

What he wanted, replied Ullman, was an employment contract that contained a clause that would compensate him for having passed up the Dayton Hudson job if Finkelstein left for any reason and Ullman wasn't named chairman.

Millstein took the issue to the board, and endorsed Ullman's request. The directors voted their approval, and Ullman rejected Dayton Hudson's offer.

Ed Finkelstein, however, was deeply upset over what he viewed as Ullman's treacherous disloyalty. And when Ullman said he wanted to announce his new contract internally, Finkelstein disagreed, saying that the timing wasn't right.

A few days later, on March 5, Macy's filed papers with the U.S. Bankruptcy Court stating that Ullman had been given a new contract. The rich new pact was made effective January 27, the day of Macy's filing. Ullman was to receive a base salary of $800,000 a year, with a guarantee of a 10 percent annual increase for the next three years. The agreement also specified that if Finkelstein "ceases for any reason" to be chief executive, Ullman would receive a new executive role within sixty days. Otherwise, Ullman would be entitled to an immediate $2.4 million payout.

It was solid endorsement at a time when some angry creditors were already suggesting that it was time for Finkelstein to leave. And since the contract also promoted Ullman to chief operating officer, Macy's now had a young successor in place.

That role had been held by Mark Handler, Macy's president. In hopes of appeasing him, Handler was named chief merchandising officer, a title that Finkelstein believed more accurately reflected his role inside the company.

Although Mike Ullman had now seemingly been anointed Macy's number two executive, Finkelstein quickly moved to end any speculation that he would soon be leaving. "I feel energetic and involved," he told reporters. "I have a responsibility to take this company out of Chapter Eleven."

He also insisted that his old friend and colleague Mark Handler was still the most likely candidate to succeed him.

The very next day, Finkelstein sent a letter to about one hundred senior executives, describing Mark Handler as "my valued partner and a leading member of Macy's senior management team for many years. His demonstrated merchandising expertise and capabilities have been invaluable to the company, and his being named chief merchandising officer appropriately reflects the role he has been playing for some time. If I were to become incapacitated, it would be my recommendation to the board that Mark be named chief executive."

"Mark and Ira both thought the letter was crazy," says Ullman. "But by then our hands were full running the Chapter Eleven. You have to work to stabilize the company, to get people on board again, to get the management team to recognize that the company isn't going to be liquidated. We didn't have time to worry about anything else."

One other Macy's executive was also rewarded with a new contract and a promotion within days of the bankruptcy filing. Mitchell Finkelstein, Ed's oldest son, was named chairman of sourcing and product development for all of Macy's, a significant step up from his prior post as president of Macy's Asia. As Macy's entered its bankruptcy period, it would have three Finkelsteins as chairmen: Dan Finkelstein, chairman of Macy's West, his brother Mitch, and their father, Ed, who continued as chairman of the corporation.

On April 20, 1992, Macy's board of directors quietly seized control of the company.

For nearly six years, the Macy's board had operated with nine Macy's executives as directors, and seven outside investors filling the remaining chairs.

But that Monday, six Macy's executives agreed to step down, including A. David Brown, senior vice president of personnel; Rose Marie Bravo, chairman of I. Magnin; Gertrude Michelson, senior vice president of external affairs; Theodore Ronick, chairman of marketing and corporate-owned brands; Arthur Reiner, chairman of Macy's Northeast; and Daniel Finkelstein, chairman of Macy's California.

Although unusual, the terms of the original leveraged buyout called for significant changes in the case of a bankruptcy filing. Only Finkelstein, Handler, and Ullman remained.

And behind the scenes, an even more dramatic and unexpected power play was beginning to unfold.

Although Ed Finkelstein had appointed his son Mitch chairman of sourcing and product development, the issue still had to be approved by the full board. In the weeks that followed, Mitch said he expected to live in Los Angeles, rather than move to New York, where the majority of Macy's sourcing and product development managers and designers worked. Although he insisted that Los Angeles would be a good geographical base for someone who would likely be spending so much time in Hong Kong, the board didn't like the idea.

More important, certain key members had lost faith in Mitch's skills. They had read stories that put some of the blame for Macy's poor performance on its private label goods, for which Mitch had significant responsibility. Nobody wanted to fire him, but a consensus gradually developed that he would perform better if he reported directly to Mark Handler—and had a less important title.

The retailer's outside directors knew that Ed Finkelstein deeply loved and believed in his son. Rather than confront the Macy's chief at the board meeting, several directors asked Ira Millstein, Macy's key outside attorney and Finkelstein's closest adviser, and Ken Heitner, a soft-spoken, good-humored Weil, Gotshal & Manges tax lawyer, to meet privately with Finkelstein in his office before the board meeting.

When they explained why they were there, Finkelstein became furious. After defending Mitch's performance as outstanding, he suggested a witch-hunt was under way to get his oldest son. The two lawyers patiently heard him out. Then they carefully suggested that Ed would have to compromise. They were his friends, they said, and they wanted the best for him. But the board was opposed to naming Mitch chairman, and Ed would have to give way. Mitch would receive a less prestigious title, they said, but he would still have a job and significant standing in the company.

Grudgingly, Finkelstein said he understood. Finally, he said he could live with the decision, and the two lawyers left.

Millstein and Heitner returned to the board room and said the matter was resolved. Mitch Finkelstein's name was never mentioned that morning.

Later that afternoon, however, Ed Finkelstein changed his mind. He wouldn't stand for it, he told Millstein. Mitch had earned the job, he'd already been given the promotion, and now, unfairly and improperly, it was being taken away.

"That's it," Finkelstein finally shouted. "I'll leave."

Millstein, stunned that Finkelstein was willing to end his career over such an issue, attempted to talk him out of it. Finkelstein, however, appeared adamant. Early the following morning, the two spoke again, and Finkelstein repeated his unhappiness with the board's decision.

As it happened, there was a Chase Manhattan board meeting that day. Finkelstein and Macy's director A. Alfred Taubman were both directors, so Millstein called Taubman, who had remained close to

Finkelstein throughout the entire ordeal, and asked him to intervene.

"We've got a problem here," said Millstein. "You're going to be with Ed all day. Talk some sense into him. Tell him to calm down."

Taubman's words, however, had little effect. Twenty-four hours later, Handler, Ullman, and Finkelstein boarded the Macy's jet for a flight to San Francisco. Handler and Ullman spent most of the trip in the front of the plane, working. Finkelstein never once mentioned his pending resignation. After they landed, Finkelstein said he would be spending the next few days with Dan.

On Thursday morning, Ira Millstein and Harvey Miller called Handler, then fifty-nine years old, and Ullman, forty-five years old, and said that in their opinion, Ed would soon resign, and that Handler and Ullman "needed to sit down and decide how you want to work together. The board has decided the two of you should run the company."

That evening, Ullman and Handler ate dinner together and then spent hours talking in Handler's room at the Clift Hotel, trying to decide what would be best for Macy's. By the time they finished, they'd agreed that if the board would approve, Handler would succeed Finkelstein as chairman, while Ullman would be named chief executive.

They then flew back to New York without Finkelstein, and met with Larry Tisch at Tisch's home in Westchester, where most of Macy's remaining directors had gathered. As the board listened, Ullman and Handler explained how they wanted to manage the company. Before the informal meeting broke up, Larry Tisch said that the board "had confidence that they would be able to run the business." It wouldn't be easy, Tisch added, but they would all have to move on.

Ullman wouldn't talk to Finkelstein again for two months.

By the start of the weekend, it was clear that events had become irreversible. On Saturday, Millstein again spoke to a number of Macy's directors, including Tisch, Taubman, and Michael Price, the portfolio manager of the Mutual Series mutual fund group, Millstein told them that Finkelstein continued to feel very strongly about Mitch, and that he wanted Mitch to have the title of chairman. Taubman said much the same, and added that Ed would resign over the issue.

But the sentiments of the board were clear: they had agreed to keep Mitch on the payroll in a key position, which meant that his life would go on pretty much unchanged. But he wouldn't be chairman. And if Ed couldn't accept that compromise, he could resign. Finally, Larry Tisch said, "Look, do whatever has to be done. If Ed has to leave, so be it."

Heitner now decided he had to begin talking to Finkelstein about his severance pay. Millstein, upset, didn't want to participate. Millstein had also been close to Marvin Traub, the former Bloomingdale's chairman, and he'd seen how Traub had ended his career with parties, celebrations, hoopla, and applause. Ed Finkelstein wouldn't be leaving on the same note, and it pained him.

At 8 P.M. Saturday evening, Heitner called Finkelstein in California and said that he had to face the reality of leaving. The Macy's board was going to set up a committee to discuss Finkelstein's severance package, Heitner said, but it would be better for them both to work on a strategy. Heitner then outlined a proposal that he thought would win board support, and which he hoped would be acceptable to Finkelstein.

Finally, on Monday morning, April 27, they met on the thirty-second floor of the General Motors building. Ed sat in Ira Millstein's office, while Harvey Miller, Ken Heitner, Larry Tisch, and Al Taubman sat in a separate room. Heitner then presented an outline, with Taubman and Tisch negotiating on behalf of the board. The two directors felt some provisions were too generous, but accepted others.

By 11 A.M., it was done. Ed Finkelstein would continue as a consultant, earning $3 million through December 1994, plus a handsome pension, and the right to share in any profits generated by the sale of his East Side carriage house, which he would have to leave by year-end. Macy's would also indemnify him against liabilities from future lawsuits.

Before the meeting ended, Finkelstein pulled Tisch and Taubman aside and voiced his doubts about Ullman's abilities to lead the company. Finkelstein also said they should tell Mark Handler that he would have to work harder if he wanted the respect of his staff. Finkelstein even suggested that they advise Handler to do less social drinking with his colleagues, since it was something they later gossiped about. Then Finkelstein made a prediction. Ullman, he said, would chew Handler up.

Ninety minutes later, the Macy's board held a conference call. Before the day's end, a press release announced Finkelstein's resignation and named Mark Handler and Mike Ullman as Macy's new co-chairmen.

Finkelstein, sixty-seven years old, didn't participate in any of that. His career was over.

Years later, one of Finkelstein's closest and most trusted advisers would offer a different explanation for Finkelstein's resignation. Whether Mitch lived in New York or Los Angeles was irrelevant, he says, as was the issue of Mitch's title.

Instead, says this former high-ranking Macy's executive, Ed Finkelstein was under such pressure that his family was concerned about his well-being. He also began to see that his continued presence at the company was an impediment. He was an easy target for unhappy creditors, while some on the board had also lost faith in him. Rather than hang on for a few more months, this executive says, Finkelstein quit because he believed he would eventually be forced out of the company. Furious at Ullman, whom he considered duplicitous, and exasperated by Mark Handler's work habits, Finkelstein was despondent and exhausted.

"Look at it this way," says this executive. "Mark Handler was a best friend sort of a guy. Ullman made fun of Handler, and looked like he was on track to take over the corporation. Given the people involved, Ed didn't see how he could get out of his situation. After the bankruptcy, it became obvious that he, too, would have to go. And it was better to get out alive, not dead."

Chapter 14

"I suggest you face up to your mistake."

In the weeks following his departure, Ed Finkelstein became increasingly bitter. Despite having earlier that year recommended that Mark Handler eventually succeed him, Finkelstein now lashed out at his colleague of nearly forty years for having accepted the Macy's chairmanship. It was disloyal, he told friends, overlooking the fact that Handler had invested heavily in the buyout and needed his large salary. Eventually the two men stopped speaking, as did their wives.

To some, Finkelstein was rapidly becoming a King Lear–like figure—angry, abandoned, bewildered. "He had a notebook that he carried with him, in which he'd written down everything that he had done well for Macy's," says Robert Miller, a former partner at Berlack Israels & Liberman, the firm that represented Macy's bondholders. "He was willing to talk all day about the things he had done. His take on the bankruptcy was that it was somebody else's fault; an act of God; a conspiracy; the recession. Somebody did it, somebody was responsible. But not him. He sounded like Richard Nixon in his last days at the White House."

And Macy's was moving ahead without him. On May 20, the company hosted a creditors meeting in which Harvey Miller, Diane Baker, and Mike Ullman answered dozens of questions, most of which involved whether the questioner would get paid or not.

Ullman made the introduction, and as he had done on many previous occasions, painted an optimistic future.

Since the date of the bankruptcy filing, Ullman said, Macy's had secured a $600 million debtor-in-possession financing that provided adequate working capital. Meetings were set up with key vendors and shipments resumed. Aging inventory was marked down; the Blackstone Group was engaged to provide investment advice; and rounds of meetings were held with various creditor groups, including the unsecured general creditors, which represented the trade, and the bondholders committee. Macy's had also decided to close five I. Magnin stores by June and shut the entire thirty-four-store Fantasies by Morgan Taylor lingerie specialty chain. Its current management had presented a final spring 1992 financial plan. In addition, Macy's was now filing monthly reports as required with the U.S. Trustee overseeing the bankruptcy.

There was other good news, too. The Sabre information system was finally installed in all Macy's stores, two years after the initial contract had been signed with Sabre's owner, Federated Department Stores. And perhaps most important, Macy's was creating a buyer/planner merchandising approach in which buyers would work directly with the market, while planners assumed responsibility for the allocation of goods at different stores.

This represented a radical change, Ullman said, one that he was confident would provide major gains in the future. He then noted that Macy's had decided to close eight of its department stores, including the former Bamberger's flagship store in Newark and the Macy's store in the Flatbush section of Brooklyn.

Finally he addressed Macy's future. The company had already filed a motion to extend its exclusivity period through November 6—the time frame in which it alone would be able to suggest a plan of reorganization necessary to emerge from Chapter 11 bankruptcy. Macy's, he said, would file a tentative business plan by September 15, so the court could ascertain that it would have a firm business plan two months later, a plan that would address the five-year period from 1993 to 1997.

The audience, which had listened patiently, now began to ask when they would be paid. Creditors owed relatively tiny amounts stood and complained the loudest, arguing that they had done work on the good faith that they would be paid.

Baker and Ullman said they would be. They simply didn't know when.

Macy's now began to dismantle the grand trappings of the Finkelstein era. On July 7, Macy's struck a deal with Starling Aviation, which agreed to pay $9.3 million for the retailer's eight-year-old Gulfstream III aircraft. The ten-passenger jet included a four-place, fixed-table conference area and six single seats that converted to full-size beds. Also on board were two coffee brewers, a toaster oven, four ice bins, flatware, linen, and china. The plane had been repainted in July 1991 with Macy's newest color scheme: white, with burgundy stripes.

Other far-reaching changes began to take place inside the stores as well. In their first few months as co-chairman, Handler and Ullman announced they were redirecting Macy's commitment to private label. Although the actual dollar spending didn't change, Macy's eliminated forty of the sixty in-house labels it was using.

Then, to add insult to Finkelstein's misery, attorney Robert Miller challenged his $3 million consulting agreement. Miller had already succeeded in eliminating a clause that would have enabled Finkelstein to share in any proceeds above the original cost of his East 77th Street carriage house.

Now he wanted the contract further reduced. Macy's had recently reported disappointing results in April and May. When the creditors realized that the company was in worse shape than expected, Finkelstein's lucrative pact was attacked as wasteful.

In July, says Miller, Finkelstein finally visited him at his law firm. "At one point he wouldn't talk to me because he thought I was the devil incarnate," says Miller. "But he came. And I said, 'Ed, you did some great things, but we don't want to reward you when your company is doing so badly.' "

One of Finkelstein's biggest problems, Miller believed, was that he'd surrounded himself with yes men during his career. He'd developed an emperor mentality. But when he failed, the real world intruded. "Do you know the movie *The Producers*?" continued Miller. "At the end, when they are singing 'Springtime for Hitler,' Zero Mostel says, 'I hired the wrong director, the wrong actor, the wrong story. Where did I go right?' It was like that for Ed. Ed did everything right. So today he believes that the mistakes and faults weren't his. It was the weather, it was the recession, but never me."

Desperate for allies, Finkelstein called Jerome Chazen, the head of Liz Claiborne, and a leading member of the trade creditors committee. Finkelstein was worried that Chazen was blocking his settlement;

Chazen told him it wasn't true. Only two days before Macy's filed for Chapter 11 bankruptcy protection, Finkelstein assured him it would never happen. Now Finkelstein was on the phone, saying that he just wanted to get on with his life. Chazen said he would do what he could.

Finkelstein, though, had little leverage. In August, he accepted a package that offered considerably less than the deal Weil, Gotshal & Manges had negotiated. The $3 million agreement was replaced with a new pact that paid him $1,747,500, or $750,000 a year from September 1, 1992, to December 31, 1994. If he was bitter, he wisely kept his feelings to himself.

When Ed Finkelstein resigned, there was immediate speculation about the future of his sons, Mitch and Dan.

Both decided to stay, despite the obvious pressure they would be under. Mitch, however, was never named chairman and had to be content with his role as president of Macy's Asia unit. And by November, he'd decided to resign. During an interview with *The Wall Street Journal* in Hong Kong, he conceded that Macy's private-label strategy may have been overemphasized.

Shortly afterward, he and his father revealed they would be joining forces to launch a new retail venture in China. His father would provide the merchandising expertise, while Mitch oversaw sourcing. (In October 1993, a three-thousand-square-foot sportswear boutique called The American Place opened on Beijing Road in Guangzhou. Inside was a sign that read: "No smoking, no food, and no bare feet." The store failed.)

Not long after Mitch resigned, his father wrote a nine-page, single-spaced letter to the three Macy's board members who negotiated his original consulting agreement: Laurence Tisch, A. Alfred Taubman, and Paul Van Orden. In it, he bared his rage and anguish over Macy's bankruptcy while warning his former colleagues never to trust Mike Ullman.

Instead of having provided the support that he needed, Finkelstein believed that Ullman and Handler failed to fullfill their responsibilities to the company, thus in large part causing Macy's collapse. Ullman in particular was at fault, Finkelstein suggested, because he had conspired to take his job. Finkelstein had once treated Ullman almost like a son. Now he warned that Macy's faced possible "liquidation" if the board allowed itself to be "flimflammed and hoodwinked" by Ullman's behavior.

It was an extraordinary attack, made all the more terrible by the fact that Finkelstein had once been so close to both. Mark Handler, after all, was the man he'd called "a hell of a partner" at the black tie party Finkelstein had hosted at the Metropolitan Museum to celebrate the Macy's leveraged buyout.

There was one other significant theme: Dan Finkelstein, he insisted, had done superb work in a difficult situation in California. Dan's efforts deserved to be rewarded, he added, despite criticism that his stores weren't performing as well as expected.

The tone was so strident and accusatory that Macy's board members decided not to show the letter to either Ullman or Handler, although both were informed about it. Two days later, however, Paul Van Orden wrote a curt reply. In it, he reminded Finkelstein that the former Macy's chairman had earlier given Ullman and Handler his blessings. Van Orden also said that he was dissatisfied with the progress of Macy's western stores, and in particular Dan Finkelstein. The brevity of his note indicated that further comment wouldn't be welcome.

When Mike Ullman was informed about Finkelstein's comments in April 1996, he said he was disappointed but not surprised by Finkelstein's charges. "We later met several times, and on one occasion, he told me that the first two years we worked together were the best two years of his life," says Ullman. Mark Handler's response was also wistful. "The letter was written in terrible anger. To say Ullman and I screwed up the company is a little unfair."

Dan Finkelstein remained at Macy's through the close of Christmas 1992. In a face-to-face meeting, Ullman told him frankly that he doubted Dan could successfully manage fifty-three stores. But Ullman also said he was willing to give him a chance, and left him in place.

That Christmas, Macy's West performed well below expectations. Same store sales in northern California fell 5 percent and declined half a percent in the southern half of the state. By comparison, same store sales at Macy's East increased 3.4 percent. To be sure, California's economy was deeply depressed, and most retailers had poor holiday seasons. But inside Macy's, there was a strong sense that a change had to be made, and on January 6, 1993, Dan Finkelstein resigned. Although he intended to run a major retailer, he said, he would be joining his family's venture in China for the near future.

Dan Finkelstein was later succeeded by Michael Steinberg, a sixty-five-year-old veteran merchant who had most recently been chairman of Foley's, the Houston-based department store company. Earlier in his career, Steinberg had headed Sanger Harris, where Mike Ullman had once served as executive vice president. Steinberg had been widely praised for his role in merging Sanger Harris into Foley's, and now Ullman was betting he could revive Macy's West. Steinberg would later be judged one of Macy's most successful merchants.

Late in 1992, one other event of note would take place. Allen Questrom, chairman of Federated Department Stores called Laurence Tisch and asked if he would be interested in merging Macy's with Federated.

Tisch said no, the timing wasn't right. The two men exchanged pleasantries and the matter was dropped. Questrom was a patient man. He would wait.

Chapter 15

"There comes a point where a rational person finally says yes to a number."

Macy's was beginning to show signs of revival, but very slowly. On March 16, 1993, the retailer reported that it had turned a small profit for the Christmas quarter ended January 27, the first such results since filing for Chapter 11 bankruptcy protection.

The company earned $9 million on $2 billion in revenues. Although sales decreased by 1 percent, Macy's had closed a number of unprofitable stores, and the fall-off had been expected. The department store retailer even slightly exceeded its cash flow target of $136 million.

Meanwhile, the partnership between Mike Ullman and Mark Handler was about to come to an end. The following month, one year after the two had agreed to serve as co-chairmen and co–chief executives, Handler announced he was retiring.

Although the two men had worked well together, it was always understood who was actually in charge. Ullman was fifteen years younger, with enormous energy and drive. In public meetings Ullman did most of the speaking, while Handler hovered in the shadows. Still, Handler had helped restore Macy's relationships in the garment industry and created a sense of stability inside the company.

Nevertheless, he was able to jump-start the merchandising side of the business. Perhaps it was his age, perhaps it was the many years he'd spent serving as Ed Finkelstein's number two, but Handler never became the partner Ullman needed.

By contrast, soon after Federated Department Stores filed for Chapter 11 bankruptcy protection, its board hired Allen Questrom, one of the strongest merchants in the country. Federated had to increase its revenues to survive the debilitating Chapter 11 bankruptcy process, which meant offering customers values they couldn't find elsewhere. Only a merchant could lift a company out of bankruptcy; expense cutting alone wouldn't be enough.

When he was asked why the board hadn't been more aggressive in finding a new senior merchant to succeed Ed Finkelstein, Laurence Tisch said there wasn't enough time. "You always come up with this question: who's around?" said Tisch. "When a company is in bankruptcy, you can't afford to spend three to six months on a search process. There were no obvious candidates inside Macy's for the job." Once again, Macy's was without a top merchant a year after filing for bankruptcy, squandering valuable time in which it should have been establishing a new merchandising direction.

And others were noticing, most important the Prudential Insurance Company of America, one of Macy's largest and most secured creditors. It was also unhappy, not only with the pace of Macy's efforts to emerge from bankruptcy, but with the flow of information from Herald Square. Prudential knew it would eventually be repaid—it just wasn't sure how long it would have to wait.

Finally, Prudential did something about it, very quietly. On May 11, at the St. Regis Hotel's ultrachic Lespinasse restaurant, Federated's top three executives—Chairman Allen Questrom, President James Zimmerman, and Chief Financial Officer Ronald Tysoe—met with a small group of Prudential executives that included Frank MacDougal, chairman of the Prudential Realty Group, and Barbara Chu, an analyst who oversaw the Macy's account.

The ties between the two companies extended back to the days when Federated and its sister division, Allied Stores, had filed for Chapter 11 bankruptcy protection. At the time, Prudential held about $350 million in loans secured by Allied real estate, and during the bankruptcy hearing that followed, requested that it receive post-petition interest payments. The move was almost unprecedented, but Federated's Ron Tysoe decided not to oppose it. Prudential's lawyers had reason to be very pleased. Now that generosity was about to be repaid.

Soon after they ordered dinner, MacDougal turned to Questrom, who was sitting next to him, and casually asked if he had considered merging with Macy's. It looked like it would be a perfect fit, he said. They would be able to merge back-office operations, greater purchasing power would result, and there were many stores that didn't overlap with one another. Back in 1988, Macy's wanted to buy Federated; perhaps Questrom should considering turning the tables.

MacDougal thought he had an idea on how they could do it: by acquiring Prudential's stake in Macy's. "They had a surprised look on their face, and the dinner became very cordial," says MacDougal. "But it was only an idea. I didn't think it was going to go anywhere." For Questrom, who had been thinking about acquiring Macy's since 1992, the suggestion was as welcome as it was unexpected.

Several weeks later, Macy's presented a revised five-year business plan in U.S. Bankruptcy Court. The retailer said it had made "significant progress" toward emerging from Chapter 11 by "implementing 21 critical buying, planning, selling and managing initiatives," decisions that would eventually restore the company to profitability.

Terms of the new plan called for Macy's to generate $817 million in cash flow by 1998, slightly more than earlier projections, on revenues of $8.5 billion. Still, when asked when Macy's would emerge from bankruptcy, Ullman said Macy's "must first build a credible program."

In July, Mike Ullman decided that he'd found his man: Roger Farah, the forty-year-old chairman and chief executive of Federated Merchandising Services, a division of Federated Department Stores.

Although Farah had a noncompete clause in his contract, Ullman wasn't concerned. As he understood it, Roger Farah felt that Allen Questrom had promised to name him heir apparent. However, when the subject had come up in a recent conversation, the Federated chief insisted that he didn't remember making such a promise. Feeling angry and betrayed, Farah expressed interest in the Macy's job as soon as it was mentioned to him by Korn/Ferry International, the executive recruiting firm. During that interview, Farah said that he'd never signed his new contract and would be free to go elsewhere after it expired in eleven months.

Korn/Ferry was so impressed with Farah that they recommended Ullman should hire him immediately as president, chief operating officer, and chief merchant—even if Macy's then had to wait until June 30, 1994, when Farah's contract expired. "They said we were better off getting out of bankruptcy with me at the helm than selecting the wrong partner," recalls Ullman. "I thought they were right."

But Federated had no intentions of letting Farah go. In prior months he had participated in high-level Federated discussions involving the possibility of taking over Macy's. Federated had already made overtures about acquiring Macy's, which Ullman swiftly rejected.

Allen Questrom was furious. He didn't believe that he'd promised Farah the top job at Federated, only that Farah would be a leading candidate in three to six years if he was successful in the post at Federated Merchandising Services. Further, Farah knew that Questrom wanted to buy Macy's, and he had also been told that if the merger occurred, it would delay the process of appointing Questrom's successor.

Federated quickly struck back. Only days after Macy's completed its negotiations with Farah, Federated filed suit, seeking to permanently prevent him from violating his employment contract. Forty-eight hours later, the retailer's attorneys asked for, and received, a temporary restraining order from a Common Pleas Court judge in Cincinnati. David Heiman, coordinator of the business practices group at Jones, Day, Reavis & Pogue, Federated's top outside law firm, says that Farah was served as he was getting onto a ferry to Nantucket. "I don't think he ever forgave us," says Heiman.

Macy's responded that it didn't expect Farah to start work before July 1, 1994, one day after his Federated contract expired.

The dispute wouldn't be resolved until late October, when Federated finally agreed that Farah could join Macy's the following July. Until then, however, he would have to sit on the sidelines—and remain on the Federated payroll.

Although Macy's executives said they were satisfied with the resolution, it was a serious blow, since Macy's would now be without a top merchant for another nine months.

In early fall, based on its apparent progress, Macy's exclusivity period was extended to March 15, 1994, by Bankruptcy Judge Burton R. Lifland, who was overseeing the case.

For Mike Ullman, it was the best possible news. "This extension is appropriate due to the size and complexity of the case, and the practical desire by our creditor groups to give Macy's adequate time to fully implement the initiatives in our revised five-year business plan," he commented.

In other words, more breathing space.

And he would need every minute of it. Although he didn't know it, the clock was ticking.

Late on New Year's Eve, Prudential Insurance Company did something nobody expected: it sold half of its Macy's claim to Federated Department Stores for $449.3 million. Terms called for a cash payment of only $109.3 million and the remainder due in three years. Federated also received an option to acquire Prudential's remaining Macy's stake at a later date.

At the time, Prudential's claim totaled more than $1 billion.

Prudential sold its Macy's interest for several reasons, including the fact that it was under serious pressure to reduce the size of its delinquent loan portfolio. By selling its Macy's debt to Federated, it immediately resolved one of its biggest problems.

Although the idea originated with Prudential's Frank MacDougal, it had been Federated's Ron Tysoe who embraced it. Once a key adviser to Robert Campeau, Tysoe specialized in real estate values. He was also willing to take big risks. "Here was Federated, barely eighteen months out of bankruptcy, and they were talking about spending $1 billion," says David Heiman, the Federated attorney. "In the beginning, Ron couldn't decide how big a stake to buy. Then we narrowed it to what we needed. He understood Prudential, he knew the store locations that they controlled, and he was absolutely confident that he could make this work."

Mike Ullman rarely had time for sports. But on that Sunday afternoon, January 2, he was sitting in front of his television set, working on his church's checkbook and preparing to watch the New York Giants take on the Dallas Cowboys when the phone rang. On the other end was Dennis Broderick, Federated's general counsel. What he wanted to know was whether Ullman would accept a call from Allen Questrom and James Zimmerman.

"I've accepted your call without knowing who you are," said Ullman. "So sure. I'll talk to them."

Half an hour later, the two Federated executives called back and explained that they had acquired half of Prudential's stake in the company. They knew it was coming as a surprise, so they didn't expect Ullman to fully understand the significance of what they'd done. However, they wanted to meet the following morning at Macy's Herald Square and discuss the possibilities of merging. They would have a significant role for him, and it didn't have to be contentious. What they wanted to avoid, they added, was a hostile takeover.

Ullman, taken by surprise, agreed to the meeting. He then called Harvey Miller at Weil, Gotshal & Manges, as well as several other senior Macy's executives.

The following morning, Questrom and Zimmerman met with Ullman at Macy's Herald Square and explained why they felt a merger would be in the best interests of the two companies.

"I told them that we were happy to listen, but that we had our own plans," recalls Ullman. "They said they expected I would say that." The meeting lasted barely half an hour.

Nobody discussed price. When Macy's filed for Chapter 11 bankruptcy, its own board valued the business at no more than $2 billion. Since then, however, Ullman had done a solid job of cutting costs, closing stores, and improving cash flow. Although Macy's still wasn't achieving the sales gains analysts believed it needed, the company was significantly stronger than in January 1992, so much so that its directors now believed it was worth at least $3.2 billion.

That Sunday afternoon, Federated put out a press release disclosing its ownership of the Prudential stake and announcing that it intended to work toward "a combination of Federated and Macy's into a single nationwide multi-billion dollar department store operation."

It would be the biggest department store company in the world, with 340 stores and combined annual sales of $14 billion. The merger would also solidify Federated's control of Florida, while giving it a major presence in California, where it didn't have any stores.

For Macy's, however, the benefits were less clear, and Ullman quickly distanced himself from the merger. "It's premature as to whether that is in the best interest of the company," he said. "My concern is for rebuilding Macy's."

But if Ullman was cool to Federated's overtures, Macy's bond-holders and other creditors were overjoyed. Within a few days, the Macy's junk debt rose significantly, based on the expectation that Federated would buy it. Federated's own stock climbed several dollars a share. Early estimates suggested Federated would be able to buy its longtime rival for $3 billion to $3.5 billion.

Federated's move also turned a spotlight on Daniel Harmetz, a money manager with Fidelity Investments' Capital & Income Fund. The former bankruptcy attorney had originally thought that the Macy's bonds were a bargain and snapped up nearly $500 million worth of bank debt. He was now Macy's second-largest creditor—behind Federated Stores Inc. He was also growing impatient.

Instead of using its momentum to lead a creditors' revolt, however, Federated surprised many by agreeing not to challenge Macy's in court. Rather, it suggested it would be willing to wait until September 15 to file its own plan of reorganization. Although senior Federated executives didn't say so publicly, they didn't want to risk alienating Mike Ullman to the point where he began searching for other bidders. Besides, Macy's still had the exclusive right to file its own plan to emerge.

For Federated, there was virtually no risk. Not only was the Prudential debt well-secured by Macy's real estate, but it would likely be awarded substantial post-petition interest as part of Macy's emergence from Chapter 11.

Allen Questrom was also convinced that a merger would create at least $125 million in savings, which meant that whatever Macy's could offer creditors as it emerged from bankruptcy, Federated would be able to pay more. And the fact that Fidelity owned such a large block of debt would only work to Federated's advantage, since it would only be interested in the highest possible price.

But Questrom believed that more than cost efficiencies were involved. The entire retailing landscape had changed in recent years. During its own stay in bankruptcy, Federated had all but eliminated its private label programs because overseas manufacturers demanded payment in advance, while domestic suppliers offered a thirty-day payment window. In Macy's, Questrom saw an opportunity to gain control of a large private label program without the necessary trial and error period.

And the entire marketplace was changing in terms of manufacturing. New York designers were handing much of their production to overseas contractors and opening their own retail shops. Other manufacturers were taking the same product they were selling to department stores, attaching different labels, and putting it in outlet stores at reduced prices. Going forward, Questrom believed, the ability to design, source, and market goods under one roof would be much more critical than it had been in the 1980s.

What's more, the customers were shopping differently. Federated's competition was no longer limited to other department store chains, such as Dillard's or May, but now included the big discounters, which had reduced their operating costs and were able to provide shoppers with lower prices. Most department store retailers didn't want to surrender their high profit margins because they had high expenses. But in Questrom's view, that didn't address the needs of the customers, only the needs of the stores. "On the outside world, we were losing shoppers, which meant we had to find ways of getting our costs down," he says. "We had to get bigger and more efficient. And it wouldn't be without pain."

Mike Ullman was now in a bind. He had to continue to improve Macy's operating performance, and at the same time win the support of creditor groups that now sensed an end to their long wait to be paid. At the same time, he was being pressured by Federated, which wanted him to accept a shorter exclusivity period.

It all came to a head on February 22, when Macy's and Federated met in bankruptcy court. A compromise had been quietly worked out that would give Macy's until August 1 to file its own plan of reorganization, a somewhat shorter period than Macy's had wanted. As Judge Lifland listened, Harvey Miller talked for nearly an hour about the progress Macy's had made in recent months. And when Miller was done, Judge Lifland stunned both sides.

Because Federated and Macy's appeared to be essentially in agreement on how to proceed, and because there now appeared the very real possibility of a plan or reorganization emerging, he wanted to ensure that it didn't unravel. As a result, he was appointing a mediator— Cyrus Vance, the former secretary of state.

All sounds ceased instantly.

As reporters rushed to the phones, small groups of lawyers and their creditors gathered together to decipher what it meant, including Harvey Miller, who offhandedly said, "I hope he does better here than he did in Bosnia," referring to Vance's latest diplomatic efforts.

His comment appeared in *The Wall Street Journal* the following day, which didn't help his face-to-face meeting with Vance.

Moments after the ruling, Federated's attorney David Heiman turned to Ron Tysoe and said, "Ron, this is great. It takes all the power away from Weil, Gotshal. We're going to mediation. The highest bid takes the bread. The exclusivity period won't mean anything."

What it meant, thought Heiman, was that Macy's was now finished. Federated had cash, and it had a $1 billion claim that it could forgive by converting it to stock.

Vance's appointment would have major consequences. Cast in a seemingly neutral role, he bridged the gap between rival creditor groups, each of which wanted the highest return. Vance would meet with each, gauge their demands, and then shuffle between separate camps attempting to find common ground. And inevitably, the only way to do that was to coax a higher price from Federated.

"You have to give him credit for bridging the gaps between the various creditors," says Tom Shull, a former Macy's executive vice president. "Eventually we were able to achieve a settlement that satisfied almost everyone, including the unsecured bondholders."

Shull had joined Macy's in June 1992 as one of Mike Ullman's most important confidants. A West Point graduate who later taught a class in leadership at the military academy, Shull met Ullman in 1981, when both were serving as White House Fellows. A former consultant at McKinsey & Co., where he specialized in cost-cutting and business strategies, Shull was initially hired to effect changes that Ullman expected Macy's Old Guard would resist. Before he was done, Shull would oversee the dismissal of 20,000 employees in a two-year period.

"We always thought they were going to win," says Diane Baker. "They had access to the banks, and they had access to the capital markets. We were a private company, one that had just lost creditors $5 billion. But because a number of board members had conflicting interests, they were able to keep the game going. And in the end, this was the only way that Macy's could create higher bids."

During the next few months, the battle for Macy's swung from side to side, Fidelity first endorsing a Macy's plan, and then seeming to favor Federated. At issue was how much Macy's was really worth. If the price was too low, Macy's bondholders would get almost nothing. But if the price was too high, Macy's secured creditors feared that the stock they received in exchange for their claims would have less value, because it would be inflated.

What made the situation even more difficult was the fact that Macy's board was now divided. Tisch, the company's most influential director, also controlled $52 million worth of Macy's bonds, which meant that he wanted the highest possible valuation placed on the company—about $5 billion. Ullman, however, initially began negotiating from a plan that valued Macy's at only $3.5 billion.

"Larry and some of the other board members thought we should value the company at the high end, and let the secured creditors suck wind until they got scared enough to accept less," says Ullman. "But the danger was that the secured creditors could do a deal without the unsecured, and negotiate directly with Federated. That was the conflict. Larry felt we were naive to think that the secured creditors would respond to negotiation without scaring them. But I didn't know how to scare them, since they had two thirds of the claims and all of the collateral. The argument wasn't about personality but strategy: who do you get the most agitated in order to get the right result?"

That tension helped drive up Macy's value a little higher each month. At the same time, the department store company continued to show small but steady gains in cash. An estimated twenty thousand employees had now been eliminated, numerous stores had been closed, and the economy was beginning to brighten.

Macy's battle to remain independent lasted all spring. But by late June, it was clear that Federated had greater financial resources, and wouldn't back off. "There comes a point where a rational person finally says yes to a number," says Ullman. "There was a market for Federated stock, they had an option to buy the second half of Prudential's claim, and they had all these synergies working which enabled them to look at a $4.1 billion bid and treat it as though it was a $3.6 billion offer. And we didn't have that option."

On July 1, Allen Questrom and Federated's top management finally met with the Macy's board for the first time and explained his proposed merger in person. The hour-long presentation included an estimate that the combined companies would save at least $100 million in expenses. Although the board didn't commit itself, Questrom left believing that he had made a compelling argument.

"They wanted to remain independent," says Questrom. "I told them I understood that. But I also pointed out that some of them were on the board in 1988 and had then supported merging with Federated. How could they not support it now? The normal reaction is to want to go your own way; we felt like that in 1988. There is a natural tendency to protect the history, and the culture, of a company. You can present facts, but that doesn't mean people necessarily buy into them. But over time, thoughtful people eventually agree."

On the same day, for the first time, Roger Farah reported to work at Macy's as the retailer's new president and chief merchant.

Thirteen days later, after Questrom raised Federated's bid to $4.1 billion, the Macy's board capitulated. The new combined company would be the sixth largest retailer in the country, by *Women's Wear Daily*'s count, ranking behind Wal-Mart, Kmart, Sears, Roebuck & Co., JCPenney Co., and Dayton Hudson Corp.

Macy's creditors, owed $6 billion, would receive two thirds of that amount, depending on their collateral.

The retailer's four-hundred-plus employee investors, however, didn't receive a cent. Their common shares were deemed worthless. In truth, that stock had always been backed only by Ed Finkelstein's promise of a wondrous future. For most, that alone had been enough to spark dreams of becoming millionaires.

As soon as Federated was crowned the winner, consumer groups began griping that shoppers would enjoy fewer sales while paying higher prices. In the New York metropolitan area, for example, Federated/Macy's would operate Stern's, Macy's, Abraham & Straus, and Bloomingdale's; thirty-nine department stores in all. New York State Attorney General Oliver Koppell raised antitrust issues. But when Federated agreed that it would "attempt" to sell six stores, the clamor quieted, and finally disappeared altogether.

In the days that followed, Mike Ullman was offered an opportunity to share the office of the presidency at Federated. He said he would mull it over. But on September 19, he announced that he was leaving the company. His severance pay was slightly more than $14 million, including an $8.4 million payment related to the increase in Macy's value, as specified in his contract. Having trimmed Macy's payroll, the size of his check created anger and bitterness among many Macy's veterans. Macy's cash flow was at or above plan for almost eighteen months. He had taken a business that was worth only $2 billion in January 1992 and doubled its value two and a half years later. "After June 1992, we added $100 million a month in increased value," he says. "If we hadn't fixed the company, Macy's wouldn't have sold for $4.1 billion."

Two days later, Roger Farah also left. Having put in three months of service, he took home an estimated $14 million because his contract, like Ullman's, provided him with participation in the event Macy's was sold.

For Federated, Macy's would become a cornerstone of Allen Questrom's aggressive strategy to dominate the department store industry. Federated's Abraham & Straus/Jordan Marsh division was folded into the Macy's East division, and analysts expected that additional Federated chains would be merged. At some point, Federated executives said, they might even convert all of their stores to three formats: Bloomingdale's for upscale brands, Macy's for moderate-priced goods, and Stern's for low-priced merchandise.

For Ed Finkelstein, the leveraged buyout had been a personal calamity. He'd lost the respect and loyalty of many former colleagues, his own sizable personal investment had been mostly wiped out, and he'd been forced to leave the carriage house on East 77th Street that he enjoyed so much.

His family also suffered. His two sons, Dan and Mitch, both resigned, leaving careers of long standing. They, too, had invested in the buyout and had suffered financial losses as well. All of his life, Ed Finkelstein had provided for his children; that he was no longer able to do so at Macy's was a bitter pill.

For Macy's, the Federated takeover was both a defeat and an opportunity. Although it had lost its independence, that freedom had meant little in the two years prior to bankruptcy, when the company performed terribly in all aspects. That it was now setting out on a new course with a seasoned team of merchants at the top, including some former Macy's executives who had since returned, suggested that there might be unexpected possibilities.

But for Macy's old guard, veterans of twenty, thirty, forty years standing, the buyout, and all that followed, destroyed a culture and a style of doing business that was irreplaceable. "The company was lost, lives were ruined," says Ken Straus, the last member of his family to work at Macy's. "People had worked so hard to build something that mattered. And then it was gone."

Epilogue

By the summer of 1996, R. H. Macy & Co. had been neatly divided into two Federated divisions, Macy's East and Macy's West.

At Macy's Herald Square, Federated chairman Allen Questrom sat in the spacious office that had once belonged to Ed Finkelstein. (Although Federated is based in Cincinnati, Questrom preferred to work in New York.) The Macy's East senior staff, including Chairman Harold Kahn, worked two floors below.

Questrom, passionate and relentless, was now one of the department store industry's greatest empire builders. In October 1995, he paid $1.6 billion in stock and the assumption of debt to buy the eighty-two department stores owned by Los Angeles–based Broadway Stores Inc., doing business as The Broadway, Weinstocks, and The Emporium. It was a rich price for a business near financial collapse, but the purchase assured that Federated would dominate California well past the dawn of the twenty-first century.

A deeply troubled company that filed for Chapter 11 bankruptcy in January 1990 because it couldn't pay its debts, Federated was now one of the world's largest retailers, with more than $15 billion in annual revenues from more than 400 department stores. Questrom had also surprised many by keeping Macy's two specialty chains, Aeropostale and Charter Club, which numbered about 150 stores, in part because Macy's sold lots of private label clothes under those brands.

Although many of Macy's former senior managers were gone—

Diane Baker, the former chief financial officer and the last of Ullman's management group, departed in January 1995—Federated was making shrewd use of some of Macy's best assets. Acknowledging Macy's superiority in private label sourcing, Federated kept much of the Macy's team. Ed Finkelstein's vision of a successful stable of brands was being realized, albeit under somebody else's direction. Federated was also absorbing parts of Macy's strategy that called for a group of planners to decide which goods should be stocked in specific stores, a savvy strategy designed to tailor items to local tastes.

But there were also striking changes. Macy's no longer had a corporate staff, its own back-office operation, or its own feisty identity. Instead, a new culture was being created, one that emphasized cost-cutting, controls, and uniformity. For shoppers, it meant that Macy's Herald Square would no longer be as free-spirited. When Ed Finkelstein returned to New York in the mid-1970s and revitalized Macy's ailing flagship, he appealed to his customer's aspirations. If Macy's sometimes stretched beyond their means, Herald Square was always entertaining.

By mid-1996, much of the glitter had disappeared, as evidenced by a casual walk-through in June. Under Federated, Macy's has emphasized clothes that can be found in dozens of chains across the country. Departments that were once exclusive to Macy's had been closed or reduced in size. Although the main floor at Herald Square remained as it had been under Finkelstein and Ullman—including the huge but faded bouquets of silk flowers that lined the aisle on the Broadway side of the building—much of what Finkelstein created had been stripped away.

Under Finkelstein, The Cellar's tiled promenade was flanked with individual boutiques, many with their own in-store windows. Now, instead of an open space, the main walkway was crammed with islands of summer goods, such as picnic baskets and scented candles. Some of the windows had been removed, creating additional selling space for pots, pans and the like. Boxes were stacked so high that it was difficult to see over them. It was less comfortable to walk here, and the boundary lines between departments were blurred.

The Marketplace had fallen on even harder times. Finkelstein created a premier food hall famed for its fine selection of sturgeon, salmon, and caviar. No longer. The shelves were dusty, and bakery signs that once would have been made of brass were instead cut from paper. The floor needed replacing, while a white metal garbage pail at the end of one aisle was filthy. Although shoppers were still invited to spend more than $300 for 14 ounces of Beluga, the modest caviar department was unmanned.

The heralded P. J. Clarke's restaurant is gone, replaced by Ottomanelli's Cellar Grill at Macy's.

It was better upstairs, on the second floor, where Macy's sells sports clothes designed by Tommy Hilfiger, Nautica, and Ralph Lauren, among others. There the displays were crisp, exciting, and spotless. Every polo shirt in the Tommy Hilfiger department was sharply folded, the array of colors dazzling. It was a stark contrast to Macy's own men's sportswear offerings, where clothes spilled off the tables onto the floor. Key suppliers, willing to share the costs, were orchestrating how their goods were sold, including the design, maintenance and staffing of their departments. It was a practice started by Macy's old regime. Still, the gap between their efforts and Macy's own merchandising offerings had widened. A nearby women's moderate-priced sportswear department, for example, had filthy carpeting and poor lighting.

There were other changes, too. The women's designer department on the third floor was gone, including the top fashions of Giorgio Armani, Calvin Klein, and Claude Montana. The bookstore on the eighth floor had been closed. And on nine, the furniture department no longer sells many of its most exclusive names, including Stanley and Drexel Heritage. In place of tasteful living room tableaus, there are endless rows of couches, chairs, and tables. Says one salesman: "We only buy furniture from the manufacturers that Federated does business with. What they have in Ohio, we have here."

The ninth-floor Corner Shop has also been dramatically scaled back. Once filled with European antiques and one-of-a-kind decorative items that Macy's own buyers scoured Milan, Paris, and London to purchase, the boutique had been a destination for decorators and their wealthy customers, giving Macy's Herald Square a cachet it otherwise wouldn't have enjoyed.

The tourists, of course, still pour into the store, as do native New Yorkers, especially when there is a major sale. And Federated executives promise to restore Macy's Herald Square to its glory days.

They will spend $60 million over three years to renovate a New York icon that hasn't been painted, fixed, or cared for in a decade. An estimated $500,000 will brighten the bathrooms. The first-floor cosmetics department will be expanded. A line of top-quality luxury linens will be added to the sixth floor. The men's designer business will be expanded. The grungy Marketplace will be closed and replaced by a New York restaurateur and gourmet food shop that will lease the space. And The Cellar, which celebrated its twentieth anniversary in 1996, will receive a major overhaul. Carpets will be cleaned, broken tiles replaced.

The tony women's designer business will never return; by all accounts, it was a big money loser. Instead, Macy's is emphasizing affordable names like Et Vous, Leon Max, Laundry, and Parallel. And the customers have apparently embraced the new strategy: sales at the Herald Square store have grown 4 to 5 percent a year since Federated took over the business. For the fiscal year ending January 21, 1997, the giant emporium is expected to top $500 million in revenues.

Whether the shoppers will continue to flock to a midpriced store that resembles every other one is less clear. Federated is betting that the Macy's customers who once bought their Giorgio Armani suits at Herald Square will now shop at Bloomingdale's, which is being positioned as a national upscale chain. A savvy move? Maybe. High-priced luxury retailers, including Tiffany & Company, Saks Fifth Avenue, Gucci, and Neiman Marcus are again thriving, as customers place greater value on character and personal attention. And Bloomingdale's, where the service has improved, may be able to do a better job than Macy's at providing a personal touch.

And there is little doubt that the department store industry had to consolidate; with Wal-Mart's sales approaching the $100 billion mark, and mass merchants like Sears doing an increasingly better job of selling men's and women's casual clothing, department stores will be under even greater pressure to operate more efficiently. Alan Millstein, publisher of the *Fashion Network Report*, says that within a few years there will only be three major department store companies: Federated, May Department Stores, and Dillard Department Stores.

Most cities, he says, will be served by a single department store company, which means less competition and higher prices. "When Allen Questrom gave up the Bullock's name in southern California, it said to me that the game is making Macy's a national name," says Millstein. "They take out layers of expense by wiping out buyers, and then expand their use of private label. It also enables them to increase their buying clout with outside manufacturers. And the Justice Department couldn't care less."

Meanwhile, many of Macy's former employees who invested in Finkelstein's leveraged buyout have found new jobs. When they reflect on their careers at Macy's, they say, they tend to remember only the many good years. They now regret that the buyout failed, but few question having bought stock in the company they loved.

Friends of Ed Finkelstein say he is markedly less bitter than in the months following Macy's Chapter 11 bankruptcy filing. "He's started to recover," says one former protégé. "Ed hasn't mentioned Mike Ullman once in the last nine months." Still, Finkelstein no longer counts as friends the select group of merchants that he nurtured for decades. Those close to him say he believes many stopped working hard when they cashed in their stock options following the leveraged buyout. "One reason he left was that he didn't feel he could replace his top merchants and start all over again," says one confidant. "It also hurt him that after he left, his cronies turned on his children, Mitch and Dan."

Others exited with heads high. Ullman pocketed more than $14 million and today has another top job in retailing. Diane Baker earned more than $3 million, and is chief financial officer at *The New York Times*. Laurence Tisch, who fought bitterly with Ullman over the value of the company when it was under attack from Federated, created at least an additional $500 million for Macy's creditors—including himself.

The biggest winner, though, was Allen Questrom. Having resigned from Federated rather than work for Robert Campeau, he now oversees the biggest department store company ever assembled in this country. "Smart? Is he ever," says Alan Millstein. "But he's been loading on lots of debt, and it may come back to haunt him."

Macy's, by surviving, has also won. Almost all of the great regional department store names that made up the Federated group will disappear; many have already vanished. Yet consumers from coast to coast still shop at stores carrying the Macy's banner, while its Thanksgiving Day parade still delights millions. And Macy's Herald Square, open for business seven days a week, is still the biggest store in the world.

Where are they now?

Diane Baker, Macy's former chief financial officer, resigned in January 1995 and joined The New York Times Co. nine months later as its chief financial officer. "Federated paid a full price, but they got a world-class brand name. Bloomingdale's is New York; Macy's is America."

Barbara Bass, the former chief executive of I. Magnin, left her job as chief executive of The Emporium, a division of the bankrupt Carter Hawley Hale Stores Inc. in 1992. She currently sits on several corporate boards. The Emporium has since been purchased by Federated Department Stores.

Daniel Bergman, the former director of stores at Bamberger's, is now a sculptor living in New York City. He works in steel, and has entered his art in shows throughout the country, including Boston and San Diego.

M. Jeffrey Branman, the former First Boston investment banker who advised Robert Campeau, resigned in March 1996 from Financo Inc., an investment banking firm, and accepted a new job as a senior vice president at Woolworth Corp.

Robert Campeau, the Canadian real estate developer who bought Allied Stores and Federated Department Stores, is believed to be living in Europe. In February 1996, Camdev Corp., which oversaw Campeau Corp.'s surviving real estate holdings, was acquired by Nan Fung Group, a Hong Kong conglomerate.

Tom Delavan, the young Goldman, Sachs analyst who fell asleep during meetings, went on to earn an MBA from Harvard Business School. He is now director of the Gramercy Art Fair, which organizes contemporary art exhibits in New York and Los Angeles.

Stephen DuBrul Jr., the former Macy's director, operates his own financial consulting firm in New York City.

Alfred Eckert, a senior Goldman, Sachs partner in charge of the Macy's buyout, resigned in 1991. He is now president of Greenwich Street Capital Partners, L.P., a merchant banking unit of Travelers Inc.

Daniel Finkelstein resigned as chairman of Macy's West in January 1993. In May 1994, he was hired as chief executive of Breuners Furniture chain in San Diego. That business was acquired eight months later by San Diego–based Arnold's Home Furnishings. The new owners didn't invite Finkelstein to stay. In June 1996 he was named chief executive of Britches of Georgetown, a chain of men's clothing stores.

Edward Finkelstein resigned as Macy's chairman in April 1992. He later opened a small retail store in China, The American Place, but it failed. He currently operates a consulting firm, Finkelstein Associates Inc., in New York City.

Mitchell Finkelstein resigned as president of Asia for Macy's product development in November 1992. He has since launched his own sourcing business called Wisetex Trading Ltd. in Hong Kong.

Robert Friedman, the former chairman of Bamberger's and Macy's South, resigned as president of merchandising for the Macy's East division in March 1992 and was named chief executive of Loehmann's, the discounter.

James Gray, the former chairman of Bullock's Wilshire, left his post as president of Burdines in October 1994 to become president and chief operating officer of Macy's East, reporting to Harold Kahn.

Mark Handler retired from Macy's as co-chairman in April 1993. Retired, he says he has put Macy's bankruptcy and the loss of his $2.1 million "in the past." He plays golf with a twenty-three handicap.

Gilbert Harrison, the investment banker who urged The Limited's Leslie Wexner to merge with Macy's, operates Financo Inc., an investment banking firm in New York City. One of his associates is Marvin Traub, the former chairman of Bloomingdale's.

Eugene Kahn, the former senior vice president of Macy's South, was named vice chairman of May Department Stores Co. in February 1996.

Harold Kahn, the former chairman of Macy's California and Macy's South, was named chairman and chief executive of Macy's East, which includes the former Abraham & Straus/Jordan Marsh division, in September 1994.

Sankar Krishnan, the former Bamberger's executive, left Macy's in June 1988. He is currently vice president of finance at Phar-Mor Inc., based in Youngstown, Ohio. Krishnan joined Phar-Mor after a massive fraud was discovered at the discount drugstore chain.

Frank MacDougal, the former senior Prudential Insurance Company of America executive who negotiated with the Tisches shortly before Macy's filed for Chapter 11 bankruptcy protection, retired in 1996.

Robert Miller, the former bankruptcy attorney at Berlack Israels & Liberman, the law firm that represented Macy's bondholders, left his practice in 1995. He is currently a partner in 32 Records, a music company based in New York City.

Rita Reid, the former Goldman, Sachs number cruncher, later sued her firm for sex discrimination when she was denied a partnership. She lost. Most recently she worked at BDS Securities Inc. in New York City.

Phil Schlein, the former chairman of Macy's California fired by Ed Finkelstein in November 1994, is a partner at U.S. Venture Partners in Menlo Park, California, a venture capital firm.

Herbert Seegal, the former president of R. H. Macy & Co. and Ed Finkelstein's mentor, is now a retail consultant living in New York City. He left Macy's in August 1980 and hasn't seen or spoken to Finkelstein in more than a decade.

Donald Smiley, the former Macy's chairman, died of a stroke in January 1995. He was seventy-eight years old.

Kenneth H. Straus, the former Macy's director, died in July 1996. At the time, he was an honorary commissioner of both the New York City Police and Fire departments. His funeral was attended by New York Mayor Rudolph Giuliani, who eulogized him as one of New York's most public-minded citizens.

Laurence Tisch stepped down as chairman and chief executive of CBS Inc. after the television network was acquired in November 1995 by Westinghouse Electric Corp. He continues as co-chairman of Loews Corp. and serves on the board of Federated.

Myron E. Ullman III resigned January 31, 1995, as president and chief executive of R. H. Macy & Co. In November of that year, he joined the DFS Group Ltd., a chain of San Francisco–based duty-free stores, as chief executive.

Investment banker James Wolfensohn, hired by Macy's old board to find a bidder to top Ed Finkelstein's buyout offer, was named president of the World Bank in March 1995.

Sources

Chapter 1

Ed Finkelstein declined on numerous occasions to be interviewed for this project. In the early summer of 1996 he explained he didn't think it would "be in my best interests" to cooperate. Daniel Finkelstein also declined comment. Otherwise, almost all of Macy's former top executives graciously consented to interviews.

I read all of the books, newspaper articles, and magazine articles cited below. They are listed chronologically, reflecting the style of the book's narration. *Women's Wear Daily, The New York Times, New York Newsday,* and *BusinessWeek* were particularly important. Also see the books mentioned in the bibliography pertaining to Macy's history.

"Jack Hersch's Estimates of Effects of Macy's Bankruptcy on Its Bonds and Shareholders." An analyst report published by M. J. Whitman, L.P., New York.

"Store Punishes Products to Safeguard Customers" by Nan Robertson. *The New York Times,* April 25, 1959.

"Personality: A Fourth Generation Retailer" by Leonard Sloane. *The New York Times,* June 23, 1963.

"Macy's Merchandise Tester Retires" by Lisa Hammel. *The New York Times,* Jan. 30, 1964.

"At Macy's: After Straus, What?" by Isadore Barmash. *The New York Times,* Nov. 29, 1967.

"Merger Theme of Macy Meeting" by Isadore Barmash. *The New York Times,* Nov. 29, 1967.

"Straus Leaving Top Macy's Post" by Terry Robards. *The New York Times*, Sept. 25, 1968.

"Ceauşescu Gets 90-Minute Macy Tour" by Andrew H. Malcolm. *The New York Times*, Oct. 22, 1970.

"Sam Walton in His Own Words." Excerpt from "Sam Walton: Made in America," published in *Fortune*, June 29, 1992.

Chapter 2

"Limited Inc. to Begin $1.1 Billion Offer of Cash and Stock for Carter Hawley Hale" by Stephen J. Sansweet. *The Wall Street Journal*, April 3, 1984.

"Limited to Raise Bid for Carter Hawley but Stock Buy-Back May Block Takeover" by Roy J. Harris Jr. and Ralph E. Winter. *The Wall Street Journal*, April 25, 1984.

"Limited Ends Its Offer for Carter Hawley but Says Control of Retailer Is Still a Goal" by Jolie B. Solomon. *The Wall Street Journal*, May 22, 1984.

"Associated Dry Goods Elects Joseph Johnson Chairman and Chief" by Hank Gilman. *The Wall Street Journal*, June 12, 1984.

"No Trivial Pursuit; Are Those Old Discounters, the Hafts of Washington D.C., Mad to Think They Can Take Over May Department Stores?" by Jeffrey A. Trachtenberg. *Forbes*, March 11, 1985.

"Why Retailing Is Ripe for the Raiders" by Gene G. Marcial. *BusinessWeek*, April 29, 1985.

"Associated Dry Goods Is in Merger Talks with May, but Negotiations Are Stalled" by Daniel Hertzberg and Scott Kilman. *The Wall Street Journal*, July 11, 1986.

"Associated Says It Would Accept Higher May Offer" by Scott Kilman and Daniel Hertzberg. *The Wall Street Journal*, July 15, 1986.

"Associated Dry Goods Accepts May Stores Bid" by Scott Kilman, Daniel Hertzberg, and Ann Hagedorn. *The Wall Street Journal*, July 17, 1986.

"Goldman Sachs's Whitehead to Resign, Leaving Weinberg as the Sole Chairman" by Scott McMurray. *The Wall Street Journal*, Aug. 16, 1984.

"Can Goldman Stay on Top?" by Jack Willoughby. *Forbes*, Sept. 18, 1989.

"All's Relatively Quiet on Haft Family Takeover Front" by L. A. Lough. *The Baltimore Business Journal*, June 17, 1991.

Chapter 3

"Macy's Gets 7 1/2% of Sales Sundays" by Isadore Barmash. *The New York Times*, Nov. 23, 1977.

"Ed Finkelstein's Marketing Miracle on 34th Street: It's the Glamorous New Macy's" by Shirley Clurman. *People*, Dec. 10, 1979.

Chapter 5

"Jack I. Straus: Guided Macy's in Major Expansion." *The Los Angeles Times*, Sept. 22, 1985.

"Jack I. Straus, 85, Macy's Leader Through 4 Decades of Expansion" by Eric Pace. *The New York Times,* Sept. 20, 1985.

"R. H. Macy Executives to Propose Leveraged Buyout for $3.58 Billion" by James B. Stewart. *The Wall Street Journal,* Oct. 22, 1985.

"Macy's Officials Plan Leveraged Buyout" by Caroline F. Mayer. *The Washington Post,* Oct. 22, 1985.

"Executives Plan $3.6 Billion Bid for R. H. Macy" by Richard W. Stevenson. *The New York Times,* Oct. 22, 1985.

"Macy's Proposed Buyout Value and Source of Financing Has Most Investors Mystified" by Dean Rotbart. *The Wall Street Journal,* Oct. 23, 1985.

"Taking Macy's out from Under the Magnifying Glass" by Amy Dunkin. *BusinessWeek,* Nov. 4, 1985.

"Macy May Cut Buyout Offer of $70 a Share" by James B. Stewart and Hank Gilman. *The Wall Street Journal,* Dec. 4, 1985.

"Macy's Management Group Cuts Its Bid for Firm to $68 a Share, or $3.48 Billion" by Hank Gilman. *The Wall Street Journal,* Dec. 20, 1985.

"When Wolfensohn Talks, Big Business Listens—Carefully" by Edwin A. Finn. *Forbes,* Dec. 26, 1988.

"Weil, Gotshal's Leaders Have Turned Their Firm Into a National Powerhouse. But It's Not a Place for the Faint-of-Heart" by Alison Frankel. *The American Lawyer,* Oct. 1992.

Chapter 6

"Macy's Board Clears Buyout for $3.5 Billion" by Hank Gilman. *The Wall Street Journal,* Jan. 17, 1986.

"Macy's Group Files with SEC on Debt for Buyout Plan" by Hank Gilman. *The Wall Street Journal,* Feb. 20, 1986.

"Management Group to Own 20% of Macy's" by Sidney Rutberg. *Women's Wear Daily,* Feb. 20, 1986.

"Macy's LBO Plan Will Give Finkelstein Control of Board" by Sidney Rutberg. *Women's Wear Daily,* Feb. 27, 1986.

"Prudential to Provide Loan of $800 Million." *The Wall Street Journal,* Feb. 15, 1986.

Chapter 8

"Federated Stores Acts to Catch Up to Rivals in Retail Revolution" by Jolie Solomon. *The Wall Street Journal,* April 5, 1984.

"Woodward & Lothrop Holders Clear Buyout by Taubman Holdings." *The Wall Street Journal,* Sept. 17, 1984.

"Federated Chooses Not to Choose" by Subrata N. Chakravarty. *Forbes,* April 8, 1985.

"Carter Hawley to Sell Wanamaker Unit to Concern Owned by Taubman Family" by Kathleen A. Hughes. *The Wall Street Journal,* Nov. 5, 1986.

"Scholars Nurture Einstein's Legacy at Institute" by Charles Hillinger. *Los Angeles Times,* Jan. 12, 1986.

"Bamberger's New Name: Macy's" by David Moin. *Women's Wear Daily,* Aug. 20, 1986.

"Allied Stores Gets Proposal of $2.74 Billion" by Steve Weiner, Jacquie McNish, and John D. Williams. *The Wall Street Journal,* Sept. 5, 1986.

"It's Official: Bamberger's Units Christened Macy's" by David Moin. *Women's Wear Daily,* Sept. 7, 1986.

"Allied Stores Corp. to Be Acquired for $67 a Share, or $3.25 Billion" by Ann Hagedorn. *The Wall Street Journal,* Oct. 8, 1986.

"Allied Stores to Be Bought by Campeau" by Ann Hagedorn and Leonard Zehr. *The Wall Street Journal,* Nov. 3, 1986.

"Macy's Tops Post-LBO Projections" by Pete Born. *Women's Wear Daily,* Dec. 29, 1986.

"Campeau Succeeds Macioce as Head of Allied Stores." *The Wall Street Journal,* Jan. 13, 1987.

"The Year's Best Sale at Macy's: Itself" by Amy Durkin. *BusinessWeek,* Jan. 12, 1987.

"Turning the Shopping Mall Upside Down" by Ann Hagedorn. *The Wall Street Journal,* May 29, 1987.

"Macy's: An Early Dip into Black Ink" by Sidney Rutberg and Pete Born. *Women's Wear Daily,* Jan. 11, 1988.

"Federated Gets Late $73.80-a-Share Bid from Macy's, Clouding Campeau's Offer" by Bryan Burrough. *The Wall Street Journal,* March 1, 1988.

"Federated's Board Studies Rival Bids Late into the Night" by Bryan Burrough. *The Wall Street Journal,* March 2, 1988.

"Finkelstein Puts Forth the Gospel of Private Label." *Women's Wear Daily,* March 23, 1988.

"Campeau's Victory Puts Robert Morosky at Helm of Federated" by Ellen Forman. *Women's Wear Daily,* April 4, 1988.

"Clothing Retailers Stress Private Labels" by Teri Agins. *The Wall Street Journal,* June 9, 1988.

"How Campeau Won Federated" by Martha Groves. *Los Angeles Times,* June 12, 1988.

"Struggling Macy's, Federated Face Crucial Test" by Sidney Rutberg. *Women's Wear Daily,* Nov. 1st, 1988.

"King of Malls" by Jonathan R. Laing. *Barron's,* June 12, 1989.

"Hooker Stumbles in Its U.S. Retail Drive" by Jeffrey A. Trachtenberg. *The Wall Street Journal,* June 20, 1989.

"Aeropostale Takes Flight" by Martha Groves. *Los Angeles Times,* July 14, 1989.

"The Biggest Looniest Deal Ever" by Carol J. Loomis. *Fortune,* June 18, 1990.

"The Kung Fu King Who Rescued Macy's" by Pete Engardio and Laura Zinn. *BusinessWeek,* June 24, 1991.

"An Era Ends as Macy's Closes Its Newark Store." *The Star-Ledger,* Aug. 8, 1992.

"A Temple of Commerce" by Lawrence Hall. *The Star-Ledger,* June 1, 1992.
Campeau: The Building of an Empire by Michael Babad and Catherine Mulroney. See bibliography.
Like No Other Store . . . by Marvin Traub. See bibliography.
Going for Broke by John Rothchild. See bibliography.

Chapter 9

"I. Magnin Names a New Chief Executive." *Los Angeles Times,* Feb. 10, 1987.
"I. Magnin Takes Off Its Velvet Gloves" by Jan Shaw. *The San Francisco Business Times,* Jan. 11, 1988.
"Macy's Gets Keys to Golden Gate" by Steve Ginsberg. *Women's Wear Daily,* April 4, 1988.
"Campeau Vows to Revitalize New Empire" by Steve Coll. *The Washington Post,* April 6, 1988.
"Three Chains, at Crossroads" by Martha Groves. *Los Angeles Times,* April 18, 1988.
"Macy Restructuring Is Seen; New Units Are a Key Factor" by Isadore Barmash. *The New York Times,* April 15, 1988.
"Top Executive Teams Reported Set at Macy" by Isadore Barmash. *The New York Times,* April 22, 1988.
"Bullock's Executives Said to Be Out in Big Reshuffling by Macy's" by Martha Groves. *Los Angeles Times,* April 22, 1988.
"Macy's Wider Losses, Weakening Condition, Mean Bad News for Big Retailer's Junk Bonds" by Linda Sandler. *The Wall Street Journal,* Nov. 4, 1988.
"Crunch Time for Federated, Macy's, Allied" by Sidney Rutberg. *Women's Wear Daily,* Nov. 11, 1988.
"Losses at Macy's Are No Surprise to Wall Street." *Women's Wear Daily,* Dec. 16, 1988.
"A New Face for Bullock's" by Martha Groves. *Los Angeles Times,* Feb. 23, 1989.
"Questrom's Quest" by Nancy Marx Better. *Manhattan Inc.,* July 1989.
"To Macy's Executive Suite Via Cincinnati, Texas and Hong Kong" by Sidney Rutberg. *Women's Wear Daily,* Sept. 13, 1989.
"Bass Is Named Emporium CEO" by Steve Ginsberg. *Women's Wear Daily,* Oct. 10, 1989.
"Can Mike Ullman Turn Macy's Around?" by Jean M. Peck. *Horizons,* July 1993.
"Bullock's Wizard Trying His Hand at Neiman Marcus" by Martha Groves. *Los Angeles Times,* Dec. 10, 1989.

Chapter 10

"Macy's California Names Dan Finkelstein Senior VP." *Women's Wear Daily,* July 23, 1986.

"Limited Makes a New Bid for Carter Hawley" by Greg Burns. *Chicago Sun-Times,* Nov. 26, 1986.

"Limited Enters Fray, May Not Buy Part of Allied" by Janet Key. *Chicago Tribune,* Nov. 2, 1986.

"DeBartolo, Limited Drop Takeover Bid." United Press International, Dec. 9, 1986.

"The Benefits of Leverage" by Subrata N. Chakravarty. *Forbes,* May 1, 1989.

"Macy May Seek an Investment from Limited" by David B. Hilder and Carol Hymowitz. *The Wall Street Journal,* May 18, 1989.

"A Reassignment of Chief Execs at Macy Units" by Pete Born. *Women's Wear Daily,* Aug. 15, 1989.

"Unexpected Stuff, Macy's Division Gets New CEO" by Laura Evenson. *San Francisco Chronicle,* Aug. 15, 1989.

"Campeau Plans to Put Bloomingdale's Store Chain on the Block, Source Says" by Judith Valente, Randall Smith, and David Hilder. *The Wall Street Journal,* Sept. 8, 1989.

"Campeau Plans Restructuring, Including Sale of Bloomingdale's Chain, to Cut Debt" by Robert Melnbardis, Teri Agins, and Carol Hymowitz. *The Wall Street Journal,* Sept. 11, 1989.

"Chairman of Saks Plans Buy-Out Bid for Unit of B.A.T" by Jeffrey A. Trachtenberg. *The Wall Street Journal,* Sept. 28, 1989.

"Discount Blitz Opens Christmas Season." *The Wall Street Journal,* Nov. 27, 1989.

"Campeau Assails Dun & Bradstreet's Advice to Clients Not to Ship It Goods" by Jeffrey A. Trachtenberg. *The Wall Street Journal,* Dec. 7, 1989.

"Campeau Posts Wider Deficit for 3rd Period" by Robert Melnbardis and Jeffrey A. Trachtenberg. *The Wall Street Journal,* Dec. 13, 1989.

"Campeau Says Stores May File for Chapter 11" by Jeffrey A. Trachtenberg and Robert Melnbardis. *The Wall Street Journal,* Dec. 14, 1989.

"Junk-Bond Prices Sustain Widespread Losses as Campeau's Woes Cast Pall over the Market" by Constance Mitchell and Anita Raghavan. *The Wall Street Journal,* Dec. 15, 1989.

"Top Factor Delays Approving Goods for Campeau Units" by Jeffrey A. Trachtenberg. *The Wall Street Journal,* Dec. 18, 1989.

"Campeau Surrenders Control of Retailing Operations at Firm He Founded, but Remains Real-Estate Chief" by Jeffrey A. Trachtenberg and Robert Melnbardis. *The Wall Street Journal,* Jan. 12, 1990.

"Campeau's Woes: Bankruptcy Petition Brings Fresh Risks for Allied, Federated." *The Wall Street Journal,* Jan. 16, 1990.

"Campeau Pins Retail Hopes on Banker, Not a Merchant" by Kathleen Deveny. *The Wall Street Journal,* Jan. 17, 1990.

"Vendors Irate" by Sidney Rutberg. *Women's Wear Daily,* Jan. 22, 1990.

"Questrom to Get $12 Million to Be Head of Campeau's Federated, Allied Stores" by Teri Agins and Jeffrey A. Trachtenberg. *The Wall Street Journal,* Feb. 5, 1990.

"Federated Finally Gets Its Man" by David Moin and Bryan Doherty. *Women's Wear Daily*, Feb. 5, 1990.

"Campeau Corp. Units Are Sued for Hiring of Allen Questrom." *The Wall Street Journal*, Feb. 13, 1990.

"Neiman's Sues Federated Over Allen Questrom" by Bryan Doherty. *Women's Wear Daily*, Feb. 13, 1990.

"Campeau Retail Units Plan to Discontinue 3 Private-Label Lines." *The Wall Street Journal*, Feb. 21, 1990.

Chapter 11

"Macy's Primps for Investors, Too, in Tough Retail Times" by Christine Dugas. *New York Newsday*, March 12, 1990.

"Macy to Post $39 Million Loss for 2nd Quarter" by Jeffrey A. Trachtenberg. *The Wall Street Journal*, March 13, 1990.

"Moody's Lowers Ratings of Macy in Three Issues" by Jeffrey A. Trachtenberg. *The Wall Street Journal*, March 15, 1990.

"R. H. Macy, Campeau Aren't in Same Boat" by Jeffrey A. Trachtenberg. *The Wall Street Journal*, March 16, 1990.

"Stemming the Losses: Trying for a Leaner Macy's" by N. R. Kleinfeld. *The New York Times*, March 18, 1990.

"Macy's Buyout Loses a Lot of Its Luster" by Christopher Power. *BusinessWeek*, March 19, 1990.

"Macy's to Use Federated Info Service" by David Moin. *Women's Wear Daily*, March 20, 1990.

"Parent of the Department Store Units of Campeau Files Under Chapter 11" by Robert Melnbardis. *The Wall Street Journal*, April 2, 1990.

"12 Bonwit's Stores to Be Liquidated; Pyramid Buys Name" by Bryan Doherty. *Women's Wear Daily*, April 5, 1990.

"Ames Files Chapter 11" by Bryan Doherty. *Daily News Record*, April 27, 1990.

"R. H. Macy Bond Prices Fall as Concern About Its Financial Condition Increases" by Jeffrey A. Trachtenberg and George Anders. *The Wall Street Journal*, May 25, 1990.

"Macy Is to Woo Credit Firms This Week as Latest Results Fail to Ease All Fears" by George Anders and Jeffrey A. Trachtenberg. *The Wall Street Journal*, May 29, 1990.

"Macy's Goes Shopping to Reduce Huge Debt" by Phyllis Furman. *Crain's New York Business*, July 23, 1990.

"Macy's Gets a Good Price for Its 1% Stake" by Floyd Norris. *The New York Times*, Aug. 3, 1990.

"R. H. Macy Sells Small Equity Stake to New York Firm" by Jeffrey A. Trachtenberg. *The Wall Street Journal*, Aug. 3, 1990.

"Cloudy Economic Outlook Turns Gloomier After Invasion of Kuwait" by Tom Herman. *The Wall Street Journal*, Aug. 14, 1990.

"Retailers Begin Belt-Tightening Early as Christmas Forecast Is Mostly Cloudy" by Francine Schwadel. *The Wall Street Journal*, Aug. 29, 1990.

"Consumers Are Likely to Start Cutting Back" by Henry F. Myers, *The Wall Street Journal,* Sept. 17, 1990.

"R. H. Macy Plans Bond Buy-Back, Executive Says" by George Anders. *The Wall Street Journal,* Sept. 19, 1990.

"Macy to Sell Its Credit-Card Subsidiary to GE" by George Anders. *The Wall Street Journal,* Oct. 12, 1990.

"Macy's Losses Said to Mount in Fiscal 1990" by Jeffrey A. Trachtenberg and George Anders. *The Wall Street Journal,* Oct. 18, 1990.

"Shaken on 34th Street," by Phyllis Furman. *Crain's New York Business,* Oct. 29, 1990.

"Factor Won't Guarantee Shipments to R. H. Macy." *The Wall Street Journal,* Nov. 1, 1990.

"Macy Lining Up Equity Infusion of $150 Million" by George Anders. *The Wall Street Journal,* Nov. 2, 1990.

"Macy's Smaller Suppliers Forced into Riskier Position" by Jeffrey A. Trachtenberg. *The Wall Street Journal,* Nov. 21, 1990.

"Macy's Sales Plunged 14% for October" by Jeffrey A. Trachtenberg and George Anders. *The Wall Street Journal,* Nov. 16, 1990.

"Macy Discloses Loss Doubled to $66 Million" by George Anders and Jeffrey A. Trachtenberg. *The Wall Street Journal,* Nov. 28, 1990.

"Macy's Bonds Face Possible Downgrading" by Jeffrey A. Trachtenberg and George Anders. *The Wall Street Journal,* Nov. 30, 1990.

"Macy's Latest Overpriced Product Is Its New Shares" by Allan Sloan. *The Washington Post,* Oct. 2, 1990.

"Macy Plans to Buy Back 'Junk Bonds' " by Leslie Way. *The New York Times,* Dec. 5, 1990.

"Macy's Ad Assails Financial Rumors" by Isadore Barmash. *The New York Times,* Dec. 5, 1990.

"Is Macy's Unraveling?" by Laura Zinn and Christopher Power. *Business Week,* Dec. 17, 1990.

"Macy Investors Get U.S. Approval to Buy New Shares" by Jeffrey A. Trachtenberg. *The Wall Street Journal,* Dec. 11, 1990.

"Macy Attracts $187.6 Million in New Capital" by Jeffrey A. Trachtenberg. *The Wall Street Journal,* Dec. 18, 1990.

"Run Run Aide Promises No Meddling with Macy's" by Paul Charles Ehrlich. *Women's Wear Daily,* Dec. 21, 1990.

"Fortune Made in Hong Kong Buoys Macy's" by Francine Brevetti. *Newsday,* Dec. 26, 1990.

"Garfinckel's Fall Changes Face of Retailing" by Susan J. Stocker. *The Washington Business Journal,* Dec. 31, 1990.

Chapter 12

"Another Chapter 11: Now It's CHH" by Sidney Rutberg. *Women's Wear Daily,* Feb. 12, 1991.

"Campeau Units' Retail Divisions May Go Public" by Jeffrey A. Trachtenberg. *The Wall Street Journal*, April 5, 1991.

"Macy's Unveils $150-Million TV Advertising Campaign" by Joyce M. Rosenberg. Associated Press, April 15, 1991.

"Finkelstein Sees Another $3.6B in Sales" by Mary Merris. *Women's Wear Daily*, May 22, 1991.

"Things Are Looking Up" by Lisa Lockwood. *Women's Wear Daily*, May 22, 1991.

"R. H. Macy Posts Record Quarterly Loss of $101 Million Amid Spending Slump" by Jeffrey A. Trachtenberg. *The Wall Street Journal*, May 29, 1991.

"Farah Charts New Course for FAMS" by David Moin. *Women's Wear Daily*, June 24, 1991.

"Macy's Confirms Plan to Consolidate Stores" by David Moin. *Women's Wear Daily*, Aug. 22, 1991.

"Macy Projects Six-Month Sales will Grow 8.3%" by Jeffrey A. Trachtenberg. *The Wall Street Journal*, Aug. 28, 1991.

"Macy's Revenue Rose in Quarter, Loss Narrowed" by Jeffrey A. Trachtenberg. *The Wall Street Journal*, Nov. 4, 1991.

"Macy Payments Lose Guarantee of Factor Firm" by Jeffrey A. Trachtenberg. *The Wall Street Journal*, Nov. 18, 1991.

"R. H. Macy Meets with Prudential for Debt Talks" by George Anders. *The Wall Street Journal*, Nov. 25, 1991.

"Macy Says Its Bankers Are Reviewing Plans to Amend Retailer's Credit Facility" by Jeffrey A. Trachtenberg. *The Wall Street Journal*, Dec. 9, 1991.

"Macy Reports Loss Widened for Quarter" by Jeffrey A. Trachtenberg and George Anders. *The Wall Street Journal*, Dec. 18, 1991.

"GM Plans to Close 21 More Factories, Cut 74,000 Jobs, Slash Capital Spending," by Paul Ingrassia and Joseph B. White. *The Wall Street Journal*, Dec. 19, 1991.

Chapter 13

"Cash Pinch Leads Macy to Delay Paying Bills and Plan Other Steps" by Jeffrey A. Trachtenberg and George Anders. *The Wall Street Journal*, Jan. 13, 1992.

"Tisch Outlines Buy-Out Bid to Rescue Troubled Macy" by Jeffrey A. Trachtenberg and George Anders. *The Wall Street Journal*, Jan. 24, 1992.

"R. H. Macy Prepares Chapter 11 Filing After Tisch Rescue Plan Falls Through" by George Anders and Jeffrey A. Trachtenberg. *The Wall Street Journal*, Jan. 27, 1992.

"Macy Files for Chapter 11, Listing Assets of $4.95 Billion, Liabilities of $5.32 Billion" by Jeffrey A. Trachtenberg and George Anders. *The Wall Street Journal*, Jan. 28, 1992.

"Macy Gives Vice Chairman No. 2 Post, Putting Him in Position to Succeed Chief," by Jeffrey A. Trachtenberg and George Anders. *The Wall Street Journal*, May 5, 1992.

"Courting Disaster," by Martin Mayer. *Worth* magazine, August/September
    1992.
"Finkelstein to Advise Macy on Real Estate." *Women's Wear Daily,* Sept. 3, 1992.
"Mitchell Finkelstein Looks Ahead to Life After Macy, Running His Own Busi-
    ness," by Jesse Wong. *The Wall Street Journal,* Nov. 27, 1992.
"Macy's Names a Temporary Successor to Finkelstein" by David Moin.
    Women's Wear Daily, Jan. 7, 1993.

Chapter 14

"Severance Deal for Ex-Macy Head" by Stephanie Storm. *The New York Times,*
    Aug. 29, 1992.
"Macy's West Names New CEO" by Louis Trager. *The San Francisco Examiner,*
    July 29, 1993.

Chapter 15

"Macy Shows Small Profit in Quarter" by Stephanie Strom. *The New York
    Times,* March 17, 1993.
"R. H. Macy Details Changes in Five-Year Business Plan" by Sidney Rutberg
    and David Moin. *Women's Wear Daily,* May 28, 1993.
"Hear Macy's Is Zeroing In on Roger Farah" by Dianne M. Pogoda and
    Jonathan Auerbach. *Women's Wear Daily,* July 29, 1993.
"Finkelstein Deal Up in Air" by Jonathan Auerbach. *Daily News Record,* July
    30, 1992.
"Macy Is Considering Farah of Federated As Chief Merchant." *The Wall Street
    Journal,* July 30, 1993.
"Federated Gets Order Stopping Farah From Taking Position at Rival Macy"
    by Teri Agins. *The Wall Street Journal,* Aug. 9, 1993.
"As Macy's Woos Farah, Federated Declares War" by David Moin. *Women's
    Wear Daily,* Aug. 9, 1993.
"Courts Could Sideline Farah for Months" by Jonathan Auerbach and David
    Moin. *Women's Wear Daily,* Aug. 10, 1993.
"Federated: We Want A Full Trial in Farah Case" by David Moin and Jonathan
    Auerbach. *Women's Wear Daily,* Aug. 12, 1993.
"Federated Fighting for Farah" by David Moin and Jonathan Auerbach.
    Women's Wear Daily, Aug. 16, 1993.
"Roger N. Farah: A Hot Property in Retail Limbo" by David Auerbach.
    Women's Wear Daily, Aug. 19, 1993.
"Federated Makes a Move on Macy's" by Lisa Lockwood and Jonathan Auer-
    bach. *Women's Wear Daily,* Jan. 3, 1994.
"Federated Bidding for Macy Through Bankruptcy Court" by Patrick M.
    Reilly and Eben Shapiro. *The Wall Street Journal,* Jan. 3, 1994.
"Macy Is Cool to Overture From Federated" by Jeffrey A. Trachtenberg and
    Laura Jereski. *The Wall Street Journal,* Jan. 4, 1994.

"On Macy, Fund Manager Speaks Loudly" by Laura Jereski. *The Wall Street Journal,* Jan. 6, 1994.

"Federated Delays Action on Macy Plan" by Jeffrey A. Trachtenberg and Patrick M. Reilly. *The Wall Street Journal,* Jan. 10, 1994.

"Vance is Named as a Mediator in Macy Case" by Patrick M. Reilly and Laura Jereski. *The Wall Street Journal,* Feb. 23, 1994.

"Federated Department Stores and R. H. Macy & Co. Agree to Merge," by David Moin. *Women's Wear Daily,* July 15, 1994.

"Farah Unfurls $14M Parachute." *Women's Wear Daily,* Sept. 30, 1994.

Bibliography

Auletta, Ken. *Greed and Glory on Wall Street: The Fall of the House of Lehman.* New York: Random House, 1986.

———. *Three Blind Mice: How the TV Networks Lost Their Way.* New York: Random House, 1991.

Babad, Michael, and Catherine Mulroney. *Campeau: The Building of an Empire.* Toronto: Doubleday Canada Ltd., 1989.

Barmash, Isadore. *Macy's For Sale: The Leveraged Buyout of the World's Largest Store.* New York: Weidenfeld & Nicolson, 1989.

Birmingham, Nan. *Store.* New York: G. P. Putnam's Sons, 1978.

Boorstin, Daniel J. *The Americans: The Democratic Experience.* New York: Random House, 1973.

Harriman, Margaret Case. *And the Price Is Right.* Cleveland: The World Publishing Company, 1958.

Harris, Leon A. *Merchant Princes: An Intimate History of Jewish Families Who Built Great Department Stores.* New York: Harper & Row, 1979.

Hart, Harold H. *Hart's Guide to New York City.* New York: Hart Publishing Company, 1964.

Hower, Ralph M. *History of Macy's of New York 1858–1919: Chapters in Evolution of the Department Store.* Cambridge: Harvard University Press, 1943.

Hungerford, Edward. *The Romance of a Great Store.* New York: Robert M. McBride & Company, 1922.

Johnson, Curtiss S. *The Indomitable R. H. Macy.* New York: Vantage Press, 1964.

Jordan, Robert H. *There Was A Land: A History of Talbot County, Georgia.* Columbus, Georgia: Privately published, 1971.

Mahoney, Tom, and Leonard Sloane. *The Great Merchants: America's Foremost Retail Institutions and the People Who Made Them Great*. New York: Harper & Row, 1974.

Raban, Jonathan. *Hunting Mister Heartbreak: A Discovery of America*. New York: HarperCollins, 1991.

Rothchild, John. *Going for Broke: How Robert Campeau Bankrupted the Retail Industry, Jolted the Junk Bond Market, and Brought the Booming Eighties to a Crashing Halt*. New York: Simon & Schuster, 1991.

Straus, Isidor. *The Autobiography of Isidor Straus*. Privately published, 1955.

Straus, Robert K. *In My Anecdotage*. Santa Barbara: Privately published, 1989.

Traub, Marvin and Tom Teicholz. *Like No Other Store . . . The Bloomingdale's Legend and the Revolution in American Marketing*. New York: Times Books, 1993.

Index